ASPA • BNA Series ②

Human Resource Planning Employment & Placement

Editorial Advisory Board

ROBERT L. BERRA, AEP
Senior Vice President
Monsanto Company

CATHERINE DOWNES BOWER
Vice President, Communications and Public Relations
American Society for Personnel Administration

STEPHEN J. CARROLL
Professor, Organizational Behavior & Industrial Relations
College of Business & Management
University of Maryland

PHILIP FARISH
Editor
Human Resource Management News

GERALD W. HOLDER, AEP
Senior Vice President (Retired)
Marion Laboratories

EDWARD H. LYONS
Vice President, Technical Services
American Society for Personnel Administration

GEORGE T. MILKOVICH
Professor, Personnel & Human Resource Studies
New York State School of Industrial & Labor Relations
Cornell University

MARY GREEN MINER
Publisher, BNA Books
The Bureau of National Affairs, Inc.

RONALD C. PILENZO, SPHR
President
American Society for Personnel Administration

JAMES H. WILKINS, JR., SPHR
Director, Personnel Accreditation Institute
American Society for Personnel Administration

ASPA • BNA Series ◇2

Human Resource Planning Employment & Placement

Wayne F. Cascio
Editor

Donald H. Sweet
Consulting Editor

The Bureau of National Affairs, Inc., Washington, D.C.

Copyright © 1989
The Bureau of National Affairs, Inc.

Library of Congress Cataloging-in-Publication Data

Human resource planning, employment & placement/Wayne F. Cascio, editor: Donald H. Sweet, consulting editor.
 p. cm.—(ASPA/BNA series ; 2)
 Includes indexes.
 ISBN 0-87179-602-3
 1. Manpower planning. 2. Recruiting of employees. I. Cascio, Wayne F. II. Sweet, Donald H. III. Bureau of National Affairs (Washington, D.C.) IV. Title: Human resource planning, employment, and placement. V. Series.
HF5549.A9574 1988 vol. 2
[HF5549.5.M3]
658.3 s—dc20
[658.3'01]

Authorization to photocopy items for internal or personal use, or the internal or personal use of specific clients, is granted by BNA Books for libraries and other users registered with the Copyright Clearance Center (CCC) Transactional Reporting Service, provided that $0.50 per page is paid directly to CCC, 27 Congress St., Salem, MA 01970. 0-87179-602-3/89/$0 + .50.

Published by BNA Books, 1231 25th St., N.W., Washington, D.C. 20037

Printed in the United States of America
International Standard Book Number: 0-87179-602-3

Preface

It has been 15 years since the first volume of the original ASPA Handbook of Personnel and Industrial Relations was published. A great deal has changed in our profession since then. No longer is PAIR (personnel and industrial relations) the accepted acronym for the management of human resources, primarily because our roles and our accountabilities are so different.

Human resource executives have been broadening their horizons and learning new ways to make a bigger contribution to their organizations. So, too, does the focus of this new HRM (human resource management) series indicate the extent to which the field has changed and how pace-setting human resource executives have been reshaping management practice. We have tried to reflect those changes in this new series.

The original series was eight volumes with a heavy emphasis on "how-to-do-it." This new series, comprised of six volumes, focuses more heavily on the why than the how, on strategy and integration rather than the specifics of execution.

The very process we used to develop this series indicates the shift in orientation. Each of the six volumes had a different well-known academician as its editor. These individuals were supported by at least one consulting editor, a senior practitioner in the HRM field whose role was to provide the "real world" perspective so necessary to this kind of project. And the overall series was guided by an editorial advisory board made up of practitioners, academicians, and representatives of BNA and ASPA. Members of the editorial advisory board are listed opposite the title page of this Volume.

Collectively, we struggled through the development of each volume and its chapters, striving to achieve the proper balance between a macro perspective of the profession and an evolutionary approach to the material presented. Our target audience—middle to upper level practitioners and those who aspire to such positions—was a constant presence during all of our discussions.

The six volumes in this series and their key players are:

1. *Human Resource Management: Evolving Roles and Responsibilities* edited by Lee Dyer, professor at Cornell University with

Jerry Holder, retired vice president of human resources for Marion Laboratories, as consulting editor. Additional consulting editors included Robert Berra of Monsanto, Leo Contois of Consolidated Foods (retired) and Garth Dimon of Bristol-Meyers.

2. *Human Resource Planning, Employment, and Placement* edited by Wayne Cascio, professor at the University of Colorado with Donald Sweet of Hawkins Associates, Inc. as consulting editor.

3. *Compensation and Benefits* edited by Luis R. Gomez-Mejia, professor at the University of Colorado with consulting editors Ray Olsen of TRW and Wes Leibtag of the University of Illinois.

4. *Employee and Labor Relations* edited by John Fossum, professor, University of Minnesota, with Jerauld Mattson of International Multifoods as consulting editor.

5. *Developing Human Resources* edited by Kenneth N. Wexley, professor, Michigan State University with John Hinrichs of Management Decision Systems as consulting editor.

6. *Managing Human Resources in the Information Age* with Randall S. Schuler of New York University as editor and James Walker of Walker and Associates as consulting editor.

This new management series reflects the coming of age of human resource management. ASPA is grateful to the individuals whose work is reflected in its pages and proud to mark this professional transition with such an outstanding series.

Ronald C. Pilenzo
Alexandria, VA
June 1988

Introduction

The first volume in this series took a "macro" view of the current and emerging field of human resource management (HRM). This volume adopts a more restricted focus, for it is concerned principally with the employment function. Topics including human resource planning, job analysis, recruitment, staffing, internal placement and career management, and outplacement fall within its purview.

As with the other volumes in this series, this one was developed with three audiences in mind: upper-level managers, whether inside or outside the HR function; HR professionals at all levels; and academics teaching and doing research in the field. Our objective is simple: to enlist the best talent currently available to document current practice and to identify future trends. Each of the authors in this volume is on the cutting edge of his or her area, each has extensive practical experience in these areas, and each is well aware of the literature that has developed in his or her area. The result is a collection of chapters that is practical and applied in orientation, that reflects the very best that the field has to offer, while preserving and building upon the intellectual foundations of each topic.

In addition to the lists of references at the end of each chapter, there is a wealth of information about other resource material that will prove useful over time. Examples include the names and addresses of journals, societies, professional organizations, and other publications that will allow the interested reader to remain up-to-date on topics of interest. In this respect, we hope that the volume will serve as more than a summary of current practice and a projection of future trends. We hope that it will serve as a professional resource to be consulted often, one whose value will increase over time.

The first two chapters provide a foundation of information for the discussion of the employment processes to follow. Here is a brief overview of the contents and topics addressed in each chapter:

Foundations

Chapter 2.1: "Societal Trends and Staffing Policies" by Wayne Cascio and Ray Zammuto

This chapter provides a broad discussion of the impact of trends on HRM in such areas as demographics, deregulation, and economic-competitive. Among the topics are: the impact of automation and education on the employment of new workers, the impact of shifts from a manufacturing to a service economy, the impact of the women's movement, the aging of the population, the continuing effect of EEO/affirmative action, and the impact of deregulation of airlines, telecommunications, trucking, and banking on staffing policies. The chapter concludes with a discussion of the impact of these trends on the employment of workers now and in the decades to come.

Chapter 2.2: "Job Analysis and HR Planning" by Ron Page and Dave Van De Voort

The theme of this chapter can be expressed concisely: given the pace of changes in organizations, and given the rapidly evolving new organizational structures stimulated by the kinds of changes described in Chapter 2.1, there must be a closer link between the strategic and tactical objectives of the business enterprise (as articulated in human resource plans) and statements of the kind of work to be done, the skills needed, and the training required of the individual jobholder (job analysis). Page and Van De Voort use company examples and computer-generated graphics to illustrate the state of the art in job analysis and HR planning. Taken together, job analyses and human resource plans provide a coherent framework for the staffing and placement decisions to follow.

Processes

Chapter 2.3: "External and Internal Recruitment" by Scott Lord

This chapter contains a wealth of practical, hands-on information that experienced recruiters will find particularly useful during the implementation phase of a recruitment program. Written by a leader in the recruitment field, this chapter outlines the organizational structure of a dedicated recruitment function, recruiting operations in a small company, staffing the recruitment function, managing and controlling recruitment, and the distinctions between executive search firms and contingency-fee agencies. For those organizations that do not have dedicated recruiters, Lord provides practical advice on how to use an executive search firm, how to select an advertising agency, and how to make the most of alternative recruitment sources. Finally, he provides guidelines for identifying and developing internal talent, plus many sources of further information.

Chapter 2.4: "Recruitment Sources" by Phil Farish

This chapter presents information needed by relative novices in the recruitment field. It provides a broad overview of the various recruitment techniques and trends, and, as is customary in this volume, illustrates the discussion with many real-life examples. There is considerable discussion of alternative sources and how to make the best use of them—e.g., executive search firms; employment agencies; college recruiting; nontraditional sources, such as alumni associations; company relations with community colleges; cooperative education programs; recruitment channels to reach unemployed youths; government sources; employee leasing for large and small companies through temporary agencies; and job posting. An overriding theme is how to fit practice to purpose, relative to client needs. Recruiting has changed, and it is likely to continue to change in the coming years in order to respond successfully to the demands of the global marketplace. This chapter looks forward, not backward, focusing on the opportunities that lie ahead in finding and keeping top talent.

Chapter 2.5: "Merit-Based Selection: Measuring the Person for the Job" by Milt Hakel

This chapter provides a broad overview of key considerations that underlie personnel selection programs. It offers an objective review of the advantages and disadvantages of alternative methods for selecting employees, including nontest methods (e.g., interviews, background/credit checks, polygraphs) as well as test methods (e.g., measures of aptitude, job knowledge, performance and personality, situational tests, and assessment centers). It emphasizes alternative strategies for demonstrating job-relatedness and nondiscrimination, and it provides practical, workable suggestions that recognize the constraints faced by organizational decision makers.

Chapter 2.6: "Tools for Staffing Decisions: What Can They Do? What Do They Cost?" by Rick Jacobs and Joe Baratta

This chapter provides a wealth of practical information regarding six specific selection techniques. These include interviews, tests, work samples, assessment centers, experience, and realistic job previews. Many of these procedures are then broken down further into specialized applications. Each of the procedures is described in terms of critical issues in application, effectiveness, cost estimates, and legal implications. In addition, the authors present a considerable amount of information on the costs and benefits of these procedures that has not been published elsewhere. In sum, the chapter is an eminently practical guide to the problem of making choices among alternative procedures in personnel selection.

Chapter 2.7: "Internal Placement and Career Management" by Marilyn Quaintance

As soon as employees are assigned to available jobs (the placement process), issues of career management arise. Career management is the joint responsibility of the employee and the organization, and it is an ongoing process that assumes different forms at different stages of the adult life cycle. The intent of this chapter is to identify key issues to be faced by employees and their organizations as careers unfold, with particular emphasis on how companies actually *do* manage careers. The chapter illustrates many key research results, such as the linking of strategic planning to executive development, through company examples involving AT&T, the Japanese career progress study, General Foods, Xerox, Motorola, Federated Department Stores, and Coca-Cola USA. The chapter concludes with a set of recommendations for strengthening the program evaluation process.

Chapter 2.8: "Outplacement" by Donald Sweet

The theme of this chapter is straightforward: outplacement is here to stay and it will assume many forms in the future. It will include attempts to salvage careers in organizations (people considered for alternative jobs if they do not work out on a given job), and it will continue to be a valuable public relations and employee relations tool to ease the trauma and emotion for the individual(s) affected. In the context of termination, one of the most fruitful activities for managers is to learn *how* to terminate employees. Sweet describes clearly the relative responsibilities of HR professionals as well as line managers, presents the advantages and disadvantages of alternative outplacement arrangements, and guides the reader through the mechanics of this process. A final section of the chapter considers the relative costs and benefits of alternative outplacement arrangements.

Literally several years' worth of work has gone into the preparation and production of this volume. Many people in addition to the authors and editors contributed to the final product, and they should be recognized. I am particularly grateful to the ASPA/BNA Advisory Board, comprised of senior HR executives plus the editors of each of the volumes in the HRM series. I found their comments and constructive criticisms to be forward-looking and progressive. To Ron Pilenzo and Cate Bower at ASPA, as well as Mary Miner and Anne Scott at BNA Books, thanks for your patience, understanding, and support. You represent the best of the HRM profession, and your uncompromising standards have deepened my appreciation of the term *human resources*.

Wayne Cascio
Denver, Colorado
February 1989

About the Authors

Chapter 2.1

Societal Trends and Staffing Policies

Wayne F. Cascio (Ph.D., University of Rochester) is a professor of management at the University of Colorado-Denver. He is a Fellow of the American Psychological Association, a Diplomate in industrial/organizational psychology of the American Board of Examiners and Professional Psychology, and a member of the editorial boards of the *Journal of Applied Psychology, Human Performance, Organizational Dynamics* and *Academy of Management Review*. He has consulted with a wide variety of organizations in both the public and private sectors on personnel matters, and periodically testifies as an expert witness in employment discrimination cases. Dr. Cascio is an active researcher, and is the author of four books on HRM.

Raymond F. Zammuto (Ph.D., University of Illinois at Urbana) is associate professor of management at the University of Colorado-Denver. His primary interests are studying how organizations create and respond to changes in their environments, interests reflected in the courses he teaches on organization theory and design and on turnaround management. Zammuto also has been a senior associate at the National Center for Higher Education Management Systems, and he has served on the *Administrative Science Quarterly* and *Academy of Management Journal* editorial boards.

Chapter 2.2

Job Analysis & HR Planning

Ronald C. Page (Ph.D., University of Minnesota) is a consultant at Hay Management Consultants. Prior to this he was a principal consultant with Control Data Business Advisors, a HR consulting company; a consultant with Control Data Corp.; and a supervisor of selection research at the state of Minnesota. At these organizations he has applied and installed computer-assisted job analysis systems to address applications including job evaluation, performance appraisal, selection procedure development, career planning, job classification, organization design, and organization effectiveness. A Senior Professional in Human Resources (SPHR) and a licensed consulting psychologist, he has authored numerous publications and presentations on the topics of job analysis and performance appraisal.

David Van De Voort (M.A., Ohio State University) is salary management practice leader at Wm. M. Mercer-Meidinger-Hansen, Inc., in Columbus, OH. He was formerly compensation and organization planning manager for Nationwide, a family of more than 100 insurance and financial service companies. As a consultant and manager, Van De Voort has contributed to all phases of large scale HR classification, compensation and incentive design, selection systems, and organization effectiveness. He has contributed two chapters to the *Handbook of Job Analysis*. He has made presentations to national, regional, and local professional and industry conferences, including the American Psychological Association, Academy of Management, Military Testing Association, Human Resource Systems Professionals, and others. He is a member of the chartering council of the Association for the Management of Organization Design and is a doctoral candidate in Psychology at Ohio State University.

Chapter 2.3

External and Internal Recruitment

J. Scott Lord (B.A., Kenyon College) is Vice-President of Travis and Co., an executive search firm in Sudbury, MA. His experience in HR management began at Raytheon Co., after which he joined Costello & Co. where he was president of the Contract Services Division. There he provided consulting services in outplacement, recruiting, training, and organizational development for clients such as GTE, Simplex, RCA, Federal Express, TASC, and GE. Lord is a frequent contributor to industry publications as well as articles for HR journals such as *Personnel Administrator* and *Personnel Journal*. He is a member of the Employment Management Association and the Northeast Human Resources Association.

Chapter 2.4

Recruitment Sources

Philip Farish (B.A., University of North Carolina; B.A., University of Oklahoma) is editor of the monthly newsletter *Recruiting Trends* and the weekly *Human Resource Management News*. Both are published by Enterprise Publications, Chicago. He also writes the column "HRM Update" for *Personnel Administrator*, the magazine of the American Society for Personnel Administration. Prior to joining Enterprise Publications he was Director of Research for Howard E. Nyhart Company, an Indianapolis-based firm of consulting actuaries and employee benefits consultants, where he prepared technical newsletters for the staff and communication projects for clients.

Chapter 2.5

Merit-Based Selection: Measuring the Person for the Job

Milton D. Hakel (Ph.D., University of Minnesota) is a professor and chair of the Department of Psychology, University of Houston. Prior to this he was a professor at Ohio State University. Hakel also serves as president of Organizational Research and Development, Inc., and publisher of *Personnel Psychology*. He is the author of the book *Making It Happen: Design Research With Implementation in Mind*, as well as the author of the chapter "Personnel Selection" in the *Annual Review of Psychology 1986*. His research interests include employee selection and promotion, job analysis, assessment centers, compensation, and executive development.

Chapter 2.6

Tools for Staffing Decisions: What Can They Do? What Do They Cost?

Rick Jacobs (Ph.D., University of California-Berkeley) is an associate professor of psychology at Pennsylvania State University. Jacobs' research interests include the role of attitudes on performance, the relationship between experience and job performance, abilities testing for personnel decision making, and craftsmanship. In addition to his responsibilities as a faculty member, he is also a principal in the consulting firm of Landy, Jacobs and Associates of State College, PA. He publishes in and participates as a reviewer for such periodicals as *Journal of Applied Psychology, Personnel Psychology, Human Performance, Applied Psychological Measurement* and *Academy of Management Journal*. He serves on the editorial board of *Test Validity Yearbook*.

Joseph Baratta (M.A., Pennsylvania State University) is a Ph.D. candidate in the department of Psychology at Pennsylvania State University. His research has looked at the role of strategies in decision making among business professionals. During the 1988-89 school year, Baratta is serving as an intern with LIMRA in Hartford, CT.

Chapter 2.7

Internal Placement and Career Management

Marilyn K. Quaintance (Ph.D., George Washington University) is assistant director for personnel research and development, Office of Personnel Management. She has had a diversified career history, working in psychological research associations, a professional association, several organizational consulting firms, and for the federal government. Her responsibilities included conducting multi-purpose job analyses, developing professionally and legally defensible selection procedures (written tests, behaviorally-based interviews, assessment centers), and designing a comprehensive training system to train embassy security officials. Quaintance has written several journal articles and co-authored the book *Taxonomies of Human Performance: The Description of Human Tasks*. She is a national officer of the Society for Industrial and Organizational Psychology and a past president of the Personnel Testing Council/Metropolitan Washington.

Chapter 2.8

Outplacement

Donald H. Sweet (B.A., Gettysburg College) is an independent consultant based in New Bern, NC. Sweet, who is a well-known figure in the outplacement and HR industry, was a consultant for Costello & Co., guiding companies in ensuring successful transitions for senior executives. He has authored several books, among them *A Manager's Guide to Conducting Terminations: Minimizing Emotional Stress and Legal Risks; The Modern Employment Function; Decruitment and Outplacement: A Positive Approach to Terminations;* and *Job Hunting for the College Graduate*, which merited an annual book award from ASPA. Sweet is a three-term president of the Employment Management Association which has named an annual award in his honor to recognize a professional practitioner's outstanding contribution to the industry.

Contents

Preface   v

Introduction   vii

2.1   Societal Trends and Staffing Policies   2-1
Wayne F. Cascio
Raymond F. Zammuto

Overview of the Employment Function   2-2
Factors Affecting Future HR Managers   2-4
Implications for HRM   2-19
Conclusion   2-30

2.2   Job Analysis and HR Planning   2-34
Ronald C. Page
David M. Van De Voort

Job Analysis as a Foundation of HRM   2-35
Job Analysis Methods   2-41
HR Planning   2-58
Conclusion   2-66

2.3   External and Internal Recruitment   2-73
J. Scott Lord

The Recruitment Process   2-74
Managing the Recruitment Function   2-78
External Recruitment Sources   2-84
Internal Recruitment Sources   2-96
Conclusion   2-99

2.4 Recruitment Sources   2-103
Philip Farish

Internal Recruitment Sources   2-103
External Recruitment Sources   2-109
Special Inducements   2-127
Conclusion   2-128

2.5 Merit-Based Selection: Measuring the Person for the Job   2-135
Milton D. Hakel

National Values and Legal Requirements   2-136
Establishing Job-Relatedness   2-137
Methods of Measuring Merit   2-139
Recommendations and Reference Checking   2-149
Choosing Measurement Methods   2-154
Combining Preemployment Information   2-155
Concluding Comments   2-156

2.6 Tools for Staffing Decisions: What Can They Do? What Do They Cost?   2-159
Rick Jacobs
Joseph E. Baratta

Interviews   2-160
Cognitive Abilities Tests   2-170
Personality and Interest Inventories   2-175
Physical Abilities Tests   2-179
Work Samples   2-182
Assessment Centers   2-186
Experience and Past Performance   2-189
Realistic Job Previews   2-192
Summary   2-195

2.7 Internal Placement and Career Management   2-200
Marilyn K. Quaintance

Internal Placement Programs   2-200
Career Management Programs   2-205
Factors Affecting Internal Placement and Career Management Programs   2-208
Examples of Internal Placement Programs   2-215
Corporate Experiences With Career Management Programs   2-220
Conclusion   2-228

2.8 Outplacement   2-236
Donald H. Sweet

What Is Outplacement?   2-236
History   2-236
Factors Promoting Outplacement   2-237
The Value of Outplacement   2-239
The Termination Process   2-242
The Mechanics of Outplacement   2-249
Conclusion   2-256

Author Index   2-263

Subject Index   2-269

2.1

Societal Trends and Staffing Policies

Wayne F. Cascio

Raymond F. Zammuto

Prior to 1960, the employment function was fairly simple. The 1950s were the "happy days"—keep employees happy, make sure everybody gets paid on time, and see that the company newspaper gets printed once a month. The nicest thing about the job then was that nobody paid much attention to it. The personnel department was an island unto itself.

Then things began to change in the 1960s. New civil rights laws came at employers right and left, upstart radicals with long hair and unorthodox ideas, minorities, women, the handicapped—you name it, they all marched through the personnel department, looking for jobs and trying to change the way things had been done for over half a century. To the surprise of many employers, if employees didn't get what they were asking for, they would claim discrimination and have some government enforcement agency come over and do a little arm-twisting on their behalf. Firms found themselves in court losing millions of dollars over standard interview practices, such as asking young women if they planned on getting pregnant in the near future.

As the job changed, so did training programs for the employment function. Some personnel managers went back to school to learn about the law and HRM, to study the research methods and statistics necessary for performing cost-benefit analyses and program evaluations that top management thought important, and to learn more about how business operates.

In the 1970s and early 1980s, the pressure for legal compliance stayed intense, but new problems entered the picture. The economy went sour and foreign competition started to become fierce in the marketplace. "Keeping competitive" and "controlling labor costs" became the watch words to live by. The "Personnel Department" became the "Human Resources Department," and top managers made it clear that they expected HR managers to be able to read the charts and tables in the annual report in order to understand the financial condition of their company.

Just as these trends have changed the employment function, the next generation of HR managers will face new challenges. They will require new ideas for attracting, retaining, and motivating employees and managers at all levels of the corporation, and consequently, they will need new ways of managing the employment function.

This chapter will attempt to identify some key developments in the environment that may affect the way the employment function operates in the coming years. It begins by considering the structure, mission, role, and goals of the employment function, and then examines the issues and what they might mean for these elements of the employment function.

Overview of the Employment Function

The employment function is concerned with the same areas as the entire HRM function, although its narrower mission places different emphasis on these issues. The entire HRM function is concerned with six areas:

- Attraction—the tasks of identifying job requirements, determining the numbers of people and the skills mix necessary to do the jobs, and providing equal opportunity for qualified candidates to be considered for jobs.
- Selection—the process of choosing the people who are best qualified to do the jobs.
- Retention—policies that sustain employees' motivation to perform their jobs effectively and to maintain a safe, healthy work environment.
- Development—programs that preserve and enhance employees' competence in their jobs by improving their knowledge, skills, abilities, and other characteristics.

- Assessment—the observation and evaluation of attitudes relevant to jobs, job performance, and compliance with organizational personnel policies.
- Adjustment—activities, such as retirement counseling and outplacement, that are intended to maintain the required number and skills levels of employees.

Needless to say, these functions can be carried out at the individual, group, or organization level. Some activities, such as recruitment efforts or management development programs, are initiated by the organization; others, like voluntary retirement or safety improvements, are initiated by the individual or group. Moreover, the functional responsibilities are highly interrelated, as Figure 1 illustrates. Together they comprise the HRM system.

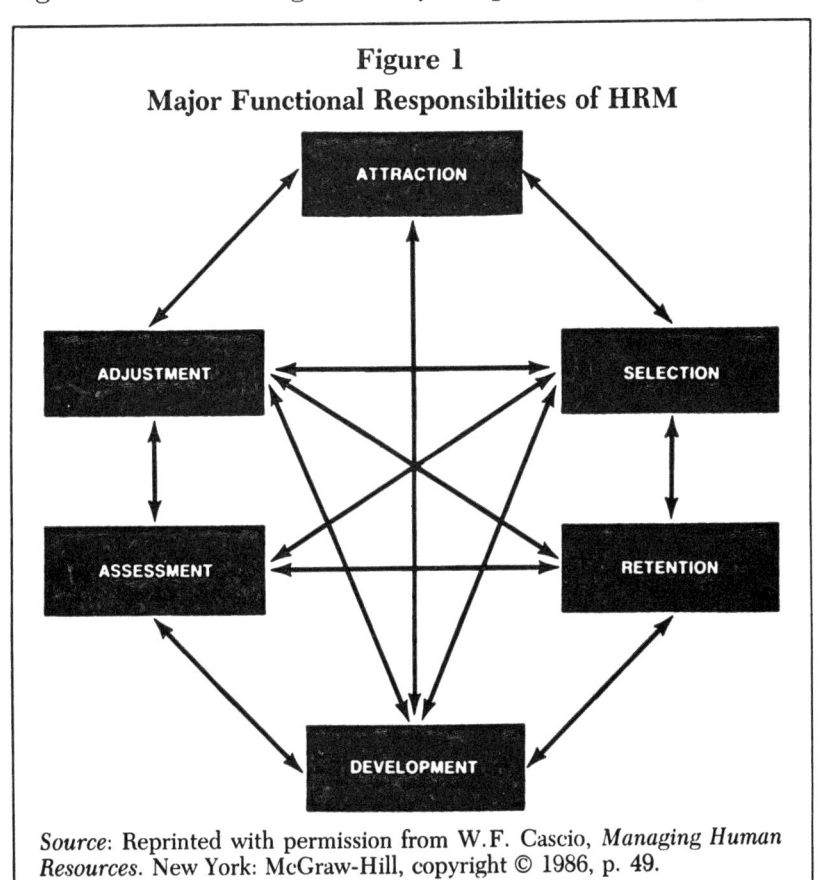

**Figure 1
Major Functional Responsibilities of HRM**

Source: Reprinted with permission from W.F. Cascio, *Managing Human Resources*. New York: McGraw-Hill, copyright © 1986, p. 49.

The employment function is responsible primarily for attraction and selection. Job analysis, HR planning, internal and external recruitment, and selection are key concerns. For the employment function, retention and development are secondary responsibilities relating to the orientation of new employees and the internal placement and career management of current employees. The employment function also is involved secondarily with assessment and adjustment, because it manages outplacement.

In short, the primary job of the employment function is to help line managers manage people effectively. To do that job, managers need to understand how the business works; they need to be able to speak the language of business, that is, dollars; and they need to adapt the strategic mission of the employment function to that of the business. These ideas are shown graphically in Table 1.

Employment managers who can do these things well will be successful; those who cannot will likely wind up in an employment function that is viewed as a "cost center" rather than a "profit center." On the positive side, however, effective employment managers have a tremendous opportunity to contribute to profits, since they are instrumental in selecting and deploying human assets. They can infuse new talent where it will contribute best, and help employees and managers at all levels to maximize their potential.

Factors Affecting Future HR Managers

Just what are the trends that have shaped this role for HR managers, and what are the implications of these trends in the future? The future, as Kenneth Boulding noted, is "irreducibly uncertain" because society evolves from complex, indeterminate dynamics.[1] While uncertain, much of the future's general outline is in place today and it has a number of implications for HR managers.

Perhaps the most important factor that will affect HRM is changing population demographics. Most people have heard about the "aging of the population" that will create a bulge in the older age group over time as the baby boom generation ages. Less obvious are the effects of changing population demographics on other segments of the potential labor force, particularly on the supply of entry-level workers. Moreover, a number of other factors, such as moves to deregulate sectors of American industry, automation, the decreasing dominance of American firms in the global market, and the

Table 1

Functional Responsibilities of Line Managers and HRM Department

Function	Line management responsibility	P/HR department responsibility
Attraction	Provide data for job analyses, descriptions, minimum qualifications, integrate strategic plans with human-resource plans at unit level (e.g., department, division)	Job analysis, human-resource planning, recruitment, affirmative action
Selection	Interview candidates, integrate information collected by P/HR department, make final decisions	Compliance with civil rights laws and regulations, application blanks, written tests, performance tests, interviews, background investigations, reference checks, physical examinations
Retention	Fair treatment of employees, open communication, face-to-face resolution of conflict, promotion of teamwork, respect for the dignity of each individual, pay increases based on merit	Compensation and benefits, labor relations, health and safety, employee services
Development	On-the-job training, job enrichment, coaching, applied motivational strategies, feedback to subordinates	Technical training, management and organization development, career planning, counseling
Assessment	Performance appraisals, morale surveys	Development of performance appraisal systems and morale surveys, personnel research and audits
Adjustment	Discipline, discharge, promotions, transfers	Layoffs, retirement counseling, outplacement services

Source: Reprinted with permission from W.F. Cascio, *Managing Human Resources*. New York: McGraw-Hill, copyright © 1986, p. 50.

increasing penetration of the U.S. market by foreign competitors, will affect managers as well.

The following discussion will review the potential impact of these factors on the labor force and suggest implications for HRM. In addition, the discussion will offer strategies that HR managers might consider implementing now to cope with and to take advantage of these changes.

Population Projections

All the individuals who might be entering the labor force by 2000 have been born. As a result, near-term population projections provide a fairly good picture of what the size and composition of the potential labor force will look like in 15 to 20 years. Beyond that time span, uncertainties crop up because of the need to make assumptions about future birth and mortality rates, migration, and similar variables. Still, projections provide some indication of what the future labor pool might look like.

The U.S. Bureau of the Census "middle series" population projection indicates that the total size of the population will continue to increase, from 228 million in 1980 to about 297 million in 2020, although the rate of growth will decline over time.[2] Overall, the projection shows a 30 percent increase in the size of the total population between 1980 and 2020.

Age Distribution

The distribution of the population by age will change dramatically during the next 30 years, as Figure 2 shows. Baby boomers will pass through middle-age, causing the proportion of the population between ages 45 and 64 to increase from less than 20 percent in 1980 to over 25 percent by 2020. In contrast, the pool of potential new entrants into the labor force, those individuals between ages 16 and 24, will decrease from 17 percent of the total population in 1980 to just over 11 percent by 2020.

Another way of looking at this is to consider that there were about 39 million 16- to 24-year-olds in 1980, and this total number will decline through the next three decades. Overall, a 16 percent decrease in the number of people in the entry pool will occur between 1980 and 2020, while the total population will increase by 30 percent. Assuming that growth in the demand for workers simply

Societal Trends & Staffing Policies 2-7

Figure 2

Population Distribution by Age Group, Ages 16–24 and 45–64

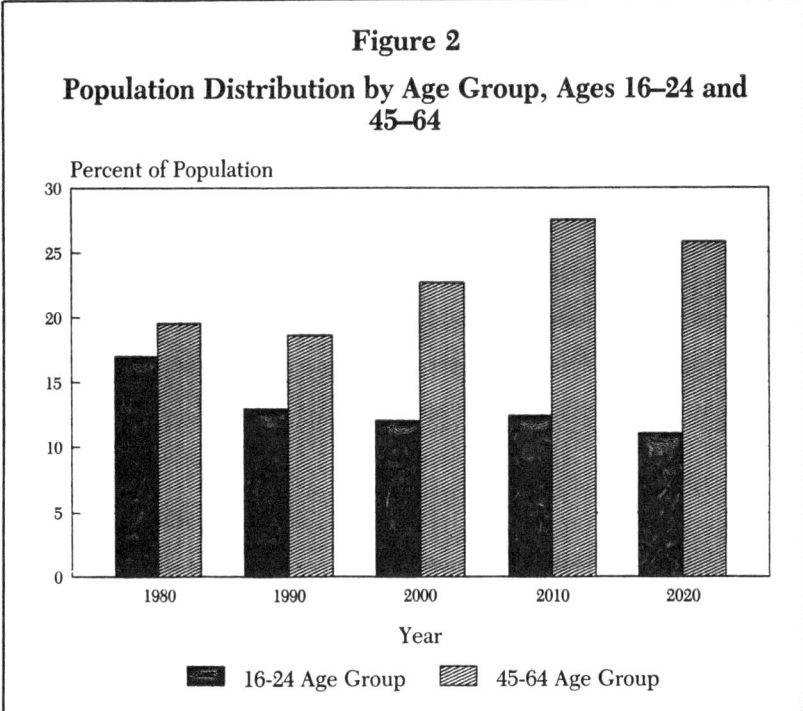

[Bar chart showing Percent of Population for 16-24 Age Group and 45-64 Age Group across years 1980, 1990, 2000, 2010, 2020. Approximate values — 1980: 17%, 19.5%; 1990: 13%, 18.5%; 2000: 12%, 22.5%; 2010: 12.5%, 27.5%; 2020: 11%, 26%.]

Sources: U.S. Bureau of the Census, "Estimates of the Population of the United States, by Age, Sex, and Race: 1980 to 1983," *Current Population Reports*, Series P-25, No. 949, May, 1984; U.S. Bureau of the Census, "Projections of the Population of the United States, by Age, Sex, and Race: 1983 to 2080," *Current Population Reports*, Series P-25, No. 952, May, 1984.

matches total population growth, the projection suggests that there will be comparatively one-third fewer potential entry-level workers in 2020 than there were in 1980.

Ethnic Composition

Other important changes will take place in the ethnic composition of the potential entry pool. As shown in Figure 3, 84 percent of the 16- to 24-year-old population in 1980 was white. This percentage will decrease to 78 percent by 2020 because of higher birth rates for blacks and other nonwhites, and because of immigration. The black proportion of the 16- to 24-year-old group will increase from

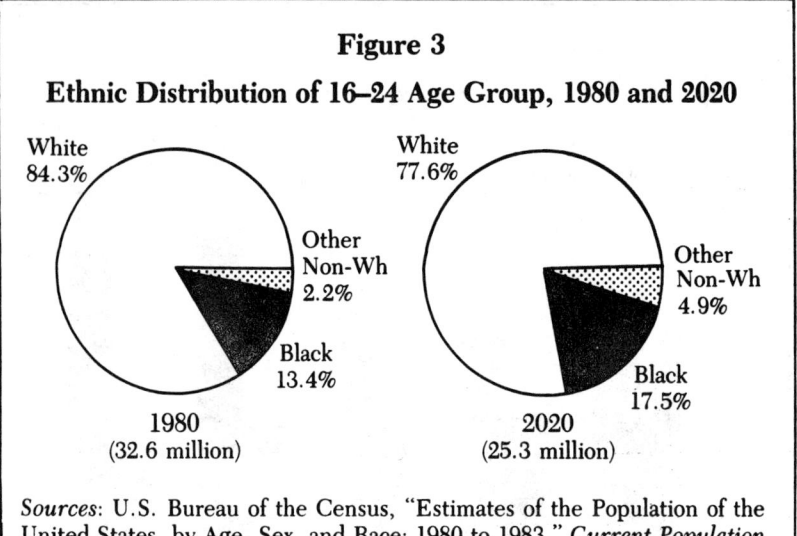

Figure 3
Ethnic Distribution of 16–24 Age Group, 1980 and 2020

1980 (32.6 million)
- White 84.3%
- Other Non-Wh 2.2%
- Black 13.4%

2020 (25.3 million)
- White 77.6%
- Other Non-Wh 4.9%
- Black 17.5%

Sources: U.S. Bureau of the Census, "Estimates of the Population of the United States, by Age, Sex, and Race: 1980 to 1983," *Current Population Reports*, Series P-25, No. 949, May, 1984; U.S. Bureau of the Census, "Projections of the Population of the United States, by Age, Sex, and Race: 1983 to 2080," *Current Population Reports*, Series P-25, No. 952, May, 1984.

13.5 percent in 1980 to an estimated 17.5 percent in 2020, and the proportion of other nonwhites will double from 2.3 percent in 1980 to 4.9 percent in 2020.

These population proportions reflect an absolute decrease in the number of white 18- to 24-year-olds, from about 33 million in 1980 to 25 million in 2020. Blacks in this age group will decrease from 5 million in 1980 to a low of 4.5 million in 1995, then increase to about 6 million in 2020. Other nonwhites in this age group will increase steadily from 870,000 in 1980 to about 1.6 million in 2020. In short, a larger proportion of the smaller pool of entry-level individuals in the future will be minorities.

Labor Force Participation Rates

In order to translate population projections into labor force estimates, civilian labor force participation rates have to be taken into account. While there are no long-term projections of future labor force participation rates, current trends are useful in speculating about the shape of the future.

Gender Composition

From 1960 to 1980, the civilian labor force participation rate for the whole population increased from 59 percent to 64 percent, largely because of the number of women entering the labor force during this period. Labor force participation for women increased from about 38 percent to 51.5 percent between 1960 and 1980, but for men, it declined from 83 percent to 77 percent. By 1995, total labor force participation should reach 66.5 percent, and the proportion of women will continue to grow.[3]

Age Distribution

Examining labor force participation rates by age and sex provides a more refined view of the composition of the labor force. The participation rates for 1960, 1970, and 1980, categorized by men and women for the entry pool and for workers between ages 45 and 69, are presented in Figures 4 and 5. Figure 4 shows a small increase in labor force participation for men ages 16 to 19, and a slightly larger decline in participation of men ages 20 to 24. In contrast, Figure 5 shows a sizable increase in participation for women ages 16 to 19, and a smaller increase in participation by women ages 20 to 24. Overall, labor force participation for 16- to 19-year-olds rose from 47.5 percent in 1960 to 56.7 percent in 1980, and for people ages 20 to 24, it rose from 65.2 percent in 1960 to 77.2 percent in 1980. These increases are expected to continue through 1995, helping to offset the small numbers of 16- to 24-year-olds.

A similar pattern is shown for the older age groups. Labor force participation for males ages 45 to 54 decreased slightly between 1960 and 1980, but decreased substantially for older males. In contrast, the participation rate for women ages 45 to 59 increased between 1960 and 1980. Participation remained relatively stable for older women, increasing slightly for women ages 60 to 64, and decreasing slightly for women ages 65 to 70. Overall, the figures show that participation by older men in the labor force decreased between 1960 and 1980 while increasing for women. Total labor force participation for older individuals should continue to decrease through 1995. This trend is partly due to the higher participation of younger workers and the increased number of 25- to 54-year-olds.

Changes in the labor force participation rates reflect changes in American society. For example, the increased rates for women

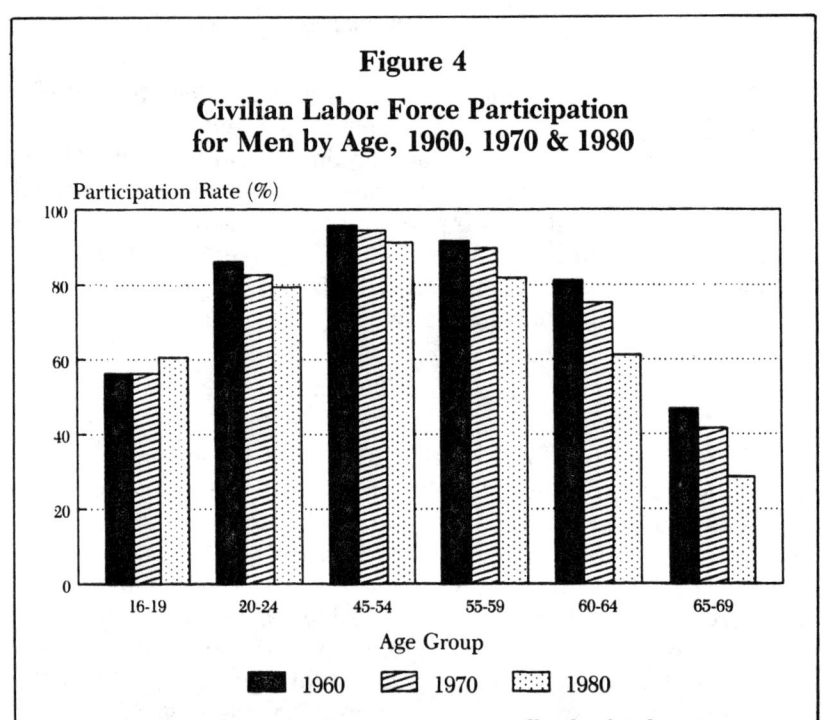

Figure 4
Civilian Labor Force Participation for Men by Age, 1960, 1970 & 1980

Sources: U.S. Bureau of Labor Statistics, *Handbook of Labor Statistics*, Bulletin #2217, June, 1985; U.S. Congressional Budget Office, *Work and Retirement: Options for Continued Employment of Older Workers*, July, 1982.

reflect their changing role in American society, the increase in single-person households, and increasing numbers of multiple earners in a family. Conversely, the decreased participation of white males in the economy reflects the effect of corporate policies toward retirement and features of private pension plans and Social Security that promote early retirement—notwithstanding the Age Discrimination Act and its ban on mandatory retirement—as well as changes in social values concerning work.

Post-1995 Trends

These projections indicate that little net change will take place over the next decade in the relative supply of labor.[4] No severe labor shortages are likely in the near term, nor is there a great likelihood that demand will increase for workers over age 65. However, spec-

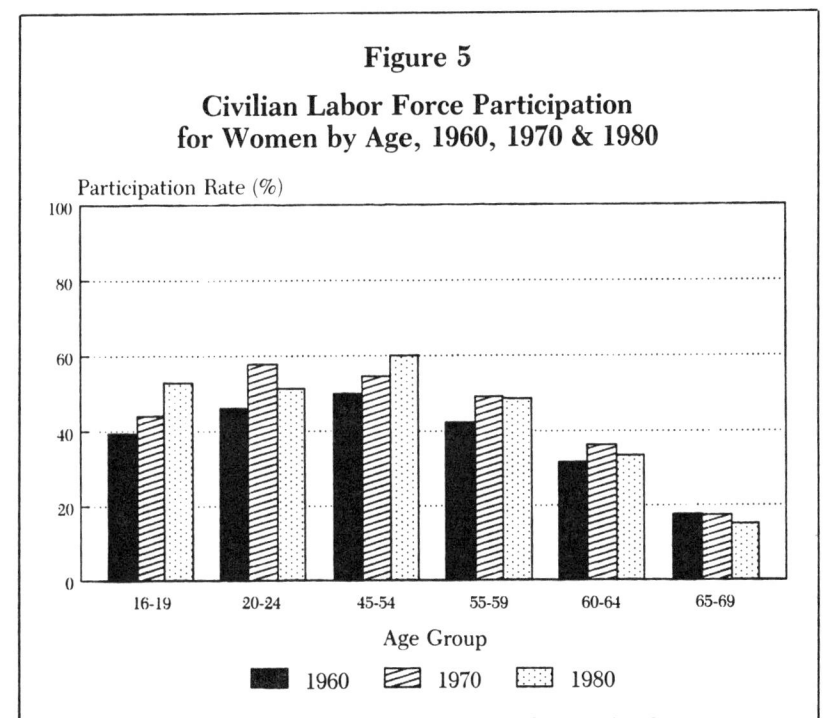

> **Figure 5**
>
> **Civilian Labor Force Participation for Women by Age, 1960, 1970 & 1980**
>
> [Bar chart showing participation rates (%) by age group 16-19, 20-24, 45-54, 55-59, 60-64, 65-69 for years 1960, 1970, 1980]
>
> *Sources*: U.S. Bureau of Labor Statistics, *Handbook of Labor Statistics*, Bulletin #2217, June, 1985; U.S. Congressional Budget Office, *Work and Retirement: Options for Continued Employment of Older Workers*, July, 1982.

ulating beyond 2000 is somewhat more hazardous. If changes in the age distribution continue into the future in line with the population projections, three observations can be made:

- Early in the 21st century, baby-boomers will reach age 55 and begin to pass through their working prime.

- The size of the cohort immediately following the baby-boomers is smaller than the one it will replace.

- Population projections indicate that the size of the 16- to 24-year-old cohort will not increase significantly.

These factors suggest that the labor force outflow is likely to exceed the inflow of new workers after 2000. Therefore, labor force shortages could appear in the first decades of the 21st century, even though shortages are not likely to arise in the near term.

Automation

One factor that may forestall the impact of changes in the labor force on industry is automation. Automation has been touted as a way to increase industrial productivity, flexibility, and product quality. It also is seen as the path to regain a competitive edge in global competition and decrease import penetration into American markets. Finally, automation offers the promise of making manufacturing less labor intensive, thus reducing the need for workers in the future.

From 1980 to 1986, investment in automation doubled to $18.1 billion, and experts project another doubling between 1985 and 1990.[5] Computer-aided design, engineering, and manufacturing already have found applications in many industries, shortening lead times for design and production tooling. Robots are used increasingly to automate tedious or dangerous jobs, such as welding and painting in the auto industry. Moreover, it now appears that computer-integrated manufacturing systems, which automate and link all functions of the production process, are technologically feasible and are now being used on a small scale worldwide. While the cost of such systems is high, the potential benefits are considerable in terms of design and production flexibility.

But the use of automation as a solution to potential manpower shortages poses three problems. These limitations become apparent when the impact of automation is examined in light of projected changes in the age distribution, training levels, and ethnic composition of the work force.

Impact of Automation on Age Groups

Much of the labor savings from automation is likely to affect middle management since automation integrates information-processing as well as production. Most middle managers are ages 25 to 54, the age group that will experience the largest increases through 2020. As a result, automation will likely have only marginal impact on the demand for entry-level workers.

Automation and Educational Trends

Another limitation concerns the highly trained workers needed to design and operate automated systems. These workers could very well be scarcer in 2020 than they are today. As the size of the entry cohort decreases, competition among organizations for new recruits will increase. One possible effect of this competition is higher wage levels for entry-level workers.

The entry-level cohort also is the pool from which colleges and universities recruit the majority of their students. Higher entry-level wages could mean that colleges and universities will have to compete with industry for individuals in this age group. Some signs indicate that this competition already is occurring. For example, the fast food industry, which depends heavily on a supply of young workers, has experienced difficulty recruiting enough young persons to meet its needs. One solution under consideration is raising wages to attract older workers. But increased wages would likely have the effect of attracting younger workers as well. Projections of increased labor force participation for younger age groups indicate that this trend may have started already.

If entry-level wages rise and the cost of a college education continues to increase at the rate it has for the past decade, the opportunity costs of college attendance will increase. If opportunity costs increase, employment will become a more attractive alternative to college enrollment. Therefore, increased competition for entry-level workers may decrease the pool of college-educated, highly trained workers needed to automate American industry. This possibility suggests that while a general labor force shortage does not seem likely in the near term, there could very well be a shortage in the supply of highly trained workers.

Automation and Ethnic Composition of the Work Force

Moreover, changes in the ethnic composition of the 16- to 24-year-old cohort could also affect the educational attainment of this age group. Figure 6 shows the proportion of individuals in the civilian labor force between 1959 and 1984 who have completed four or more years of college. Over this 25-year period, the proportion of college graduates in the labor force doubled, from about 10 percent to 21 percent. The figure also shows an uneven distribution of college-educated members of the labor force when sex and ethnicity are considered. White males historically have been the most educated segment of the labor force, with white females next while blacks and Hispanics trail far behind. While the proportion of college-educated black men and women in the labor force has increased almost three fold over the 25-year period, only 11 percent of black men and 13 percent of black women in the labor force had

Figure 6
Percent Civilian Labor Force With Four or More Years College

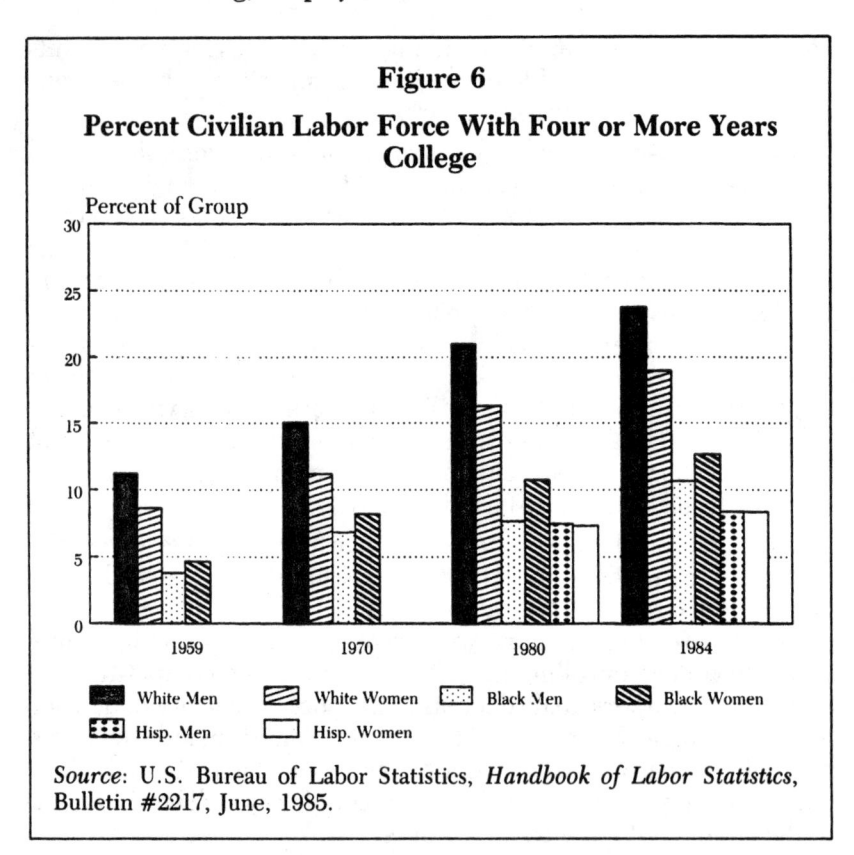

[Bar chart showing Percent of Group (0-30) for years 1959, 1970, 1980, 1984, with bars for White Men, White Women, Black Men, Black Women, Hisp. Men, Hisp. Women]

Source: U.S. Bureau of Labor Statistics, *Handbook of Labor Statistics*, Bulletin #2217, June, 1985.

completed college by 1984. The proportion of Hispanics with four or more years of college was lower: 8 percent both for men and for women in 1984.

Given that the ethnic composition of the 16- to 24-year-old group is shifting to a higher percentage of minorities, these educational differences are cause for concern. Colleges and universities generally have not been successful in recruiting minority students,[6] and they have found it difficult to retain the minority students they have recruited. The smaller pool of entry-level workers and the potential for increased competition with industry means that unless colleges and universities do a better job of recruiting and retaining minorities, the supply of highly trained, entry-level workers may not keep pace with future demand. And the more efforts industry makes to recruit workers from the declining entry-level pool, the more likely the possibility that the number of highly trained, entry-level workers will decrease.

The Shift From Manufacturing to Service Industries

The third factor that may decrease the impact of automation on a potential shortage of entry-level workers is the long-term shift in the economy from manufacturing to service industries. Manufacturing is the most likely economic sector to benefit from automation. But manufacturing's share of the employment sector has decreased from 33.7 percent in 1950 to 20.5 percent in 1983.[7] As a result of this erosion of manufacturing's position within the economy, automation may make manufacturing more productive and flexible, but it is not likely to have a major impact on the availability of entry-level workers. In fact, since most service industries are relatively labor intensive and less amenable to automation, the recruitment of entry-level workers into service jobs, in particular, may be a major source of competition with colleges and universities for enrollments. As noted above, a reduced number of college graduates could hamper manufacturing's efforts to recruit highly trained workers to automate production.

Moreover, the decline in manufacturing employment could accelerate. In response to growing foreign competition, many U.S. manufacturers have moved production operations off-shore to take advantage of lower wage rates in other countries. Hence, many firms are disaggregating the production process, selling off capacity, and contracting with suppliers, many of which are overseas, for goods and services they had produced internally. This arrangement is the opposite of past industry trends, where manufacturers vertically integrated to assure a steady supply of materials and parts for production, and to achieve economies of scale. Whether this trend continues is dependent on many complex factors: international political stability, U.S. foreign policy, domestic industrial policy, and the relative values of national currencies. The rapid devaluation of the U.S. dollar during 1987, for instance, slowed the outflow of manufacturing facilities. Some manufacturers have, in fact, brought production back to the United States because of shrinking wage differentials, and because of the difficulties of coordinating operations across national boundaries.

A new organizational form that reflects this trend toward disaggregation is appearing with greater frequency in industry.[8] This new form, labelled the "dynamic network," is a temporary collection of firms working together to produce a product through each firm specializing in one part of the production process. For example, one firm might specialize in the design of a product, another in its manufacture, and yet another in marketing the finished good. In the typical dynamic network, the design, marketing, and coordinating functions have been handled by firms within the United States, while overseas firms complete the production.

The net effect of dynamic networks is likely to hasten the erosion of manufacturing's overall share of employment in the economy. Continuation of this trend depends on many uncertain factors, such as the value of the dollar, the impact of protectionist legislation and import barriers, and the extent to which foreign competitors automate as well.

Deregulation and Decentralization

Another factor likely to affect HRM is the deregulation of many industries, such as air transportation, banking, and telecommunications. Deregulation has made the markets of firms in affected industries less certain because of increased competition. A common organizational response to uncertain markets is to decentralize, which moves decision-making authority downward to lower organizational levels. This move allows an organization to respond more quickly to changing market conditions, and assures that decisions are made by individuals who are closer to and have better information about the situation requiring a decision.

Impact on Staffing Needs

The most common reason that decentralization occurs in industries undergoing deregulation is cutbacks in management. For example, the breakup of AT&T was accompanied by a massive restructuring of the regional phone companies, which consisted largely of shrinking headquarters staffs. Such moves reduce the levels of management, which results in faster decision making at lower levels in the organization.[9]

A more subtle form of decentralization which is becoming common in many industries is worker involvement, or quality of work life, programs. Techniques such as job redesign, job enrichment, quality circles, and participative management result in decentralization because they place more decision-making power at lower levels in the organization. Production-related decisions formerly made at a supervisory level are placed directly in the hands of line workers. The resulting reduction in the levels of management should in turn increase the speed and quality of decisions.

As with automation, decentralization reduces the number of personnel needed by an organization. But these reductions will occur primarily in the ranks of middle managers, who are drawn from the 25 to 54 age group. Like automation, decentralization has the potential to reduce staffing needs, but it is unlikely to have much impact on the demand for entry-level workers, where shortages of personnel are most likely.

Effect of Older Work Force

An important factor that will affect the success of decentralization in improving the quality and speed of decision making is the aging of the work force itself. A major intent of decentralization is to improve the ability of organizations to innovate by giving individuals closest to the situation the authority to make decisions. If an organization has an ample inflow of new workers, decentralization can make an organization more adaptive because new workers bring new ideas with them. In other words,

> innovation and adaptation require the importation of new ideas into the organization. This introduction of new perspectives and new concepts is facilitated by the introduction of new people not bound by past commitments within the social structure, not previously subjected to the organization's perspective and information, and not subject to the same set of social expectations and role demands . . . [As a result,] organizations characterized by more senior demographic distributions may, other things equal, be less capable of change, innovation, and adaptation.[10]

This need for new workers suggests that the aging of the work force in itself may have a dampening effect on innovation in American industry, since long job tenure produces stability that is not conducive to change:

> An organization characterized by long-tenured persons is less likely to change policies, and this stability in the organization's policies and procedures encourages stability in employment within the organization, which in turn helps ensure a continued stability in organizational practices and so forth. One of the reasons why organizations are so difficult to change may be precisely this feedback process in which organizations that are stable produce processes that facilitate continued stability.[11]

One piece of evidence supporting this argument is the distribution of the median tenure of male workers for a number of industries, which is presented in Table 2. For example, a strong inverse correlation appears between the median years on the job in an industry and the industry's reputation for innovativeness and adaptability. Service industries with long-tenured employees, such as railroads and the postal service, are known for a seeming inability to adapt as their environments change. In manufacturing, the domestic market shares of the automotive, chemicals, mining, and electrical machinery industries have been severely eroded in recent years by intense foreign competition. These industries have the highest median level of years on the job for male workers. In contrast, other industries that have a history of adapting to rapid changes in their environments, such as wholesale and retail trade and entertainment, have low median job tenure. In short, the aging of the work force may hamper American industry's ability to innovate, to adapt to changing circumstances, and to implement

Table 2

Median Years on Job by Industry for Male Workers

Industry	Median Years on Job
Railroads and railway express	19.6
Agriculture	11.5
Postal service	10.3
Federal public administration	7.6
Automobile manufacturing	7.0
Chemical and allied products manufacturing	6.8
Mining	6.4
Electrical machinery manufacturing	5.7
Communications	5.2
Instrument manufacturing	5.1
Food and kindred products manufacturing	5.1
Finance, insurance, and real estate	4.0
Rubber and plastics manufacturing	4.0
Medical and other health services	2.8
Construction	2.7
Wholesale and retail trade	2.6
Entertainment and recreation services	1.9

Source: Reprinted with permission from J. Pfeffer, "Some Consequences of Organizational Demography," in S.B. Kiesler, et al. (eds.), *Aging: Social Change*. New York: Academic Press, copyright © 1981, p. 305.

decentralization, unless firms can maintain an inflow of new employees as the entry-level cohort shrinks.

Summary

The discussion up to this point can be summarized as follows:

- The population growth through the next few decades will be accompanied by major shifts in the population's age distribution and in the ethnic composition of younger groups.
- The proportion and number of younger workers will decrease while the number and proportion of workers over age 25 will increase significantly.
- In the short run, no major labor shortages are expected for entry-level workers because increased labor force participation rates for individuals ages 16 to 24, and the larger number of workers ages 25 to 54, will likely offset the decline.
- Shortages may occur for certain types of workers, primarily highly trained individuals with current technological skills, because of competition between industry and higher education for individuals in the entry-level age group.
- Shortages of highly trained workers could stymie the ability of manufacturing to automate, which would hamper efforts to improve industrial flexibility and productivity and to blunt the effects of foreign competition.
- The aging of the labor force may also reduce the ability of organizations to adapt to changing markets by decreasing the flow of new ideas into those organizations.

Implications for HRM

The previous discussion makes it clear that aging of the population is likely to have many impacts on American industry which in turn will have many ramifications for the practice of HRM. The remainder of this chapter will explore a number of those implications, using the framework of HRM described in Figure 1.

Attraction

By the year 2020, the traditional entry-level pool will comprise comparatively one-third fewer individuals than it did in 1980, and more of these individuals will be female and nonwhite. These changes have several important implications with respect to the attraction of new workers.

Minority Recruitment

One likely consequence will be a lesser need for government involvement in affirmative action to hire and promote members of disadvantaged and protected groups—those that have historically been the victims of illegal discrimination. This outcome seems likely since members of those groups will constitute progressively larger proportions of the work force in most firms as companies face growing economic pressure to find and retain top talent from the shrinking entry-level pool. Progressive firms will take steps now, if they haven't already, to build and strengthen ties with the female and minority populations. As a senior vice president at Travelers Corporation noted:

> It's the right thing to do economically. In 1990 more of the work force is going to be minorities—Hispanics, blacks—and women. The companies that started building those bridges back in the 1970s will be all right. Those that didn't won't.[12]

In many cases, recruiting minority workers may not be easy. A series of studies has found that the majority of black youths are serious about seeking jobs. They want the same kinds of jobs at the same wages that other young persons receive, but they have trouble in getting those jobs. Indeed, the major difference between unemployed black and white youths is that blacks face greater difficulties in obtaining work, while their ability to hold a job is comparable to whites.[13] In short, firms that are serious about attracting minority workers must seek new recruitment methods to reach these populations.

Impact of Single-Parent and Two-Earner Households

Another consequence results from the increase in single-parent heads of households and two-paycheck families in the work force. This trend will increase pressure for employer-sponsored child care, flexible work schedules, and flexible benefits options to ensure employee equity.

While these features may attract potential employees and help to retain current employees, they may have little effect on productivity. For example, claims that employer-sponsored child care reduces absenteeism or tardiness, or that it increases productivity or job satisfaction, are not supported by well-controlled research.[14] Likewise, flexible work schedules have been shown to improve work-group and superior-subordinate relations and decrease absenteeism,[15] but their impact on productivity has been mixed. In general, flexible work schedules improve productivity only when work group members must share physical resources, such as a computer system.[16]

Effect of Organizational Restructuring

A final consequence stems from the pace of changes in organizations and the rapidly evolving new organizational structures stimulated by the shifts toward deregulation, decentralization and dynamic networks. As a result, the identification and specification of job requirements is becoming a more important aspect of attraction. Businesses need clearer links between their strategic and tactical objectives, and HR plans must parallel and promote these strategic objectives. HR planning has clear and direct links to attraction and selection, since job analysis serves as the foundation for all personnel decisions. Job analysis provides a statement of the kind of work to be done, the skills needed, and the training required of the individual job holder. It only makes sense to recruit and select individuals after job analysis information has been specified—information about task requirements and information about people requirements.

Selection

A major theme of the 1986 World Congress on Human Resource Management focused on the changing role of the HR manager, a role that will continue to evolve in the face of shrinking boundaries, merging cultures, conflicting government regulations, and increased international trade. HR managers' major responsibilities will be to select, to prioritize, and to allocate resources. As a result, the impact on employment of new technology to automate production will become a key consideration for HR managers.

Effect of Automation

Fortunately, automation has not had as great an impact on employment as had been predicted, nor has it caused massive replacement of human labor by machines. Through the 1990s, experts predict that such replacement will be gradual, rather than sudden.[17] For example, General Motors' 1986 announcement of plans to close four U.S. assembly plants affected 30,000 workers. However, the company also identified a three-year time horizon, which gave workers until 1989 to retrain for new jobs. As one union leader noted:

> The real issue is whether the lack of technological change destroys even more jobs. . . . Today's trade unions accept technological change, but equally and properly require that the introduction of change be planned and provide for full consultation with workers and their unions at all stages.[18]

The garment industry provides another example of the impact of new technology on employment. In the United States, scientists have now developed a machine that can do what no machine has been able to do before: automatically construct the sleeves for a coat and sew them onto the body of the jacket. In Japan, government planners foresee bolts of fabric entering one end of a robot assembly line and emerging at the other end as finished business suits—all done with a minimum of human assistance. And in Europe, companies are developing space-age machinery, such as lasers and ultra-high pressure water jets to cut fabric to computer-controlled patterns.[19] The garment industry is one of the most labor-intensive in the world, but unions and management believe that automation must happen in order to prevent further losses of jobs to Hong Kong, China, South Korea, and other low-cost sources of labor. In the United States, the Amalgamated Clothing and Textile Workers Union saw its membership drop a full 20 percent, from 450,000 in 1980 to 360,000 in 1986. Instead of fearing further job loss from automation, one union spokesman said: "If we don't go this route, the jobs will be wiped out. It'll save what is left of a much smaller industry."[20]

This example gives us a clear lesson to learn: Automation does not cause unemployment as much as it changes the allocation of the work force. This lesson suggests an important shift in the goal of the employment function, which currently focuses on selecting employees who have the skills to perform a single job. Instead, the real challenge will be to use selection tools that will identify persons who have the intellectual ability and personal flexibility to learn continually and to change jobs, even functional specialties, if necessary. This kind of proactive approach can contribute directly to the competitive advantage of an organization.

Trend Toward Temporary Workers

A final issue related to selection decisions is the use of temporary workers—so-called "employee leasing." Employee leasing also may provide a way to lessen the impact of potential shortages of highly skilled workers in the future. The number of employees working under leasing arrangements has grown from 300,000 per month in 1978 to almost 800,000 per month in 1986, a trend that is expected to increase whether the economy contracts or expands.[21] For example, First Chicago Corp., a bank holding company, contracts out the architectural, design, and property-management work that its staff once handled. Polly Bergen Jewelry, Inc. contracts for temporary bookkeepers to help relieve pressure on regular staff. Hospitals all over the country now meet extra staffing needs by hiring registered nurses on a day-to-day basis.

The use of temporary workers will affect selection criteria for full-time employees. Organizations that regularly use a large number of temporary workers, and hence hire fewer full-time workers, will need those full-time workers to possess well-developed communication and management skills. Permanent employees will need communication skills to specify the work to be done, and to set clear standards of performance. They will need well-developed management skills in order to direct the temporaries, to provide quality control, and to solve problems through active-listening. All of this involves a decentralization of authority and responsibility down to lower levels. Needless to say, any such strategic decisions should be conscious rather than haphazard, and they should mesh with general business strategy.

Retention

A new phenomenon in business, albeit a small-scale one is the networked corporation. This type of corporation maintains a small core staff of full-time employees and farms out manufacturing and other jobs to contract workers and to organizations that have a cadre of mobile workers with flexible work schedules. These workers are teleworkers or telecommuters. Telework is distinguished from telecommuting as work done at a remote site that does not necessarily involve or require computer equipment; for example, knitting wool sweaters at home by an employee of a sweater company.[22]

Not surprisingly, a number of myths surround this kind of work. One prevalent misconception is that telecommuting only involves low-skill jobs that appeal to people who can't leave their homes. In fact, telecommuting may appeal more to higher-skilled workers, who, for whatever reason, prefer to work at home. The personal computer has created an explosion of telecommuting opportunities, for as more jobs depend on personal computers, the responsibilities lend themselves to mobile working conditions.

Benefits to the employer include improved recruiting and retention of competent people, reduced costs for office space, and increased productivity. However, there are potential problems as well. As one observer has pointed out, "Telecommuting tends to be exploitive if there are no guarantees, especially for clerical workers, because it puts more power and information in the hands of management."[23]

Enhancing Retention of Telecommuters

Planning and monitoring is the key to successful use of telecommuters. Although telecommuters are often classified as independent contractors and moved on and off the payroll as work permits, firms that have implemented telecommuting successfully keep such employees on the payroll to maintain a sense of loyalty. Obviously, however, this strategy increases labor costs, thus offsetting some of the cost savings associated with the use of telecommuters.

Isolation from co-workers is often raised as another potential disadvantage of telecommuting. One company, Pacific Bell, has found ways to avoid this problem.[24] The telecommuting program is voluntary, and includes a mandatory screening process and training program to ensure that employees choosing to telecommute will be comfortable in the new work environment. To facilitate communication, managers also receive training on how to supervise remote workers, and Pacific Bell has a private voice mail system that all employees, including telecommuters, use. Telecommuters must report to the office at least once a week to meet with co-workers, to check mail, and to do other tasks that require a physical presence in the office. This example is typical of other companies' programs as well, for the majority of telecommuters do not work at home full time. "Mix and match" programs that let workers and managers prearrange a schedule of days spent at home and in the office are the most common and popular telecommuting arrangements.

Telecommuting is not for everyone. Research indicates that about 15 percent of the U.S. work force is favorably disposed to working alone or independently.[25] Other potential telecommuters include 10 million physically handicapped people, as well as workers who want to live in certain geographic locations. Still, the number of firms with formal telecommuting programs is very small, and experts predict that no more than 5 percent of the work force will be telecommuting by 1995.[26]

Nonetheless, one thing is certain: Telecommuting can only succeed through careful planning, screening, training of workers and their supervisors, and monitoring. If telework or telecommuting opportunities present themselves, HR managers should not make the programs mandatory and they should be flexible in their approach.

Applying Communications Technology to HRM

Executives have long complained that poor coordination among far-flung operations hurts productivity. However, as the rise of two-career marriages makes many professionals more reluctant to relocate, companies are trying harder to link offices electronically rather than to uproot employees.

So far, most efforts have been directed at formal, not informal communications. Offices can swap electronic mail, using computers or facsimile machines, and executives in different cities can hold teleconferences. Xerox Corp. is one company that is trying to enhance informal as well as formal communications among geographically separate offices. Through its "linked-office" experiment, the firm is studying the sociology and technology of office communications. All-day video and audio connections at Xerox offices in Palo Alto, California and Portland, Oregon permit the offices to relate casually as well as formally. For example, a scientist in Portland recently strolled into a common area, noticed an engineer in Palo Alto, and shouted a quick question about a technical camera problem. People in both cities regularly eat lunch on camera, chatting with one another on the screens. By examining life in this environment, Xerox hopes to learn how to combine the links into one super work station.[27]

Developments like the networked corporation are exciting, but they also suggest changes in the design of jobs and job requirements. For example, a manager's span of control may increase vastly as a result of the new organizational arrangements. Job analysis and selection systems must remain current in order to ensure that the kinds of people who will be successful in these environments can be identified and retained.

Accommodating the Shift to Service Jobs

What impact the shift to a service economy will have on retention depends on whether the service economy generates high-quality or low-quality jobs. Service jobs generally include wholesale and retail trade, finance and insurance, personal and business services, transportation, public utilities, education, health care, and government. The popular image of the service industry may be the fast-food restaurant, but the key growth fields actually have been finance and business-related professional services. This diverse group includes the securities markets, banking, advertising, management consulting, data processing, temporary personnel, building maintenance, the law, and accounting.[28]

The major shift has been toward better jobs with better pay and better prospects for personal development. While the fields are diverse, they do have several things in common. Jobs in these fields require education and training, usually at the college or technical institute level, plus continuing study. They also provide broad latitude for creativity, independent thought and action, career advancement potential, and opportunities for greater recognition.

The shift toward these kinds of jobs is not without problems. Workers need to start with fundamental literacy, number and communication skills, and the ability to learn, to reason, to draw conclusions, to express ideas, and to exercise judgment. These skills are, and will continue to be, key predictors of success in the kinds of jobs created as the service sector continues to expand. It would be a mistake not to consider them carefully in almost all staffing decisions.

Handling Corporate Reorganizations

Throughout the 1980s, the rate of mergers, acquisitions, and plant closings has been spectacular. Over half the firms on the *Fortune* list of the 1,000 largest U.S. corporations underwent some form of significant reorganization between 1980 and 1987.[29] Financial considerations are the primary motivation for these activities, but 82 percent of the executives in one survey ranked people problems as more important to the long-term success of a merger than financial considerations.[30] Indeed the people issues create complex, wrenching personnel problems for the individuals and organizations involved.

Plant closings pose even more serious problems because many of the affected workers have skills that do not transfer readily to other jobs. In an era of rapid industrial change, serious gaps in coverage have hampered the retraining of workers for newly created jobs. According to the U.S. Department of Labor, from 1977 to 1984, 1.2 million workers received basic trade readjustment benefits in the form of payments to workers in distressed industries. Only 70,000 of those workers began retraining, and of the 28,000 who completed their courses, fewer than 4,500 found jobs that used their new skills.[31]

The "Make" vs. "Buy" Debate. What does this mean for the employment function? It creates options. As an example, consider the classic "make versus buy" question. In firms that choose to "buy" workers who can contribute to productivity immediately, selection will play an important role. In firms that "make" workers, selection will focus on candidates' basic aptitudes and desire to work, but training will play a greater role in the development of specific skills. If the number of qualified applicants for a group of jobs exceeds the number of vacancies, then the best route is to emphasize "buying" talent. On the other hand, firms facing shortages of qualified talent might consider "making" workers qualified. If either strategy is feasible, the best decision is to "buy" rather than to "make," since the higher caliber workers selected can be retrained faster if necessary, and they can contribute immediately.

Regardless of the strategy chosen, selection decisions should focus on finding workers with the kinds of basic knowledge and skills noted earlier—fundamental literacy, number and communication skills, and the like. Change, growth, and development are facts of organizational life today. Learning and relearning, training and retraining, are lifelong affairs. As a result, staffing policies and staffing decisions should emphasize:

- candidates' qualifications for current jobs
- ability to develop new job competencies over time
- personal flexibility to adapt to changes in management style or organizational culture

Assessment and Adjustment

Foreign competition, deregulation, technological change, and disinflation have forced managements in many organizations to cut costs. Budget trimming often has been done by downsizing the work force, either through voluntary resignations, early retirement programs, or layoffs.[32] Firms that have tried to maintain "business as usual," even in the face of economic adversity, often have not survived.

Consider People Express airline, for example.[33] From its inception, the company sought to become a counterculture airline, and its philosophy reflected that orientation: minimal bureaucracy, group organization of workers, rotation of staff through a variety of jobs, salaries tied in large part to company profits, and "manager" titles for everyone. Each operating group of 250 people decided how it would carry out its assigned tasks. Employees moved from job to job, sometimes daily. Flight attendants often would track lost bags; pilots would take tickets or run computer operations. And everyone had to deal with customers.

The company doggedly resisted a more formal management structure with performance standards and tighter controls, even as its financial condition deteriorated. This resistance compounded the problems, because the committee-style decision making meant no single individual could be held accountable for a given problem. Academics, management consultants, and operating executives alike generally agree that any given management style or organization structure may not be appropriate for an organization throughout its lifetime. Despite the appearance of great flexibility among its employees, People Express was incapable of changing its management style to fit economic realities. This rigidity contributed in large part to its downfall.

The lesson for employment managers is clear. Despite the inportance of selecting employees whose style and temperament "fit" the organization's culture, excessively rigid styles or cultures limit an organization's ability to adapt. And firms must adapt, given the current pace of change, if they are to survive. HR managers should avoid hiring people whose past behavior indicates that they are unable to adapt.

Managing the Human Side of Downsizing

Downsizing the work force is a trend in many companies, even among those who traditionally have had full employment policies.

From 1985 to mid-1986, over 300 companies in a broad range of industries slimmed down. Among them: Apple Computer, Bank of America, CBS, DuPont, Ford, Kodak, Exxon, Monsanto, and Merck.[34] There is little question that downsizing can cut short-term costs sharply, and that powerful economic forces have compelled companies to do so.

But these cutbacks no doubt came at high cost in employee loyalty. Some firms handled the cutbacks adroitly through outplacement services and generous severance packages. For example, Exxon offered retirement planning, financial counseling for those ineligible for retirement who had been offered incentives to leave, help for those leaving Exxon in finding jobs, and stress counseling to help both departing and remaining employees to cope with the upheaval.[35] Some observers felt that the cultural fabric of the corporation had been torn, that its image as a paternalistic organization was shattered. Others noted that Exxon was generous to those asked to go, and in doing so it tried to show survivors that the company still was committed to its people even if it had to "surplus" some of them.

What will be the long-term effects of cashing in the firm's human assets, of promising only 5 to 10 years of work where once firms promised lifetime employment? No one knows for sure yet. In some industries, such as broadcasting and movies, the lack of corporate loyalty has not prevented the growth of successful companies, and may even have helped.

Still, the prospect of downsizing does not change the rules governing "make" or "buy" employment decisions. In industries where qualified labor is in short supply, firms may not have any choice other than to invest in training. For those firms that do have a choice, technological developments will make some training necessary. In fact, U.S. firms are spending an astounding $30 billion per year on formal courses and training programs for workers, and a further $180 billion annually for such unstructured training as supervision and learning on the job.[36] There are no signs that these trends will abate any time soon.

Firms make considerable investments in their employees through wages, benefits, overhead, and lifetime training and development activities. The staffing function can exercise a direct impact on productivity by establishing job requirements and performance standards, as well as by encouraging supervisors to "tell it like it is" during performance reviews and to fire laggards. To play this role, staffing managers must establish closer ties to operating managers, and they must understand the nature of their firms' businesses.

Conclusion

The next three decades pose a major challenge to HR managers. They face an aging work force and a shrinking entry-level employee pool—with potentially fewer highly educated and technically skilled employees—at a time when their organizations need to become more innovative and responsive. The challenge to HR managers is to build and maintain work forces that enable their companies to adapt to technological change and increasingly competitive global markets as the labor force changes.

The key to this challenge is *flexibility*, attracting and maintaining *flexible* work forces through *flexible* employment practices. To build flexible work forces, HR managers will have to modify existing selection processes, from selection solely on the basis of an employee's fit with a specific, existing job to selection on a broader range of knowledge, skills, and abilities: fundamental literacy and communication skills, an ability to learn and reason, draw conclusions, express ideas, and exercise judgment. Flexible work forces will aid organizations in adapting to rapidly changing and increasingly competitive markets, and in designing and operating the new, technologically sophisticated production and support systems that those markets will require.

Attracting and retaining a flexible work force as the labor force changes will require flexible employment systems. HR managers need to develop more effective methods to attract and retain women and minority employees, and employment practices will need to better accommodate both employee and employer needs. Flexible work schedules, employer-sponsored day care, flexible benefit plans, telecommuting, networked corporations, and employee leasing are some of the employment practices pioneered in the last decade that will be important HR tools in coming years.

In conclusion, building and maintaining human capital will become more important as the labor force changes. And because of these changes, HRM will assume a more critical role within business organizations. HR managers who can meet this challenge will make significant contributions to the ability of their organizations to become and remain competitive in the future.

Notes

1. Boulding.
2. U.S. Bureau of the Census.
3. See Fullerton for projections discussed in this section.
4. Morrison.
5. *Business Week.*
6. Hodgkinson.
7. *Time*, 1987b.
8. Miles and Snow.
9. Peters.
10. Pfeffer, pp. 304–305.
11. Pfeffer, p. 307.
12. Johnson, in Kiechel, p. 100.
13. Freeman.
14. Miller.
15. Narayanan and Nath.
16. Ralston, Anthony, and Gustafson.
17. *Resource*, 1986a.
18. Kelty, in *Resource*, 1986b, p. 7.
19. *Wall Street Journal*, 1986b.
20. Ibid.
21. Serrin.
22. Needle.
23. Len Siegel, author of *The High Cost of High Tech: The Dark Side of the Chip*, in Needle, p. 45.
24. Nye.
25. Needle.
26. Needle.
27. *Wall Street Journal*, 1986a.
28. Ehrenhalt; *Time*, 1987b.
29. *Time*, 1987a.
30. "Labor Letter," Aug. 26, 1986.
31. Barron.
32. Ropp.
33. Carley.
34. *Business Week*, 1986b.
35. Sullivan.
36. American Society for Training and Development, 1988.

Editor's Note: In addition to the References shown below, there are other significant sources of information on societal trends and staffing policies.

Articles

American Society for Training and Development. 1986. "Serving the New Corporation." (October).

Bennett, A. 1986. "Airline's Ills Point Out Weaknesses of Unorthodox Management Style." *Wall Street Journal* (August 11): 15.

Morgan, P.V. 1984. "International HRM: Fact or Fiction?" *Personnel Administrator* 31 (Summer): 43.

Resource. 1986. "How HRM Can Help Sharpen Competition." (October): 6.

Resource. 1986. "Pace of Change Is Challenge for HRM, Analyst Says." (October): 3–4.

References

American Society for Training and Development. 1988. "Gaining the Competitive Edge." (April).

Barron, J. 1986. "Gaps in Retraining Are Seen in Era of Industrial Change." *New York Times* (August 10): 1.

Boulding, K.E. 1982. "Irreducible Uncertainties." *Society* 20: 11–17.

Business Week. 1986a. "High Tech to the Rescue." (June 16): 100–108.

_____ 1986b. "The End of Corporate Loyalty?" (August 4): 42–49.

Carley, W.M. 1986. "New Flight Plan: Struggling to Survive, Peoples Express Alters Operations and Image." *Wall Street Journal* (Sept. 30): 1; 19.

Ehrenhalt, S. 1986. "Taking a Look at Job Quality." *New York Times* (August 13): 2D.

Freeman, R.B. 1986. "Cutting Black Youth Unemployment: Create Jobs That Pay as Well as Crime." *New York Times* (July 20): 2F.

Fullerton, H.N. Jr. 1985. "The 1995 Labor Force: BLS' Latest Projections." *Monthly Labor Review* (November): 17–25.

Hodgkinson, H.L. 1983. *Guess Who's Coming to College: Your Students in 1990.* Washington, DC: National Institute of Independent Colleges and Universities.

Kiechel, W. III. 1986. "Living With Human Resources." *Fortune* (August 18): 99–100.

Labor Letter. 1986. *Wall Street Journal* (June 24): 1; (August 1): 1; (August 26): 1.

Miles, R.E. and C.C. Snow. 1986. "Organizations: New Concepts for New Forms." *California Management Review* 28 (3): 62–73.

Miller, T.I. 1984. "The Effects of Employer Sponsored Child Care on Employee Absenteeism, Turnover, Productivity, Recruitment or Job Satisfaction: What Is Claimed and What Is Known." *Personnel Psychology* 37 (Summer): 277.

Morrison, M.H. 1983. "The Aging of the U.S. Population: Human Resource Implications." *Monthly Labor Review* (May): 13–19.

Narayanan, V.K. and R. Nath. 1982. "A Field Test of Some Attitudinal and Behavioral Consequences of Flexitime." *Journal of Applied Psychology* 67: 214–218.

Needle, D. 1986. "Telecommuting: Off to a Slow Start." *Infoworld* 19 (May): 43.

Nye, D. 1988. *Alternative Staffing Strategies*. Washington, DC: BNA Books.

Peters, T. 1985. "Why Smaller Staffs Do Better." *New York Times* (April 21): 1F, 14F.

Pfeffer, J. 1981. "Some Consequences of Organizational Demography: Potential Impacts of an Aging Work Force on Formal Organizations." In *Aging: Social Change*, ed. S.B. Kiesler, J.N. Morgan, and V.K. Oppenheimer. New York: Academic Press, 291–329.

Ralston, D.A., W.R. Anthony and D.J. Gustafson. 1985. "Employees May Love Flexitime, But What Does It Do to the Organization's Productivity?" *Journal of Applied Psychology* 70: 272–279.

Resource 1986a. "Technology vs. Unemployment." (October): 10.

_____ 1986b. "Unions Must Adapt in Order to Survive." (October): 1.

Ropp, K. 1987. "Downsizing Strategies." *Personnel Administrator* 32 (February): 61.

Serrin, W. 1986. "Part-Time Work New Labor Trend." *New York Times* (July 9): 6.

Sullivan, A. 1986. "Exxon's World-Wide Job Cuts Hit Home." *Wall Street Journal* (July 9): 6.

Time. 1987a. "Rebuilding to Survive." (February 16): 44–48.

────── 1987b. "Why Is Service So Bad?" (February 2): 48–57.

U.S. Bureau of the Census. 1984. "Projections of the Population of the United States, By Age, Sex, and Race: 1983 to 2080." *Current Population Reports*, Series P-25, No. 952 (May).

Wall Street Journal. 1986a. "In This Futuristic Office, Intimacy Exists Between Workers Separated by 500 Miles." (June 27): 29.

────── 1986b. "Robots: Next Step for Garment Makers." (August 7): 24.

────── ♦ ──────

2.2

Job Analysis and HR Planning

Ronald C. Page
David M. Van De Voort

Job analysis and HR planning are two fundamental processes that form the basis for a modern human resource management (HRM) system. In particular, these processes provide the means by which an organization may improve profitability by better utilizing employees, integrate HR programs to optimize cost effectiveness, and align HR programs and business plans to enhance the use of human resources and obtain competitive advantage. In these ways, job analysis and HR planning play an integral role in strategic business management and contribute to an organization's overall effectiveness.

The importance of job analysis and HR planning has emerged from the redefinition of the traditional personnel function into what is now called human resource management. Once a control-oriented supplier of employees, the personnel function has expanded into an operation concerned with the planning, development, performance, motivation, and productivity of the work force.[1]

Businesses now recognize that their survival depends on utilizing their human resources as effectively as their capital and physical resources.[2] In fact, the work force is seen as the only resource that produces output greater than the sum of its parts.

However, until recently, strategic management of human resources has been woefully lacking in many organizations. As organizations respond to changes in the business environment, this neglect of human resources seems likely to change:

> The greatest change ahead for the personnel function may be in its mission. The personnel department as we know it dates back to World War I, that is to a time when nine out of ten employees were "labor" doing undifferentiated, unskilled work. Then "labor" was a "cost";

and the first job of personnel was to keep costs down. But in today's business—even in the smokestack industries—at most three out of ten employees fit the "labor" category. The rest do highly differentiated and, in most cases, specialized work. They are not "labor"; they are "resources"—and resources have to be managed for optimum yield rather than for minimum costs.[3]

Job analysis and HR planning provide the foundation for translating employees into resources enabling effective management. Job analysis provides decision-support information that enables better-informed decisions to be made in virtually all HR applications. HR planning provides focus and direction to HR programs, ensuring that they are aligned with business plans. Together these processes form the starting point for sound personnel decisions and the development of most HR programs.

In the following sections, the discussion will describe how job analysis and HR planning can contribute to the goal of managing human resources for optimum yield.

Job Analysis as a Foundation of HRM

A job analysis documents fundamental information to support practically all HRM activities. Generally speaking, a job analysis is not an end in itself. Instead, it supplies the information needed to make better-informed HRM decisions and to build HR action programs which support HR plans.

Components of Job Analysis

When conducting a job analysis, HR managers should remember that the purpose is to provide an objective description of the job, not the person performing the job. Job analysis is a systematic process for gathering, documenting, and analyzing information about three basic aspects of a job:[4]

- *job content* describes the duties and responsibilities of the job in a manner that can range from very global statements of duties and functions, to very detailed descriptions of tasks and procedural steps.
- *job requirements* identify the knowledge, skills, abilities, and personal characteristics that employees need in order to perform the content of the job in a particular situation or context.

- *job context* refers to situational and supporting information regarding the particular job: its purpose; where it fits within the organization; scope data such as the magnitude of financial, human, or material resources managed; the availability of guidelines; the potential consequences of error; the amount of supervision received or provided; and the work setting, cultural context, physical demands, and working conditions.

In analyzing jobs, there are two primary perspectives: a *work-oriented* approach and a *worker-oriented* approach. Work-oriented approaches describe what gets done—the duties, activities and tasks of the job. This approach focuses on the use of action verbs (what is done) and end results (what gets done). In contrast, worker-oriented approaches, sometimes called behavior-oriented approaches, are concerned with basic human behaviors that are required to perform a job activity. A work-oriented approach, therefore, may describe a particular job component as "assembles circuit boards," and a worker-oriented analysis may indicate that the job "requires finger dexterity." The former approach concentrates on job content, and the latter focuses on job requirements.

Applications of Job Analysis Information

Job analysis, along with HR planning, is at the core of most HR programs. Figure 1 presents a conceptual overview of the relationship between job analysis/HR planning, selected HR programs, and the HRM functions that typically have responsibility for these programs.

This figure conveys three important concepts. First, it shows that job analysis and HR planning are core processes that provide information that drive multiple HR applications. A shared base of job analysis and planning information can integrate diverse HRM functions that too often stand alone. Second, Figure 1 shows that 12 HR programs are interrelated, providing a dynamic system. The displayed order approximates the chronological flow of a new job or employee through the organization's HR system. In practice, many of these programs interact concurrently or in ways that do not necessarily reflect the sequential ordering shown in Figure 1. Finally, Figure 1 shows the functional units that typically have responsibility for each of the 12 HR applications. This representation reflects functional responsibility and is not a prescribed or presumed model of organization structure.

Figure 1 can be used as a guide for the following descriptions of these HR applications and the contribution of job analysis information to each.

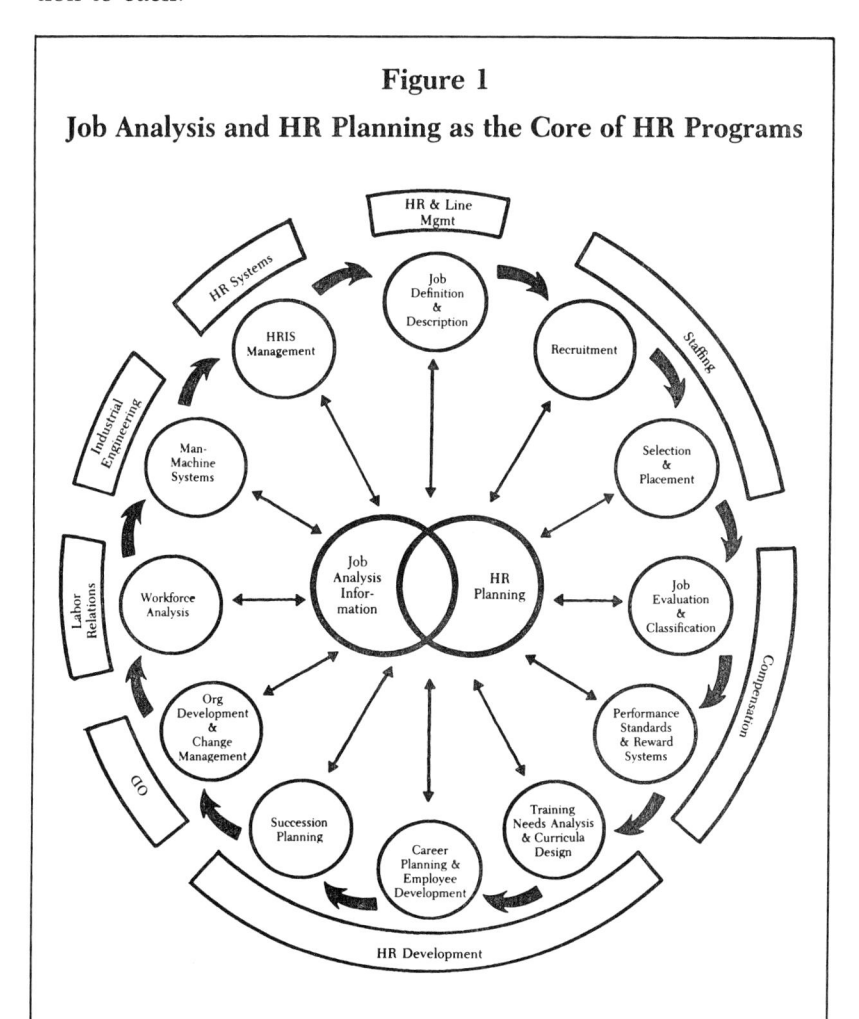

Figure 1

Job Analysis and HR Planning as the Core of HR Programs

Note: The overlapping circles in the center represent the core programs. The 12 surrounding programs represent HR end applications that interact with these programs. The outer ring represents the functional areas that typically have responsibility for the applications.

Job Definition and Description

Job descriptions are compilations of job analysis information that define the content, requirements, and context of a job. Job descriptions help managers and their employees arrive at a mutual understanding of what work is to be accomplished, and by whom.

In aggregate, a firm's job descriptions are a map of the organization's work domain. This map describes relationships and interdependencies that should be key considerations as the organization reacts to, or acts to change, its business environment.

Technology, world competition, and government de- and re-regulation are just a few influences that cause jobs to be frequently and continuously altered, eliminated, or newly created. The need for job clarification has never been greater, yet rapid change makes it increasingly difficult to obtain and maintain accurate, up-to-date documentation of job content, requirements, and context.

Recruitment

Job analysis information helps recruiters attract a better pool of applicants in a more efficient manner. The job description information helps identify how and where to recruit, and establishes the job requirements that applicants must meet. It also provides the information needed to create realistic job previews which can help ensure that a new employee's job expectations match actual job content.

Selection and Placement

Job analysis information is used to help develop job-related selection procedures, such as work samples, job simulations, written exams, and interview protocols. It also can be used to validate selection procedures, either directly, through content or construct validity designs, or indirectly, through establishing performance measurement criteria in a criterion-related design. Detailed information on job content, requirements, and context can help optimize placement by matching new hires or trainees to available positions.

Job Evaluation and Classification

Job information serves as the foundation of an organization's taxonomy of jobs—its classification structure. By understanding their similarities and differences, jobs may be grouped into job families. Furthermore, job information is needed to evaluate the worth of a job to the organization and to develop a job hierarchy or grade structure. Job analysis information is also the basis for intercompany surveys used to compare salaries paid for similar jobs in different organizations. As a result, job information helps ensure that compensation practices are both internally equitable and externally competitive.

Performance Standards and Reward Systems

Job analysis information is critical to an organization's ability to establish performance standards and to implement reward systems. Job analysis information defines upper and lower limits for job performance standards, and provides a basis for mutual performance planning and goal setting by managers and their subordinates. This process is frequently called work planning and review.

Performance appraisal rating forms should also reflect job-related performance standards, and incentive and reward systems should be based on the employee's performance relative to these standards. If an organization has an effective pay-for-performance policy and uses merit-pay increases, it must have job analysis information in order to establish job-related standards. In incentive compensation plans, a job analysis can define performance measures and criteria by clearly defining performance which is normal and expected within a job in contrast to performance beyond normal expectations, the latter being eligible for incentive payments.

Training Needs Analysis and Curricula Design

By defining key job knowledges and skills, job analysis information helps identify training objectives and course content. It is used extensively to develop technical or vocational training and is used to help design on-the-job training and employee development programs. For example, Nationwide Insurance uses computer-supported, multidimensional job analysis information to provide a direct link between objectively defined job performance dimensions and the company's training curriculum for supervisors and managers.

Career Planning and Employee Development

The definition of jobs and job requirements gives employees a better understanding of their career options, and allows them to develop relevant career movement plans. Matching employees' skills to the job requirements of targeted jobs produces a gap analysis that is used in career planning. The availability of job information enables employees to develop realistic career objectives and plans, by matching their skills with appropriate career options.

Succession Planning

By identifying job requirements for key positions, an organization can better identify appropriate succession candidates. A careful analysis of position responsibilities and requirements can help formulate appropriate succession plans and management development programs.

Organization Development and Change Management

Organization development (OD) seeks to enhance an organization's effectiveness through an organization-wide process of data collection, diagnosis, action planning, intervention and evaluation. Using applied behavioral science techniques, OD focuses on the congruence between organizational strategy, structure, process, people and culture.[5] As such, it uses information about organization structure and job definition. By understanding who has responsibility for what, as defined by job analysis, members of the organization may better understand the relationship between strategy, structure, processes, and people.

Work-Force Analysis

Job information can address a number of employee relations issues, such as job overlap, pay treatment, exemption status, and working conditions. Job information helps business management make proactive, informed decisions about critical employee relations issues. Moreover, job information may support the development of an appropriate equal employment action strategy, and provide data to support the legality of an organization's personnel practices. It can assure the validity of selection, transfer, and performance appraisal systems, and their conformance with the goals of the Civil Rights Act of 1964. It may also support employment practices related to the Equal Pay Act, the Fair Labor Standards Act, and the Occupational Safety and Health Act.

Man-Machine Systems

Job information is used extensively to determine methods and procedures for increasing efficiency and safety. Through a job analysis, managers can study physical layouts, work flows, and standards for worker and equipment capacities. In addition, job analyses that use procedures such as statistical quality control can help identify methods to improve the quality of an organization's products and services.

HR Information Systems

HR information systems store and report information to help managers in optimally managing their human resources. Many of these systems track information on such variables as skill requirements, job evaluation scores, positions held, and key responsibilities. This information supports a variety of HR program areas, such as staffing, relocation, benefits, and training programs. Information systems also provide data needed to produce governmental reports such as affirmative action planning reports. This data can support other HR planning activities by establishing expense ratios, cost estimates, and budget control.

Job Analysis Methods

Several different methods and approaches can be used to conduct a job analysis. Which method and approach is most appropriate depends on several aspects of the particular analysis situation.

Table 1 lists several variables that may be used to identify an appropriate job analysis method. Relevant aspects include the purpose of the job analysis, types of information collected, sources of information, methods of information collection, and primary forms of data analysis and reporting. Once the key project objectives and relevant job analysis variables have been identified, HR practitioners can select the optimal job analysis strategy. The following discussion examines seven possible strategies that are summarized in Table 2.

Table 1
Considerations for Selecting Job Analysis Methods

I. Purpose of Job Analysis
   1. Strategic HR Management
   2. Staffing
   3. Compensation
   4. Human Resource Development
   5. Labor Relations
   6. Industrial Engineering
   7. HR Systems

II. Type of Information Collected
   1. Job Content (work-oriented behavior, tasks, etc.)
   2. Job Requirements (worker-oriented behaviors, KSAs, traits, etc.)
   3. Job Context (Supporting Information on purpose, setting, discretion, etc. of the job)
   4. Machines/Equipment Used
   5. Critical Incidents

III. Source of Information
   1. Archival Information
   2. Incumbent
   3. Supervisor
   4. Subject Matter Expert
   5. Job Analyst
   6. Instruments/Machines (i.e., cameras)

IV. Method of Information Collection
   1. Observation
   2. Interview (individual or group)
   3. Reviewing Sample Documents, Work Outputs, Literature
   4. Diaries and Logs
   5. Open-ended Questionnaires
   6. Structured Questionnaires
   7. Recordings of Work (films, mechanical/electronic tracking, etc.)
   8. Participation (job analyst does the job himself)

V. Form of Data Analysis and Reporting
   1. Qualitative
   2. Quantitative

Observation/Interview

A survey done for the American Management Association found that almost all organizations (136 of 142 surveyed) use position descriptions when conducting job analyses.[6] In the vast majority of cases, some variation of observations and interviews form the method of job analysis used to develop position descriptions.

The observation process gathers job information by watching employees as they perform their jobs. The interviewing process collects information by questioning people who are familiar with the job being analyzed. The methods used to conduct observations or interviews range from casual to highly structured and sophisticated. A recommended procedure is to use a checklist of questions or interview protocol to increase the completeness and reliability of the information obtained.[7]

Observations and interviews have the advantage of putting the job analyst in direct contact with the work, thus supplying the richness of detail that only first-hand exposure can provide. The methods are adaptable to almost all job situations, can be learned fairly quickly, and yield a product—the position description—in a narrative format that is familiar to most users of job information. However, these methods require many hours of direct contact with the work, and involve writing, compiling, and analyzing prodigious amounts of narrative text. Consequently, the observation/interview method may be prohibitively labor-intensive, especially for large-scale applications.

Critical Incident Technique

The critical incident technique is a worker-oriented job analysis method that is particularly effective for identifying those behaviors that lead to success or failure on the job.[8]

The first step when using the critical incident technique is to determine the general objectives of the job. Supervisors, incumbents, and others who are in a position to observe and evaluate job behavior then provide specific on-the-job incidents that illustrate effective or ineffective behaviors for accomplishing those objectives.[9] The key elements of an incident are the circumstances that led up to it, what the jobholder actually did, and why the behavior was effective or ineffective. Incidents are categorized to define

Table 2
Summary Comparisons of Seven Job Analysis Methods

Method	Most Common Purpose	Type of Information Collected	Source of Information	Off the Shelf	Standard-ization	Required Amount of Job Analyst Training	User/Respondent Acceptability	Cost
1. Observation/Interview	Job Evaluation, Selection, Career Planning	Responsibilities, job Requirements, job Context and Tasks	Trained job analysts Interviewing/Observing Incumbents	No	No	Moderate	High	Moderate/High
2. Critical Incidents	Selection, Performance Appraisal, Performance Standards	Specific job behaviors/Critical Incidents	Incumbents and Supervisors	No	No	Moderate	High/Moderate	Moderate/High
3. Ability Requirements Scales	Selection, Classification	Tasks according to human abilities	Incumbents, Subject Matter Experts	In Part	Yes	High	Moderate	Moderate
4. Functional Job Analysis	Job Description, Selection, Classification, Compensation, Career Planning	Tasks by data, people, and things	Supervisors, Incumbents	In Part	No	High	High	Moderate/High
5. Position Analysis Questionnaire	Job Evaluation, Selection	194 worker-oriented job elements (requirements)	Trained job analysts Interviewing incumbents	Yes	Yes	Moderate	Low/Moderate	Low/Moderate
6. Job Element Approach	Selection	Knowledge, skills, abilities, and personal characteristics	Subject matter experts	In Part	No	Moderate/High	Moderate	Low/Moderate
7. TI/CODAP	Job Description, Training, Selection, Classification, Performance Standards, Compensation	Task statements with "relative time spent"	Incumbents	No	Yes	Low	Moderate/High	Moderate/High

Source: Adapted, in part, from H.J. Banardin & R.W. Beaty, *Performance Appraisal: Assessing Human Behavior at Work*. Boston: Kent-Wadsworth, 1983 and H.S. Field & R.D. Gatewood, "Matching Talent with the Task," *Personnel Journal*, 66 no. 4 (1987): 113–126.

effective and ineffective dimensions of job performance and, thus, define a composite picture of the job's behavioral requirements.[10]

This method requires a trained analyst and is extremely labor intensive. The analysis deals, by definition, with critical or extreme work behaviors, while many job analysis applications require measures of "typical" or "average" job performance. Although the technique can be used to elicit "typical incidents," incumbents and supervisors may find this difficult.

The critical incident technique is a general process for analyzing work behavior; it is not a packaged job analysis system. While it does not produce a job description in the conventional sense, it does develop performance checklists that target desirable and undesirable work behaviors. It is the preferred method for defining key performance requirements and for diagnosing performance problems. For these applications, and when used in combination with other methods, the critical incident is an elegant and powerful job analysis tool.

Ability Requirements Approach

The ability requirements approach to job analysis developed from a long-term research program aimed at describing human performance through the abilities required to perform tasks.[11] A key feature of this approach is the distinction between abilities and skills.

A skill is a performance capability, specific to a particular task or to a defined set of tasks, and is usually measured by the incumbent's demonstrated level of proficiency. To achieve a particular skill level on any given task, an individual must possess related basic abilities. For example, typing is a skill. The extent to which typing skills can be developed in an individual is a function of some basic abilities, such as finger dexterity.

The ability requirements method has been used to validate strength and agility requirements for public safety forces in many public-sector jurisdictions, notably the District of Columbia.

Functional Job Analysis/Department of Labor Method

These two closely related methods both originated from the effort to develop the Dictionary of Occupational Titles—a compendium of standardized descriptions of more than 20,000 U.S. occupations, organized by occupational group and by industry.[12] Functional job analysis is a refinement of the basic Department of Labor procedure.[13]

Both methods have been presented as "complete" job analysis systems which include both behavior-oriented and task-oriented features. Both methods require trained analysts to describe job tasks and duties. Task analysis consists of rating tasks and/or whole jobs on a variety of scales that index the task characteristics and worker behaviors required to perform the job.

The methods are well-documented and intuitively appealing. They are, however, labor intensive and difficult to use and defend, compared to more objective approaches.

Job Element Approach

Another job analysis approach with roots in public-sector personnel administration is the job elements approach. This approach was developed for the U.S. Civil Service Commission to use in selecting tests for trades in the federal service.[14]

Groups of job-knowledge experts brainstorm to identify job elements important to success on a job. These elements cover skills, abilities, knowledge, interests, and personal traits/motivational factors. Several raters then evaluate each job element on four dimensions: importance to achieving minimum acceptable job performance; importance to achieving superior job performance; amount of "trouble" that would be caused by ignoring the element in selection decisions; and practicality of using the element in filling the job.

Ratings of all job elements then are combined using a scoring scheme composed of those elements most likely to identify successful performers from a group of job applicants. Tests and other assessment devices that use similar ratings, or that are specifically constructed to test particular job elements, are also combined and weighted based on the job element ratings.

The Position Analysis Questionnaire

The Position Analysis Questionnaire (PAQ) is a commercially available job analysis instrument and scoring/reporting service. The structured job analysis questionnaire is "based on a statistical analysis of primarily worker-oriented job elements and which lends itself to quantitative statistical analysis."[15] The instrument was developed to measure those generalized work behaviors which are essential to performing all types of work.[16]

The 194 questions are logically organized around five basic facets of work: information inputs, mental processes, work outputs, relationships with others, and job context. Jobs are described by rating the items on one of several scales, such as extent of use (for example, of short-handled tools) and importance to the job. The questionnaire is typically completed by a trained job analyst, based on interviews, observation, or other means of gathering job information.

Jobs are summarized on 13 overall dimensions and 32 division dimensions. A job's profile across these dimensions may then be used to compare it to other jobs. Using a large database of comparison jobs, as well as extensive research results, the PAQ has been used for many purposes, including: job evaluation, employee selection and placement, performance appraisal, assessment center development, identifying job families, vocational counseling, career development, identifying training needs, and developing training curricula.[17]

Advantages of the PAQ include: it is relatively cost-effective; it may be implemented rapidly; it has several applications; and several of its reports compare a job to a normative database of job information. Disadvantages include: data must be computer-processed by a vendor; interpretation of reports generally requires a background in statistics; and job descriptions are in terms of worker-oriented behaviors, rather than the duties and responsibilities of the job.

Task Inventory Method/CODAP

Within the past two decades, the task inventory approach has become more popular, especially since development of the Comprehensive Occupational Data Analysis Programs (CODAP).[18] CODAP is an acronym that refers both to a job analysis method and to the software package used to compile and analyze the job data. Developed by the military and used by a number of federal, state and local government organizations, CODAP more recently has been used by some firms in private industry.

The primary military application has been to identify career ladders and develop training programs. Government jurisdictions and agencies have used it extensively to develop and validate work performance criteria and employee selection programs. Government and industrial applications also include job classification, job description, and job evaluation.

The software package gathers job data via comprehensive inventories of tasks performed on a job or within a general job family. Incumbents rate the tasks in terms of the relative time they spend performing each task. Statistical analysis converts the ratings into estimated percentages of work time spent on each task. The computer program may then generate task-based job descriptions on current jobs and, through cluster analysis, may identify empirically-based classification structures.

Advantages of CODAP include: a very large number of positions can be analyzed in a relatively short period of time; the specificity of the resultant job descriptions; it is cost-effective for very large organizations; detailed job descriptions are produced; and similarities and differences in jobs can be specifically identified. Disadvantages include: the user must be computer-literate to run the software package; and the development of task inventories customized to the organization requires time and resources.

Comparison of Methods

Choosing between the numerous and divergent methods of job analysis may pose a dilemma for the HR practitioner. Which method is best has been a topic of some controversy.[19] However, various researchers have suggested that the best procedure is to use several methods of job analysis to gather a comprehensive perspective of job content, especially when used to validate selection procedures.[20]

One study that systematically compared various job analysis systems included the last six methods described above.[21] Ninety-three experienced job analysts evaluated different methods in terms of their utility (for 11 organizational purposes) and in terms of practicality (on 11 indicators). The results showed that job analysis methods were rated differently in terms of effectiveness and practicality across the 22 dimensions. Task inventory/CODAP and functional job analysis methods were rated highest for the purpose of job description, job classification, and job design. These two methods, as well as the PAQ method, were rated as the most standardized and reliable. The PAQ method was also rated highest for use "right off-the-shelf." Ratings show that the PAQ and the ability requirements approach were rated as requiring the least amount of calendar time for completion.

In summary, the best method for a particular organization will depend on: the purpose of job analysis; the time and resource constraints; the utility of the results to management; the desire to make multiple applications of the data; and availability of incumbents, supervisors, and subject matter experts.

Emerging Multi-Method Approaches

With recent advances in computer technology and greater sophistication in quantitative methods of job analysis, new systems of job analysis are emerging. Several common elements of these emerging systems include the following:

- They use multidimensional perspectives on the source of job information, type of data analyzed, and response scale formats.
- They are designed to concurrently support multiple HR applications.
- They use structured questionnaires that are completed by incumbents, supervisors, and/or subject matter experts.
- They employ user-friendly computer systems that may perform complex multivariate statistical procedures but also provide graphics-quality reports for ease of data interpretation.

These methods use an eclectic approach to job analysis. They borrow from the task inventory approach, but also blend in features of other systems as well as multivariate statistical procedures. As with the task inventory approach, they can efficiently analyze a geographically dispersed work force, track and document rapidly changing job content, and will cost less per employee for large organizations.

In addition, these methods have the advantage of supporting the development of an Integrated Personnel System. This type of system is defined as:

> A comprehensive set of personnel management procedures based on job content in which the components are linked to achieve effective utilization and development of human resources. A systematic and comprehensive job analysis methodology serves as the integrating medium for personnel system components. By using the same foundation of job information, human resource planning, selection, job

evaluation, classification, performance appraisal, training and career and succession planning may be better integrated.[22]

Examples of Integrated Personnel Systems

An integrated personnel system fosters synergy between the various functions within personnel and promotes an integrated approach to managing human resources. This integration occurs because the same base of information is used to define jobs. The following examples show the actual operation of integrated personnel systems in different organizations.

JobScope. In 1979, the Nationwide Insurance Companies began developing an integrated personnel system.[23] The system, currently called the Career Directions Program, used job analysis information collected on more than 10,000 positions to improve and integrate compensation, selection, training, appraisal, and HR planning systems.

A four-phase approach, as shown in Figure 2, was used to develop and integrate a total HR system. In designing the program, Nationwide recognized that all aspects of the integrated system would directly relate to the task content of the work. Consequently, an extensive job analysis formed the first step in developing a personnel system. Phase 2 used this job analysis information to develop compensation, selection, appraisal, and training systems. Phase 3 formulated job-related succession and career planning systems using information collected from the personnel systems established in Phase 2. The final phase involved the development of a process to integrate the HRM system with strategic business planning so as to advance the corporate mission. The specific personnel programs developed as a part of Career Directions are identified at the sides of the funnel in Figure 2.

The job analysis system used in this effort is called JobScope. Through computer-analyzed, structured questionnaires, it identifies and profiles jobs on different sets of dimensions that have been specifically designed for different applications. For example, different sets of job dimensions have been identified for selection, performance appraisal, assessment center, succession planning, training program, executive appraisal, and compensation applications.

A sample microcomputer-generated report, designed for compensation applications and called the Factor Profile, is presented in Figure 3. This profile evaluates the job of an employee relations

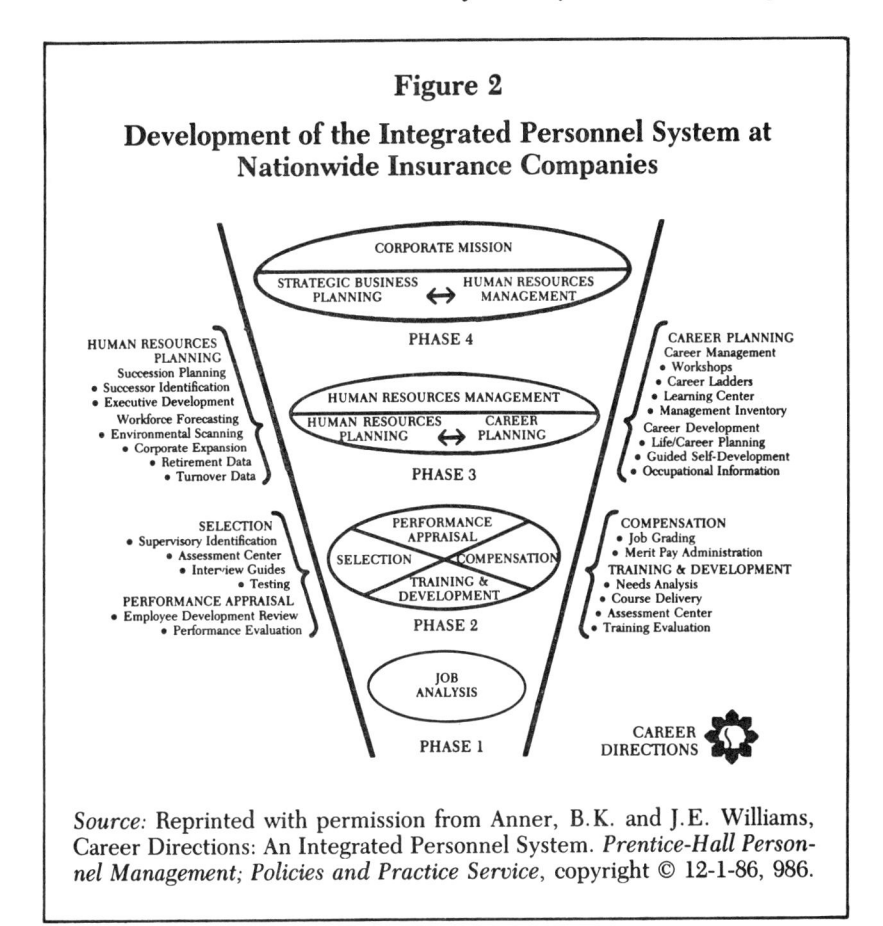

Figure 2
Development of the Integrated Personnel System at Nationwide Insurance Companies

CORPORATE MISSION
STRATEGIC BUSINESS PLANNING ↔ HUMAN RESOURCES MANAGEMENT

PHASE 4 — HUMAN RESOURCES MANAGEMENT
HUMAN RESOURCES PLANNING ↔ CAREER PLANNING

PHASE 3 — SELECTION, PERFORMANCE APPRAISAL, COMPENSATION, TRAINING & DEVELOPMENT

PHASE 2 — JOB ANALYSIS

PHASE 1 — CAREER DIRECTIONS

HUMAN RESOURCES PLANNING
- Succession Planning
- Successor Identification
- Executive Development
- Workforce Forecasting
- Environmental Scanning
- Corporate Expansion
- Retirement Data
- Turnover Data

SELECTION
- Supervisory Identification
- Assessment Center
- Interview Guides
- Testing

PERFORMANCE APPRAISAL
- Employee Development Review
- Performance Evaluation

CAREER PLANNING
- Career Management
- Workshops
- Career Ladders
- Learning Center
- Management Inventory

Career Development
- Life/Career Planning
- Guided Self-Development
- Occupational Information

COMPENSATION
- Job Grading
- Merit Pay Administration

TRAINING & DEVELOPMENT
- Needs Analysis
- Course Delivery
- Assessment Center
- Training Evaluation

Source: Reprinted with permission from Anner, B.K. and J.E. Williams, Career Directions: An Integrated Personnel System. *Prentice-Hall Personnel Management; Policies and Practice Service*, copyright © 12-1-86, 986.

---

manager on six job factors and identifies the overall estimated job grade. Moreover, job description factors are profiled for task activities, decision-making responsibilities, financial responsibilities, and knowledge areas. These factors were defined through a factor analysis of questionnaire data. Both the Factor Profile and the Diagnostic Report, a quality control report, provide information to support the interpretation and assure the quality of the evaluation decisions emerging from this system. Other JobScope reports address job description, job requirements, appraisal, training, career development, and work-force forecasting.

Many of the benefits of JobScope and Career Directions are qualitative and intangible. For example, compensation analysts no longer act primarily as gatherers and compilers of data—standard-

Figure 3

Nationwide Executive & Management Factor Profile

NATIONWIDE EXECUTIVE & MANAGEMENT FACTOR PROFILE

Title: EMPLOYEE RELATIONS MGR
Job Code: H116CA
Number of NPDQs Comprising Report: 1
Range of Completion Dates: Jul, 1981 to Jul, 1981

Questionnaire's Coverage of
Overall Job Elements: 100%
Critical Job Elements: 0%
Task Activities: 100%

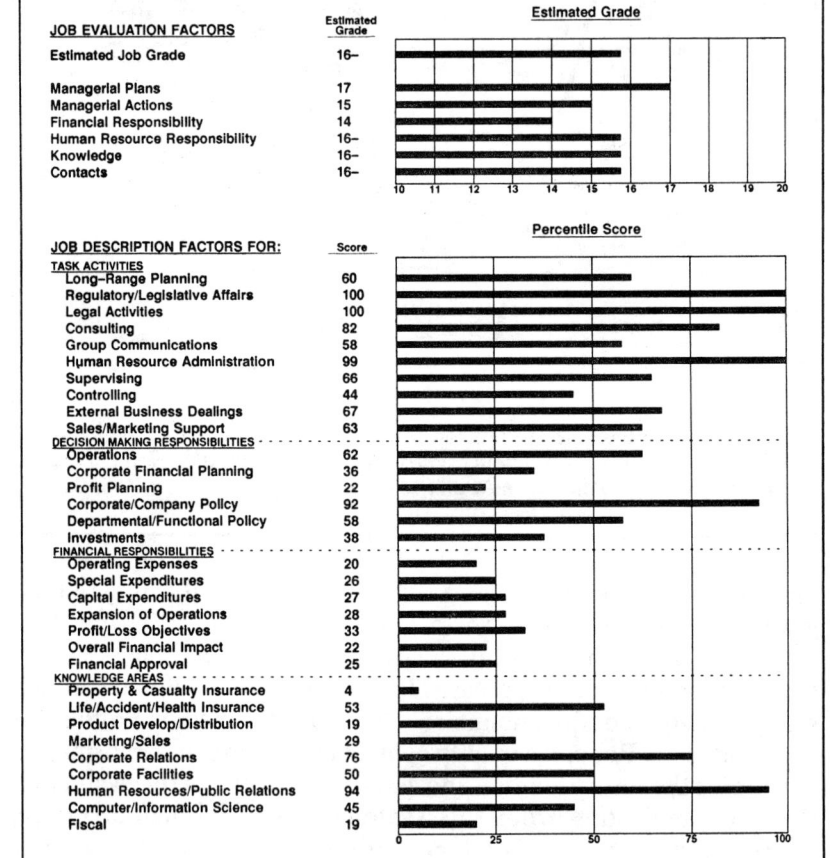

JOB EVALUATION FACTORS	Estimated Grade
Estimated Job Grade	16–
Managerial Plans	17
Managerial Actions	15
Financial Responsibility	14
Human Resource Responsibility	16–
Knowledge	16–
Contacts	16–

JOB DESCRIPTION FACTORS FOR:	Score
TASK ACTIVITIES	
Long–Range Planning	60
Regulatory/Legislative Affairs	100
Legal Activities	100
Consulting	82
Group Communications	58
Human Resource Administration	99
Supervising	66
Controlling	44
External Business Dealings	67
Sales/Marketing Support	63
DECISION MAKING RESPONSIBILITIES	
Operations	62
Corporate Financial Planning	36
Profit Planning	22
Corporate/Company Policy	92
Departmental/Functional Policy	58
Investments	38
FINANCIAL RESPONSIBILITIES	
Operating Expenses	20
Special Expenditures	26
Capital Expenditures	27
Expansion of Operations	28
Profit/Loss Objectives	33
Overall Financial Impact	22
Financial Approval	25
KNOWLEDGE AREAS	
Property & Casualty Insurance	4
Life/Accident/Health Insurance	53
Product Develop/Distribution	19
Marketing/Sales	29
Corporate Relations	76
Corporate Facilities	50
Human Resources/Public Relations	94
Computer/Information Science	45
Fiscal	19

Source: Reprinted with permission from Nationwide Insurance Cos.

ized questionnaires and computer software now do this—but now are true analysts of information. Human judgment remains the key to job evaluation, and the job of the judge is enriched by the data collection tool.

One quantifiable benefit of JobScope is realized from the well-documented accuracy of the JobScope Job Evaluation process. Using extremely conservative assumptions, one study has demonstrated that increased job evaluation accuracy is saving more than $60,000 in salary and benefits expenses each year.[24] Thus, the JobScope system has paid for itself in less than two years of operation, with actual savings probably far in excess of the very conservative estimate. Projected savings over the estimated life span of the system could total more than $3,000,000.

HR FOCUS. Control Data Corporation began developing a questionnaire-based and computer-analyzed job analysis system in 1975. The system was initially designed to address job description, job classification, and job evaluation by assessing job content, job requirements, and job context data.[25] Subsequently it has been used to identify job classification structure (using cluster analysis), FLSA exemption status, training needs assessment, performance appraisal, and selection system design and validation. Since its installation, more than 15,000 company positions have been analyzed using HR FOCUS job analysis questionnaires.

Various descriptions of HR FOCUS indicate that it offers several report formats.[26] Figure 4 presents a portion of the management Position-Tailored Performance Appraisal Form. This individually tailored form is produced by microcomputer analysis for individuals who complete job analysis questionnaires. The bulleted statements define and anchor the meaning of each of the job-family-specific factors and are identified by the employee as being crucial to his or her job. This type of performance appraisal permits managers to rate employees on job-related dimensions that have been defined by the employee. The appraisal is also drawn from the same questionnaire that produces the Position Description and Position Factor Profile reports used in compensation. Therefore, the same job documentation may serve as the foundation of job evaluation and merit pay increases based on appraisal ratings.

The Multidimensional Job Profile, as shown in Figure 5, is produced by the same system that produces six other reports: the Position-Tailored Performance Appraisal Form and the position description, job description, position evaluation, job evaluation, and job comparison reports. The job comparison report contrasts the similarities and differences in job content and is used for selection and career planning applications.

In a high-technology marketplace, Control Data finds a key benefit of the system is that it can track job changes in a fast-moving environment and quickly produce up-to-date descriptions. The system also can compile surveys of positions in a common work group to produce a composite description of the "job" performed by the work group. An additional benefit derived from using a single database of job information is the increased communication and synergy between compensation, training and development, and staffing.

HAY VALUE. A third example of a multimethod, multidimensional approach is HAY VALUE, which has been developed by Hay Management Consultants. Structured questionnaires are completed by incumbents, supervisors, and subject matter experts, and through mainframe and microcomputer analysis, HAY VALUE produces reports that address job description, job evaluation, classification structure, external equity, organizational analysis, performance management, and staffing.[27]

A common application of the HAY VALUE system is for job description and evaluation. Employees complete questionnaires consisting of a structured list of activities and short, open-ended questions. Computer analysis produces job descriptions that summarize the key activities of the job. Figure 6 presents a sample page from a computer-generated job description. Using this job description, as well as their knowledge of subordinate jobs, supervisors may then define job content on a short job-family-specific questionnaire. Using microcomputer analysis, total Hay job evaluation points are determined, assessing the same job content elements that are assessed by a traditional committee-based application of the Hay Guide-Chart Profile Method of job evaluation. Using market-pricing data, the software may then provide information on base salary and total compensation for various breakdowns of comparable jobs.

Job description data is also used for several other applications. Cluster analysis is used to identify empirically-based job classification structures for organizations. Questionnaire activities are used to generate performance standards. Figure 7 presents an example of a computer-generated form that lists a job's most important duties and projects, as rated by an employee. The supervisor then uses this form for performance planning, discussion, and review. Using

Job Analysis & HR Planning 2-55

Figure 4
Example Section of Computer-Generated Position-Tailored Performance Appraisal Form

MANAGEMENT
POSITION - TAILORED
PERFORMANCE APPRAISAL FORM

Page 2
ARNOLD H. SMITH
Questionnaire Date 9 / 7 / 84

SECTION III – PERFORMANCE FACTORS

This section helps describe how this employee goes about accomplishing typical work assignments. Nine performance factors with definitions and significant sample activities are listed below. Use the space provided for a tenth performance factor if there is an additional dimension on which this employee should be rated. Rate this employee on each of the performance factors by:

1) Reading the definition and sample activities associated with each factor. The sample activities listed are behavioral examples of each factor that this employee rated as most significant to the position.

2) Indicating this employee's typical level of effectiveness during the appraisal period by marking the appropriate shaded box with an "X".

3) Noting examples of behavior that illustrate this employee's typical level of performance in the Comments section.

FACTOR DEFINITIONS AND ACTIVITIES	RATINGS AND COMMENTS
1. MANAGING WORK: Manages work flow and resources; monitors and documents information; ensures timely completion of products/projects. * Establish personal work priorities. * Monitor the total sales volume of my operating unit. * Track and adjust activities to ensure that objectives/commitments are met in a timely fashion. * Track expenditures to budget/forecast and determine how to make the best use of funds. * Keep detailed and accurate records on projects, personnel, costs, schedules, and/or equipment. * Monitor subordinate's progress toward their objectives.	Not Effective | Somewhat Effective | Effective | Very Effective | Extremely Effective Comments:
2. BUSINESS PLANNING: Establishes and implements effective plans and strategies for achieving objectives. * Develop wide-ranging programs that result in substantial savings to the company. * Anticipate/initiate action in response to new/changing demands for products/services/technologies. * Determine the strategic business plan of an operating or staff unit. * Develop implementation plans for introduction of new/improved products, services or programs. * Determine implementation methods for meeting operational objectives established by others.	Not Effective | Somewhat Effective | Effective | Very Effective | Extremely Effective Comments:
3. PROBLEM SOLVING/DECISION MAKING: Analyzes technical or business problems/needs; makes decisions and identifies appropriate solutions or innovations. * Consider the long-range implications of decisions. * Evaluate the costs/benefits of alternative solutions to problems before making decisions. * Make decisions which could result in the savings or loss of a large amount of money. * Provide creative solutions to key problems facing your organization. * Make decisions concerning the future direction of operations. * Make decisions without hesitation when required.	Not Effective | Somewhat Effective | Effective | Very Effective | Extremely Effective Comments:
4. COMMUNICATION: Communicates effectively, thoroughly and accurately; appropriate sharing or exchange of information. * Share information with Executives. * Share information with Group Managers. * Share information with Managers. * Share information with Supervisors. * Share information with Prof./Admin. Exempt employees. * Share information with Clerical or Support staff (Nonexempt). * Influence Executives to act/decide according to your objectives. * Influence Managers to act/decide according to your objectives. * Influence Supervisors to act/decide according to your objectives.	Not Effective | Somewhat Effective | Effective | Very Effective | Extremely Effective Comments:

Source: Reprinted with permission from Control Data Business Advisors, Inc., copyright © 1984.

2-56   HR Planning, Employment & Placement

Figure 5
Example of Multidimensional Job Profile

MULTIDIMENSIONAL JOB PROFILE
PERFORMANCE AND COMPETENCY FACTORS

Job Title:	MANAGER	Number Surveyed for this Job:	11
Functional Area:	HUMAN RESOURCES	Average Percent of Job Described:	87%
Organization:	CONTROL DATA	Range of Dates Completed:	9/6/84 TO 4/3/85

Average Level of Significance

PERFORMANCE FACTORS	Average Signif.
Managing Work	1.5
Business Planning	1.4
Problem Solving/Decision Making	2.0
Communication	2.2
Customer/Public Relations	1.0
Human Resource Development	1.7
Human Resource Management	1.7
Organizational Support/Interface	2.3
Job Knowledge	1.8

Scale: Not a Part (0) — Minor (1) — Moderate (2) — Substantial (3) — Crucial (4)

Average Level of Proficiency

KNOWLEDGE, SKILLS & ABILITIES	Average Rating
Leadership	2.7
Coaching & Developing	2.7
Motivating	2.8
Delegating & Monitoring	2.5
Planning	2.5
Allocating Resources	2.0
Administrative Skills	2.2
Personal Organization/Time Mgmt.	2.3
Human Relations/Sensitivity	3.0
Coordination	2.9
Group Process Skills	2.1
Negotiation	2.5
Conflict Management	2.3
Influencing/Persuading	2.9
Customer/Public Relations	2.4
Oral Expression	3.3
Presentation Skills	2.5
Active Listening	3.0
Written Composition	2.4
Information Management	2.7
Analytic Ability	3.1
Judgement/Decision Making	3.2
Mathematical Skills	2.3
Innovation & Resourcefulness	3.1
Professional/Technical Knowledge	3.2
Organizational Practices	2.1
Sales/Marketing Knowledge	1.6
Economic & Business Trends	1.4
Legislative Trends	1.0
Company Products & Services	1.8
Computer Usage	1.9

Scale: Not Required (0) — Basic (1) — Fully Adequate (2) — Superior (3) — Outstanding (4)

Source: Reprinted with permission from Control Data Business Advisors, Inc., copyright © 1984.

Figure 6

Example Section of Hay Value Position Description

JOB DESCRIPTION
XYZ CORPORATION

INCUMBENT:	Joan Brand
JOB TITLE:	Market Analyst
DEPARTMENT:	Marketing
SUPERVISOR'S NAME:	Elliot Butler
SUPERVISOR'S TITLE:	Director of Marketing
DATE:	02/26/88

SUPERVISOR'S APPROVAL _____ **DATE** _____

GENERAL INFORMATION

There are broad precedents and practices that the incumbent uses as guidelines to determine how this job is performed. This position requires at least 3 years of relevant work experience.

The incumbent frequently exchanges information with senior management, outside consultants and infrequently with top management.

JOB DIMENSIONS

    Operating budget accountable for: $300,000 - 1,500,000

The incumbent does not have accountability for people but does oversee 1 - 2 employees on a project basis.

NATURE AND SCOPE

Note: This position involves the activities listed below. The activities in bold faced type are the most critical for this job. The activities marked with an asterisk (*) are those on which the incumbent spends the most time.

    Marketing Research, Planning and Strategy

    The incumbent directs others who:

* **Conduct sales research to determine current market conditions**
  Evaluate market reactions to product pricing, technology innovation, etc

    The incumbent is personally responsible to:

* **Analyze results of market tests**
* **Direct market research studies**
* **Manage market tests for new products**
* **Prepare reports on research studies**
  Keep abreast of marketing methods within the industry

Source: Reprinted with permission from The Hay Group.

employee input to produce individually tailored forms helps ensure discussion of job-related behaviors and participation by employees in the appraisal process.

HR Planning

The fundamental objective of all organizations is to thrive in a prosperous and self-sustaining manner. Several current trends are making this objective increasingly challenging:

- Increasing competition from a shift to a global economy, which has led businesses to emphasize long-term commitments over short-term profitability, so as to gain market share
- Changing work-force demographics and changing attitudes toward careers as "baby boomers" mature and compete for career growth opportunities
- Legal and regulatory conditions addressing issues such as employment discrimination, pay equity, data privacy, and business deregulation
- More sophisticated consumer markets in which product life cycles are growing ever shorter, and greater marketing efforts are required to establish a presence in the marketplace
- Shift to service-based economy in which employees deliver the organization's "product" via direct customer contact

To cope effectively with these trends, managers will need to make fundamental changes in how human resources are managed.

As the world becomes more complex, business management planning becomes more important, yet more difficult. As a result, organizations have a critical need to integrate HRM and business strategy formulation. However, several studies indicate that the two functions have not become fully integrated in contemporary organizations.

One recent study surveyed 252 heads of strategic planning and HRM in 168 companies.[28] Ninety-two percent of the respondents indicated that their companies performed at least a moderate amount of strategic planning. However, approximately 78 percent indicated that strategic planning activities had been introduced only within the previous 10 years. In addition, the respondents reported

Job Analysis & HR Planning 2-59

Figure 7
Example of a Hay VALUE Performance Appraisal Form that is Generated from Job Description Questionnaire Results

NONEXEMPT SALARIED
PERFORMANCE PLAN AND APPRAISAL

NAME	SOCIAL SECURITY NUMBER
Sally T. Watkins	154-98-1237
COMPONENT	DEPARTMENT
	National Compensation
POSITION TITLE	PERFORMANCE PERIOD	DATE
Administrative Assistant	FROM / / TO / /	/ /

PART I. PERFORMANCE PLAN (Attach additional sheets if more space is needed)

MAJOR JOB DUTIES AND PROJECTS List major duties and projects. To be jointly agreed upon each year	PERFORMANCE MEASURES AND STANDARDS	PERFORMANCE RESULTS Complete below anniversary date based on results for previous year
1. Review and edit final copy of outgoing reports		
2. Correct punctuation or grammar in material received from others		
3. Communicate executive's instructions to various individuals and/or departments		
4. Review format of reports to ensure conformity to standard format		
5. Take telephone messages for others		
6. Verify accuracy of typed copy against the original		
7. Obtain data from reference materials		
8. Assemble or collate documents		
9. Proofread and correct or mark for correction		
10. Coordinate the production of slides, graphics or other visual aids		

a desire to see HR activities play a much more prominent role in the strategy implementation process: 83 percent felt their companies made insufficient use of HR tools in planning strategy, and 95 percent reported that they would like to see a greater use of HR tools in implementing strategies.

Another study sheds further light on the desire for further integration of HR and business strategy planning.[29] This survey of 282 major corporations found that 62 percent currently develop HR strategies and only 6 percent develop HR plans prior to, or concurrently with, the business cycle.

These results indicate that although some movement toward integrating HR and business plans has occurred, the two planning processes are far from integrated at the present time. Numerous writers have shown that an HRM system which is integrated with the organization's strategic planning and which optimizes productivity through systematically developing employees or controlling employee costs is critical to the organization's overall performance and competitiveness.[30]

Changing Role of HRM

With labor comprising the major component of production costs in many contemporary business, managers need to view "people" expenditures as investments in business strategies. One consequence of this view is a new role for modern HR managers in which they directly advise executives on managing complex organizational issues that only people can resolve.

Effective HR planning is the vehicle and catalyst that can transform the personnel manager into the HR manager. The transformation occurs through working closely with executives to mobilize the work force toward common goals and strategic change. If successful in this role, HR managers can shed the image of incidental administrators and become valued partners in the core management team.

Figure 1 presents a conceptual overview regarding how HR planning, along with job analysis, may form the core of an effective human resource management system that may achieve these objectives.

Definition of HR Planning

HR planning is both a process and a set of plans which deals with jobs and people. It can focus on one position or on the entire work force. It addresses how an organization intends to implement its business plans from an HR perspective. It is the process through which an organization determines its HR requirements and develops plans for how these resources can best be acquired, deployed, developed, and managed.[31] HR planning addresses the demand for and supply of workers and creates action plans whenever a gap arises between the two. Moreover, the process enables senior managers to identify and to address major HR issues that can either jeopardize the success of the organization or create significant competitive advantage.

This definition has several key points. First, HR planning focuses on the congruence between jobs and people. Second, HR planning deals with the overall organization or its major segments; it is not a microanalysis of a single business segment. Third, HR planning is tied to the overall business plans of the organization, but it is a line responsibility that supports the business planning of core management. Lastly, HR planning is not a unidimensional program—it is neither succession planning, career development planning, nor planning for the HR function—but a process by which business and HR strategies are integrated.

Thus, HR planning is as an eclectic process which combines traditional approaches with newer concepts from a number of disciplines, including HRM, economic theory, mathematics, and the behavioral and computer sciences.[32] This "melting pot" of disciplines has produced various models and techniques for identifying and addressing HR planning needs.

Implemented effectively, HR planning leads managers and HR professionals to develop formal action plans and programs to accomplish key strategic objectives. For example, HR planning has been used to focus and provide direction to the following activities:

- Projecting recruitment needs
- Planning training and development efforts
- Controlling staffing levels and expenditures
- Developing career planning/management programs
- Assuring the continuity of management
- Developing compensation strategies
- Building employee relations programs
- Developing employee communication strategies
- Improving HR information systems

2-62 HR Planning, Employment & Placement

HR Planning Process

Figure 8 presents an overview of the HR Planning process and its four stages: situation analysis, HR demand analysis, HR supply analysis, and risk analysis and strategy development.

Situation Analysis

A situation analysis identifies and defines the context of the organization, its strategy, and its general HR issues. It monitors, assesses, and, at times, defines various aspects of the organization: its mission and core businesses, its strategic plans and parameters, its organizing concepts and structure, its corporate culture, and its HR challenges.

At this first stage environmental scanning is conducted "to gather information about trends and anticipated developments in external and internal environments and discern their relevance for human resource strategy making."[33] An environmental scan may address a number of external factors: economic, social, and political trends and developments in labor markets; labor relations; governmental affairs; and HR policies and practices in other firms. Internal factors are assessed by such things as grievance analyses, special meetings with employees, opinion or attitude surveys, or special studies that address such issues as employee values and expectations, and current and potential problem areas.

The situation analysis assists strategy makers in addressing HR issues before the strategy-making process begins. The ultimate goal is to improve the quality of strategic business decisions by ensuring an appropriate match between human resources, capital resources, and physical resources.

Various resources provide information for environmental scanning. The Environmental Scanning Association annually investigates new trends. The Hay Group annually publishes a free report called the *Environmental Scan*.[34] Other good sources are listed in the environmental scanning chapter in Volume 1 of this handbook series.

HR Demand Analysis

The second stage in HR planning involves the performance of a demand analysis of future HR requirements. Typically handled by line management, a demand analysis translates strategic plans developed in the first stage into organizational plans. These organizational plans help identify appropriate job definitions consistent with the business objectives.

Demand forecasts reflect business factors, such as sales or product volume, and concomitant HR needs. However, demand forecasts are beset with multiple uncertainties, such as consumer behavior, technology, and the general economic environment.[35]

Demand forecasts frequently involve analyzing past trends and productivity levels, linking business plans to productivity levels, and projecting future needs.

HR Supply Analysis

The third HR planning stage is a supply analysis. Its purpose is to determine what human resources will likely be available over the planning period. It develops an inventory of current talent through assessments of performance and potential. Moreover, it forecasts such things as the attraction, movement, and development of employees, as well as the effectiveness of past HR programs.

With this information in hand, specific plans and programs can be developed to address any imbalance between the demand and supply of people and/or skills. The resulting gap analysis serves as the foundation of the final stage in the HR planning process.

Risk Analysis and Strategy Development

The fourth stage in the HR planning process is risk analysis and HR plan development. The first three stages have provided diagnostic information; in this final stage, HR strategy formulation and action programs are designed.

A risk analysis begins with integration of information gathered in the previous steps. First, key HR issues are extracted from the situation analysis. Next, the demand and supply analyses are compared to identify any gaps or surplus of talent. Then, key HR objectives that the organization must accomplish before implementing the strategic business plan are defined. This final step is called a risk analysis because the organization's plans and programs are at risk unless the necessary HR resources are available. If the organization's strategic or business plans are at risk, then basic HR strategies must be adopted and executed.

Four types of basic HR strategies are to acquire, develop, manage, or divest. The strategy chosen depends on the organization's market attractiveness; that is, the opportunities and threats it faces, as well as its competitive strength—namely, its resources and capabilities.

A HR plan translates the risk analysis and the four basic HR strategies into action programs to help achieve the overall goals of the organization. Table 3 presents an overview of the linkages between the four basic HR strategies and various HR action programs.

Applied Examples of HR Planning

A number of organizations have begun to recognize the benefit of integrating the HR function with business strategies. As a result, some companies have developed HR planning processes, and new tools to facilitate HR planning have become available.

Control Data. Control Data Corporation, a diversified computer products and services company, uses an integrated HR planning strategy. The process allows Control Data to continually monitor HR needs as its businesses evolve; and to match HR action programs to each unit's strategy. This integration of HR and business planning helps Control Data cope with the rapid growth and short life cycles common in high-technology companies, thus maintaining and optimizing its competitive advantage.[36]

IBM. At IBM, HR planning begins with line managers in each division developing annual "commitment plans."[37] These plans include quarterly projections of volumes, revenues, and costs, plus action plans designed to carry out the targeted business strategies.

The Personnel Department's role in this process involves five activities: 1) deciding on the kinds of personnel information to be submitted by the operating divisions, and the necessary time frames; 2) assisting divisional managers in preparing divisions personnel plans; 3) assessing divisional business and personnel plans; 4) developing corporate personnel (functional) plans; and 5) evaluating selected actions against plans and giving feedback on evaluation results to line managers who have the authority and responsibility to exercise control.

Corporate staff identifies informational needs on such topics as management development, compensation and benefits, personnel services, employee relations, personnel research, resource utilization, employment (hiring and relocation), and equal opportunity. Personnel assists divisional managers in developing data and plans

Table 3
Linking HR Strategies to HR Programs

STRATEGY	FOCUS	ACTION PROGRAMS
Acquire	Recruitment	• Recruitment • Selection and Placement • Promotion and Transfer • Compensation Policy & Programs
Develop	Development	• Training • Management Development • Career Planning/Management • Succession Planning • Assessment Centers
Manage	Productivity and Performance Improvement	• Performance Management • Incentive Compensation • Productivity Improvement • Organization Development • Quality of Work Life (Climate)
Divest	Capacity Reduction	• Early Retirement Incentives • Workforce Alternatives/Job Sharing • Hiring Freeze • Workforce Resizing/Staff Reductions/Outplacement

Source: Adapted from T.B. Wilson, *A Guide to Strategic Human Resource Planning in the Health Care Industry.* Chicago: American Hospital Association, copyright © 1986.

regarding such matters as recruiting, relocations, and equal opportunity.

Once the personnel data submitted by the divisions are approved, they become standards against which the divisions are measured as they implement commitment plans. Personnel tracks potential imbalances between work loads and staffing levels, with special emphasis on imbalances that may necessitate either mission revisions or personnel redeployments. This process helps ensure linkages between the business and HR plans. It also commits personnel staff to various functional activities that support the business plans of the divisions in which they operate.

Developments in HRM Software. Computerized data-base management systems are being introduced to provide guidance in

Figure 8
Human Resource Planning Steps

```
                    SITUATION ANALYSIS
                    • Environment
                    • Strategy
                    • Structure
                    • Culture
                    • HR Challenges
                   ↙                ↘
     HR DEMAND                          HR SUPPLY
     • Determinants                     • Internal
     • Requirements                     • External
     • Summary                          • Summary
                   ↘                ↙
                 RISK ANALYSIS AND HR PLAN
                    • Key Issues
                    • Strategy
                    • Plan
              ↙       ↙        ↘        ↘
         (ACQUIRE) (DEVELOP) (MANAGE) (DIVEST)
```

Source: Reprinted with permission from Hay Management Memo, Number 340. Philadelphia: The Hay Group, copyright © 1986.

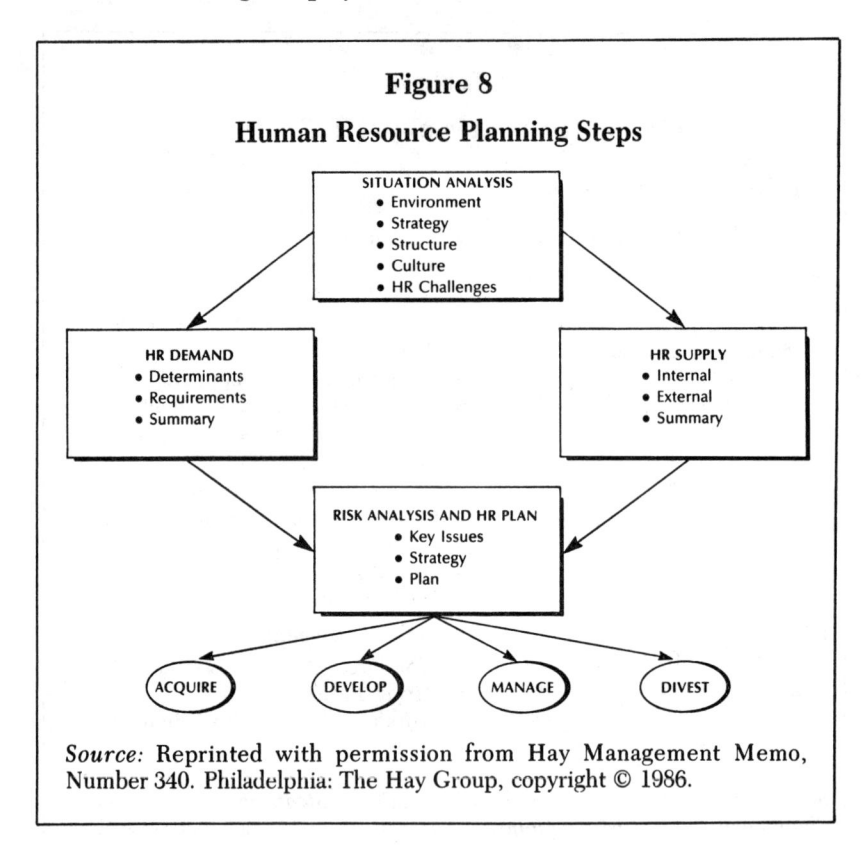

the HR planning process. For example, OASIS (Organizational and Strategy Information Service) is a system being used by organizations such as General Electric, Chase Manhattan, Pacific Telesis, and Sara Lee to identify expected performance outcomes of various strategic and HR initiatives.[38] Through a data base of various strategic and HR issues across a large number of business units, OASIS identifies relationships between initiatives and performance as measured along such dimensions as return on investment, productivity, market share growth, product quality, and innovation.

Conclusion

Many benefits can be realized from implementing job analysis and HR planning programs. Together, the two processes contribute to increased competitiveness in a variety of ways:

- They enable organizations to respond proactively to technological, organizational, and economic change.
- They improve employee morale by encouraging greater participation in and understanding of HR programs.
- They ensure that the culture of the organization and the organization's business strategy are compatible.
- They foster better integration of business and HR strategies.

Along with increased competitiveness, organizations can gain other advantages from job analysis and HR planning programs. These benefits are discussed in more detail below.

Increased Productivity

Job analysis and HR planning also promote increased productivity by better matching people and jobs. By providing thorough definitions of job requirements, job analysis enables managers to select, place, develop, train, appraise, and reward employees in a job-related manner.

HR planning provides an even broader perspective of the job-person match. By matching its future HR requirements to the projected HR supply, the organization can increase work force productivity and the quality of its products and services.

Improved Compliance With Governmental Regulations

Using job information not only makes good business sense; it also enables an organization to conform with certain governmental guidelines. Job analysis information demonstrates the job-relatedness of selection, promotion, and performance appraisal systems as required by the Uniform Guidelines on Employee Selection Procedures. It also documents compliance with the Equal Pay Act of 1963, which requires that jobs of equal skill, effort, responsibility, and working conditions have equal pay. A third law, the Fair Labor Standards Act of 1938, addresses numerous employment issues such as the payment of overtime. It contains complex considerations and criteria for identifying jobs and situations that are exempt from the protection and provisions of the law. The criteria for these exemptions require documentation of the types of work performed, the responsibilities exercised, and the context in which work is performed—in other words, job analysis.

Enhanced Communication

Communication improves when supervisors and subordinates are able to focus on specifically defined job requirements when reviewing performance or evaluating whether particular training opportunities will improve an employee's ability to meet specific job requirements. The reasons for promotion or failure to promote can be described in terms of specific job requirements. Building a job-related system provides a common focus and a common language for employees, managers, and the HR staff to discuss and carry out HRM activities.

Increased Synergy Among HR Programs

Finally, an effective program of job analysis and HR planning supports an integrated approach to managing human resources. Job analysis provides precise definitions of jobs and their requirements and supports all of the HR functions shown in Figure 1.

As demonstrated at Control Data and Nationwide Insurance, a systematic system of job analysis supports the integration of various HR programs. Using a common language about jobs, these organizations have established linkages between their selection, performance appraisal, compensation, and development programs. These linkages have streamlined employee movement in the organizations and have led to richer support programs.

Future Directions

In the future, the personnel function and its role as a control-oriented supplier of employees will continue to evolve into a HRM function concerned with the planning, development, performance, motivation, and productivity of the work force. This evolution has several implications for the role of job analysis and HR planning:

- Job analysis and HR planning will be increasingly used to "target" the implementation of specific HR programs and to provide the necessary information for ensuring that job-related programs are implemented.
- To facilitate the development of the HRM function, there will be continued evolution and use of integrated personnel systems and computers, along with the development of real-time data bases of job and people information.

- HR and business management will continue to evolve and become integrated. By ensuring that HR programs meet critical business needs, HR managers will be drawn into core business management.

◆

Notes

1. Ross.
2. Peter Drucker, perhaps more than anyone, has been largely responsible for this broader definition of HRM and of people as resources.
3. Drucker, p. 30.
4. Bemis, Belenky, and Soder, p. 1.
5. Beer.
6. Wortman and Sperling.
7. Hudock; Roy; Wortman and Sperling.
8. See Flanagan for full description of the critical incident technique.
9. Bemis, Belenky, and Soder.
10. Cascio.
11. Fleishman (1964, 1966, 1975); Theologus, Romashko, and Fleishman.
12. U.S. Department of Labor (1972).
13. Fine and Wiley.
14. Primoff.
15. Cascio, p. 141.
16. McCormick, Cunningham, and Gordon; McCormick, Cunningham, and Thornton; and McCormick, Jeanneret, and Mecham (1972).
17. McCormick, Jeanneret, and Mecham (1977).
18. Christal.
19. McCormick; Moore.
20. Brumback; Prien.
21. Levine.
22. Page (1986).
23. Avner and Williams.
24. Ibid.
25. Tornow and Pinto.
26. Page (1986 and 1987); Page and Caskey.
27. Berger.
28. Tichy, Fombrun, and Devanna.
29. English.
30. Berger and Glass; Gatewood and Rockmore.
31. Wilson.
32. Cascio.
33. Dyer, p. 12.
34. Berger and Ochsner.
35. Cascio.
36. Cascio; Burack and Mathys, p. 3; Manzini and Gridley; Walker.
37. Dyer and Heyer.
38. Geller.

◆

References

Avner, B.D. and J.E. Williams. 1986. "Career Directions: An Integrated Personnel System." *Prentice Hall Personnel Management: Policies and Practices Service* (December 1): 985–992.

Beer, M. 1980. *Organization Change and Development: A System View*. Santa Monica, CA: Goodyear Publishing Company.

Bemis, S., A.H. Belenky, and D.A. Soder. 1983. *Job Analysis: An Effective Management Tool*. Washington, DC: BNA Books, 1983.

Berger, L.A. 1986. "Using the Computer to Support Job Evaluation Decision-Making," *Journal of Compensation and Benefits*, 2 no. 1:

Berger, L.A. and H.E. Glass. 1986. "Linking Business and Human Resource Strategy." *Planning Review* 11 (6): 26–30.

Berger, L.A. and R.C. Ochsner. 1987. *1987 Environmental Scan*. Philadelphia: The Hay Group.

Brumback, G.B. 1976. "One Method Is Not Enough: An Overview of Selection Oriented Job Analysis Methodology." Paper presented at the Selection Specialist's Symposium of the International Personnel Management Association, July, Chicago.

Burack, E.H. and N.J. Mathys. 1979. *Human Resource Planning: A Pragmatic Approach to Manpower Staffing and Development*. Lake Forest, IL: Brace-Park Press.

Cascio, W.F. 1987. *Applied Psychology in Personnel Management*. 3rd ed. Englewood Cliffs, NJ: Prentice-Hall.

Christal, R.E. 1974. "The United States Air Force Occupational Research Project." AFHRL-TR-73-75. Springfield, VA: National Technical Information Service; *JSAS Catalog of Selected Documents in Psychology*, 4 (MS. 651): 36.

Drucker, P.F. 1986. "Goodbye to the Old Personnel Function." *The Wall Street Journal* (May 22): 30.

Dyer, L. 1983. "Strategic Human Resource Management and Planning." In *Research in Personnel and Human Resource Management*, vol. 3, eds. K.M. Rowland and G.R. Ferris. Greenwich, CT: JAI Press.

Dyer, L. and N.O. Heyer. 1984. "Human Resource Planning at IBM." *Human Resource Planning* 7: 111–121.

English, J.W. 1984. "Human Resource Planning: The Ideal Versus the Real." *Human Resource Planning* 7: 67–72.

Fine, S.J. and W.W. Wiley. 1971. *An Introduction to Functional Job Analysis: A Scaling of Selected Tasks for the Social Welfare Field*. Kalamazoo, MI: W.E. Upjohn Institute.

Flanagan, J.C. 1954. "The Critical Incident Technique." *Psychological Bulletin* 51: 327–358.

Fleishman, E.A. 1964. *The Structure and Measurement of Physical Fitness*. Englewood Cliffs, NJ: Prentice-Hall.

———. 1966. "Human Abilities and the Acquisition of Skill." In *Acquisition of Skill*, ed. E.A. Bilodeau. New York: Academic Press.

———. 1975. "Toward a Taxonomy of Human Performance." *American Psychologist* 30: 1127–1149.

Gatewood, R.D. and B.W. Rockmore. 1986. "Combining Organizational Manpower and Career Development Needs: An Operational Human Resource Planning Model." *Human Resource Planning* 9:81–96.

Geller, A. In press. "Organizational Characteristics of Successful Business Units." In *Handbook of Business Strategy*, ed. H. Glass. New York: Warren, Gorham & Lamont.

Hudock, A.W. 1984. "Describing Salaried Jobs." In *Handbook of Wage and Salary Administration*, 2nd ed., ed. M.L. Rock. New York: McGraw-Hill.

Levine, E.L. 1983. *Everything You Always Wanted to Know About Job Analysis*. Tampa, FL: Mariner Publishing Company.

Manzini, A.O. and J.D. Gridley. 1986. *Integrating Human Resources and Strategic Business Planning*. New York: AMACOM.

McCormick, E.J. 1979. *Job Analysis: Methods and Applications*. New York: AMACOM.

McCormick, E.J., J.W. Cunningham, and G.C. Gordon. 1967. "Job Dimensions Based on Factorial Analyses of Worker-Oriented Job Variables," *Personnel Psychology* 20: 417–430.

McCormick, E.J., J.W. Cunningham, and G.C. Thornton. 1967. "The Prediction of Job Requirements by a Structured Job Analysis Procedure." *Personnel Psychology* 20: 417–430.

McCormick, E.J., P.R. Jeanneret, and R.C. Mecham. 1972. "A Study of Job Characteristics and Job Dimensions as Based on the Position Analysis Questionnaire (PAQ)." *Journal of Applied Psychology* 56: 347–368.

———. 1977. *Technical Manual for the Position Analysis (PAQ)*. (System II). Logan, Utah: PAQ Services.

Moore, B.E. 1976. *Occupational Analysis for Human Resource Development*. Research Report No. 25. Washington, DC: Department of the Navy, Office of Civilian Manpower Management.

Page, R.C. 1986. "Developing and Implementing Compensation Applications Within an Integrated Personnel System." In *State-of-the-Art Applications of Job Analysis: Integrated Personnel Systems*, symposium conducted at the annual convention of the American Psychological Association, August, Washington, DC.

———. 1987. "The Management Position Description Questionnaire." In *Handbook of Job Analysis*, ed. S. Gael. New York: John Wiley.

Page, R.C. and D.T. Caskey. 1987. "Computer Programmer Job Analysis." In *Handbook of Job Analysis*, ed. S. Gael. New York: John Wiley.

Prien, E.P. 1977. "The Function of Job Analysis in Content Validation." *Personnel Psychology* 30: 167–174.

Primoff, E.S. 1965. "Test Selection by Job Analysis: The J-Coefficient." Assembled test technical edition. Washington, DC: U.S. Civil Service Commission.

Ross, J.D. 1981. "A Definition of Human Resources Management." *Personnel Journal* 60 (10): 781–787.

Roy, T.S. Jr. 1984. "Collecting Data Through Interviews and Observations." In *Handbook of Wage and Salary Administration*, 2nd ed., ed. M.L. Rock. New York: McGraw-Hill.

Theologus, G.C., T. Romashko, and E.A. Fleishman. 1973. "Development of Taxonomy of Human Performance: A Feasibility Study of Ability Dimensions for Classifying Human Tasks." MS. 326. *JSAS Catalogue of Selected Documents in Psychology* 3: 29.

Tichy, N.M., C.J. Fombrun, and M.A. Devanna. 1984. "The Organizational Context of Strategic Human Resource Management." In *Strategic Human Resource Management*, ed. C.J. Fombrum, N.M. Tichy, and M.A. Devanna. New York: John Wiley & Sons.

Tornow, W.W. and P.R. Pinto. 1976. "The Development of a Managerial Taxonomy: A System for Describing, Classifying, and Evaluting Executive Positions." *Journal of Applied Psychology* 61: 410–418.

U.S. Department of Labor. 1972. *Handbook for Analyzing Jobs*. Washington, DC: U.S. Government Printing Office.

Walker, J.W. 1980. *Human Resource Planning*. New York: McGraw-Hill.

Wilson, T.B. 1986. *A Guide to Strategic Human Resource Planning for the Health Care Industry*. Chicago: American Hospital Association.

Wortman, M.S. Jr. and J. Sperling. 1975. *Defining the Manager's Job*, 2nd ed. New York: AMACOM.

2.3

External and Internal Recruitment

J. Scott Lord

The recruitment process has grown increasingly important and complex during the past decade, and it promises to become the most critical element of a successful HR function in years ahead. Organizations have recognized that recruitment is a form of business competition: Just as corporations vie to develop, manufacture, and market the best product, so they must vie to identify, attract, and hire the most qualified people. Recruitment is a business, and it is big business.

This view of recruitment evolved gradually during the late 1970s and early 1980s as the labor pool began to shrink. Organizations expanded employment budgets to reflect stiff competition for employees, and recruitment managers became heroes or scapegoats depending on their ability to provide corporations with the right number and mix of employees within strict time constraints. Recruiters sharpened their business skills, became more proactive, and developed a keener business sense, changes that are here to stay.

Despite this business emphasis, recruitment is an art, not a science. The results of recruitment can be measured scientifically and defined readily—such measurements appear in exhibits and figures throughout this chapter. But the thrust of this chapter is the artistic element: those attributes, partly innate and partly acquired, that distinguish recruiters as state-of-the-art professionals. Along with examining the current state of the recruitment function, the chapter will explore areas for improvement and ways to achieve these changes.

The Recruitment Process

Reduced to its lowest common denominators, employment is a series of requisitions, résumés, invitations, interviews, offers, and acceptances. The outcome of each aspect of recruitment can be measured, but tracking numbers is not enough. Interpreting data, controlling the flow, and influencing the outcomes at every step are far more important. This section addresses methods that can help recruiters manage each phase effectively.

Handling Requisitions

The recruiter's job begins with receipt of a requisition. While this billet for a new employee requires various levels of management authorization, the employment manager should control final approval. As key players in the strategic planning process, HR managers are best equipped to evaluate any requisition against forecasted staffing needs.

The requisition should provide a detailed job description and the basic prerequisites for candidates, such as education, years of experience, and salary range. Since personal chemistry is one of the most important ingredients of job success, recruiters should supplement written requirements through personal meetings with managers who initiate requisitions. This interview can help assure positive chemistry between a candidate and the hiring manager, as well as supply information that may prove vital to the recruitment process.

To help identify job qualifications and prioritize needs, recruiters should discuss the following issues with the hiring manager:

- Which of the job specifications are flexible?
- What qualifications are critical and which are merely desirable?
- Who is performing a similar job now?
- What is a potential career path for this position?
- Does the position require teamwork or individual initiative?
- Do certain other companies employ this type of person?
- What type of personality will mesh with current employees?
- How urgent is the need?

External & Internal Recruitment   2-75

Finally, recruiters should track the progress of each open requisition and inform managers of its status by memo and in person. The more personal contact with line supervisors, the more information recruiters have to augment official job descriptions. Some companies ensure that recruiters have this type of information by including recruiters in weekly staff meetings or providing them with a cubicle in each line organization.

Managing Résumé Flow

In today's business world, the recruitment process is as much a marketing tool as traditional promotional techniques. Companies duel for candidates using marketing methods once reserved for top corporate headhunters. However, few of these techniques are new—just improved, glamorized, more expensive, and more widely utilized. What has changed are the controls that recruiters use to manage the process and all forces, internal and external, that affect résumé flow.

External Controls

External controls over the flow of résumés depend largely on the resources committed to this process. In general, increasing the flow of résumés requires more time and money than diminishing it.

To attract more résumés, companies must convey their message externally. The process can involve placing advertisements, informing third parties, holding open houses, and/or conducting direct mail campaigns. Specific techniques include sophisticated, multimedia advertising campaigns; job fairs for secretaries, scientists, and software engineers; open houses featuring glittering corporate displays, shrimp, door prizes, and instant employment offers; and a proliferation of computerized employment services and executive search firms.

To decrease résumé flow, organizations can restrict their use of outside sources, or advertise selectively in specific geographic locations or particular publications. Incoming résumés will also drop if candidates learn that the company treats current or prospective employees in a less than professional manner. Recruiters should be aware of this last possibility and should avoid its occurrence, regardless of the organization's hiring needs.

Internal Controls

Internal management of the résumé flow requires prescreening large numbers of résumés, saving the best, and assuring that line managers regularly review current résumés. This final element, ongoing review by managers, often gets overlooked, but it is critical to the recruitment process. Since successful recruitment ultimately depends on hiring decisions made by supervisors, getting line managers involved from the start can greatly improve recruiters' effectiveness.

One method that some innovative companies have adopted is the résumé review room. This room, usually located within the employment department, contains all current résumés for line managers to review against their current openings. Recruiters prescreen incoming résumés and classify them by source (direct, such as advertising, employee referral, or indirect, such as third-party recruitment) and by discipline. A sign-in log of individuals who use the résumé room can help recruiters identify which manager's requisitions need active recruitment and which might easily be filled by résumés already on file.

To maintain interest in résumé reviews, recruiters should regularly replace aged résumés with new ones. Résumés obtained from direct sources should usually be pulled after one month; those obtained from indirect sources should be withdrawn after two weeks.

Arranging Invitations and Interviews

Recruiters can increase and control the flow of invitations for interviews by taking full advantage of procedures that keep line managers involved in the recruitment process. Regular contact allows recruiters to educate résumé reviewers on how to look past idiosyncracies, accept the lack of a perfect résumé, and identify the best prospects.

The résumé room concept described above is one possible way to promote this involvement. However, recruiters in larger organizations should recognize that reviewing a daily stack of résumés can become a burden to individuals with other responsibilities. In such instances, encouraging each department to appoint a résumé reader on a revolving basis can build stronger ties without overburdening one person.

Timely follow-ups on written invitations and scheduling of interviews is an important factor for recruiters to control. Good résumés have an extremely limited "shelf life," so effective recruiters must move quickly on promising candidates to avoid discovering that they are no longer available. Once again, timeliness depends on close coordination with line management to assure prompt decisions on which candidates to interview.

Policies to assure proper treatment of interview prospects will also promote recruitment efforts. If written invitations are sent, recruiters should carefully examine the wording used. Orientation should provide enough exposure to different managers and sufficient time for candidates to form favorable impressions. Interview schedules should ensure timely processing of prospects, proper assignment of candidates to hiring interviewers, and designated replacements for absent interviewers. Recruiters should also set up a cost-effective system to provide out-of-state candidates with transportation, accommodations, directions, and hospitality. All these procedures enhance the company's reputation among prospective employees, thus contributing to recruiters' overall effectiveness.

Controlling Offers and Acceptances

Successful control over offers and acceptances depends on a recruiter's rapport with line managers. In the short term, good communication expedites hiring decisions and decreases the likelihood of candidates accepting positions elsewhere. In the long run, a good rapport with hiring managers can facilitate employee selection and retention with resulting benefits to recruiters.

To assure timely employment offers, the organization should set deadlines for making hiring decisions and formulating job offers. Line managers should be able to decide on candidates within 24 hours of completing interviews. Another three days should suffice for recruiters to prepare and present job offers to good prospects.

Expedience, however, does not justify eliminating important steps in the offer cycle. Recruiters must have input as supervisors review candidates and decide which to hire. By pushing good candidates and preventing employment of poor prospects, recruiters can reduce turnover and better control their work load. In similar fashion, recruiters who thoroughly check references within the three days prior to making a job offer will prevent potential problems later on.

Following the presentation of a job offer, recruiters should interview candidates to determine their reasons for declining or accepting the position. This information can enhance effectiveness by identifying positive factors to emphasize and negative influences to eliminate in future recruitment efforts.

Managing the Recruitment Function

Besides its importance to an organization, effective recruitment is the cornerstone of a well-designed HR function. Without qualified employees within the organization, the HR activities of training, development, compensation, and planning lose their value. As a result, internal management of the recruitment process should form the starting point in any HRM analysis. By assuring the recruitment function is properly staffed, structured, and equipped, HR managers can improve the effectiveness of recruitment and the HR function.

Assessing Recruitment Needs

A key question facing HR managers is whether to assign recruitment duties to current HR staff, or make recruitment a separate function. The current rule of thumb is to set up a separate recruitment function—perhaps just one recruiter—if the company experiences sustained annual hiring requirements for 50 to 100 exempt-level professionals. However, a number of variables can influence how well this rule of thumb works.

Factors Affecting Recruitment Needs

A recent survey of employment and staffing managers at more than 500 companies indicates how different factors can affect a company's recruitment needs.[1] The source of résumés, the type of opening, and geographic location all can influence recruiters' success at filling requisitions.

Source of résumés. On average, managers surveyed judged only about 7 percent of incoming résumés to be worth routing to hiring managers. However, several respondents found that using employment agencies generated *better* (more qualified) résumés than making general inquiries or placing employment ads.

Type of position. While the median number of routed résumés that received invitations to interview equalled only 26 percent, managers reported invitation rates ranging from 8 percent to 60 percent. A follow-up inquiry revealed that candidates for technical and lower-level positions had the highest invitation rates, and that the invitation rate fell as the level of the position rose.

The type of position also influenced the rate of offers and acceptances made to employment candidates. Approximately 40 percent of individuals interviewed received job offers, with candidates for lower-level positions earning the highest offer rates. In contrast, non-technical positions generated twice as many acceptances (82 percent) as technical positions (41 percent).

Geographic location. Finally, positions requiring relocation generated lower acceptances to interview requests and fewer employment offers. Approximately 78 percent of local candidates agreed to come in for interviews, while about 65 percent of out-of-state candidates responded positively to interview invitations.

Time. The factors cited above indicate that adequate assessment of recruitment needs starts with accurate staffing analysis and forecasting. Organizations that experience unexpected terminations and attrition may face critical employment needs and will place unrealistic time demands on recruiters. Although time frames differ from job to job and industry to industry, three months from the receipt of a requisition to the new employee's start date is considered an acceptable time period for recruiting a journey-level professional.

Structuring the Recruitment Function

Once HR managers have assessed their recruitment needs, they need to establish a structure for implementing the recruitment function. The number of employees and levels of responsibility in the recruitment area should reflect the volume of recruitment requirements and the organizational resources committed to the recruitment function.

Hiring Demands and the Recruitment Function

In smaller companies with sporadic recruitment needs, the recruiter is an HR generalist, juggling employment with other HR activities. Successful recruitment under these constraints requires

2-80 HR Planning, Employment & Placement

that HR staffers schedule regular times for handling only employment activities. For example, welcome and entry interviews could take place from 8 a.m. to 10 a.m., Monday through Thursday, without detracting from other HR duties. Likewise, telephone screening can take place in the early evening hours, when candidates have returned home from their current jobs.

Organizations with a high volume of requisitions will need a separate recruitment function within the HR department. Figure 1 shows one possible framework for a dedicated recruitment function.

In this example, the employment manager oversees four recruiters and a data processing clerk, and handles all executive

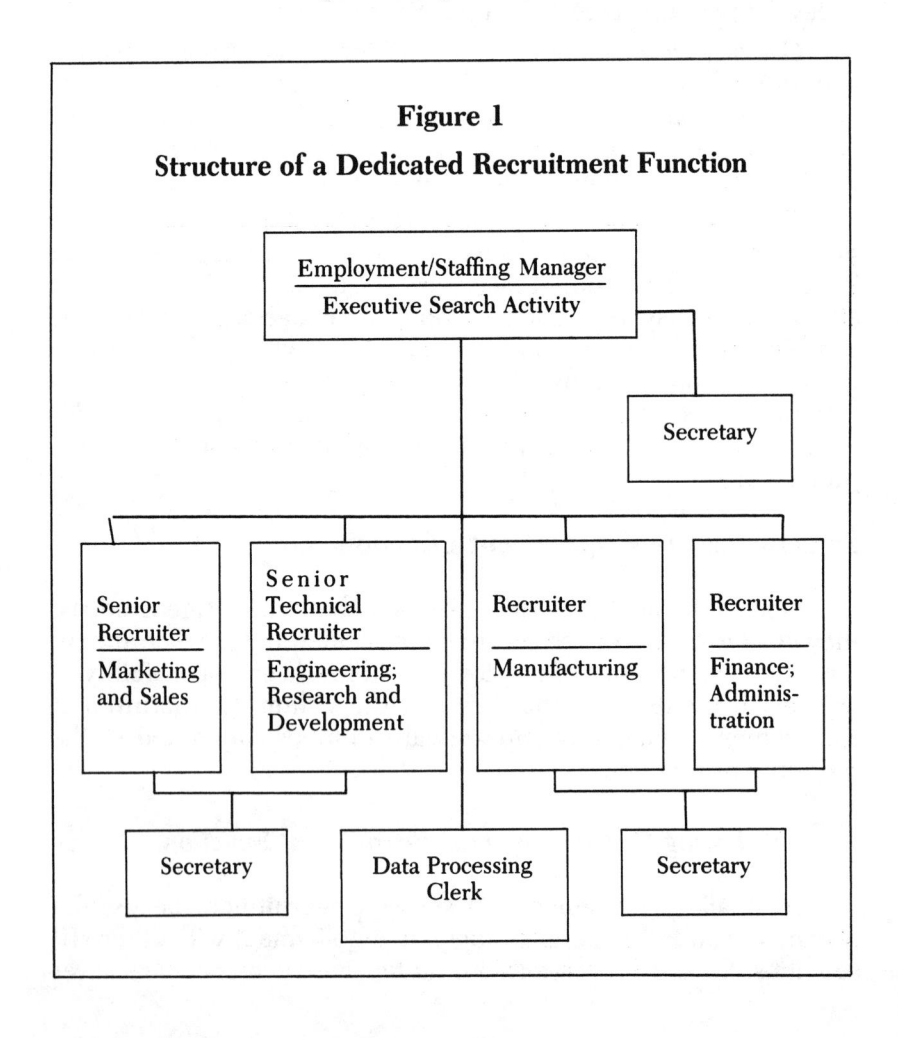

Figure 1

Structure of a Dedicated Recruitment Function

```
                    ┌─────────────────────────────────┐
                    │  Employment/Staffing Manager    │
                    │  Executive Search Activity      │
                    └─────────────────────────────────┘
                                     │
                                     ├──────────────┐
                                     │              │
                                     │         ┌─────────┐
                                     │         │Secretary│
                                     │         └─────────┘
         ┌──────────┬──────────┬─────┴────┬──────────┐
         │          │          │          │
    ┌────────┐ ┌─────────┐ ┌────────┐ ┌────────┐
    │Senior  │ │Senior   │ │Recruiter│ │Recruiter│
    │Recruiter│ │Technical│ │        │ │        │
    │        │ │Recruiter│ │Manufac- │ │Finance;│
    │Marketing│ │Engineer-│ │turing  │ │Adminis-│
    │and Sales│ │ing;     │ │        │ │tration │
    │        │ │Research │ │        │ │        │
    │        │ │and Devel│ │        │ │        │
    │        │ │opment   │ │        │ │        │
    └────────┘ └─────────┘ └────────┘ └────────┘
         │                      │           │
    ┌─────────┐        ┌──────────────┐ ┌─────────┐
    │Secretary│        │Data Processing│ │Secretary│
    │         │        │    Clerk      │ │         │
    └─────────┘        └──────────────┘ └─────────┘
```

search activity. Each recruiter covers requisitions for a specific discipline: finance and administration, research and development, marketing and sales, or manufacturing. The data processing clerk programs recruitment figures and generates analysis reports, while two other clerks handle recruiters' secretarial work.

Despite differing areas of responsibility, this structure requires close coordination among its members. When conducting an executive search, the employment manager should work closely with the recruiter assigned to that particular department. In addition, each recruiter should be familiar enough with at least one other discipline to serve as a back-up to another recruiter. Such a policy prevents backlogs during vacations and absences, and broadens each recruiter's perspective of the organization.

Companies with recruitment requirements that fall somewhere between these two examples still require some type of separate recruitment function. Placing one or two recruiters with appropriate support staff under the HR director or employment manager will produce better results than hiring additional HR staff and dividing recruitment duties among them.

Resources Committed to the Recruitment Function

The number of staff needed in the recruitment function can vary depending on the amount of resources an organization offers to support recruitment efforts. The company that hopes to compete successfully for qualified employees will have to arm its recruiters with the same tools it gives its marketing and sales staff: attractive displays, appealing literature, audiovisual presentations, and similar tools.

Developing and acquiring these recruitment tools requires financial commitment from the organization. However, cost-conscious recruiters should look inside their companies before going outside to purchase marketing tools. In-house departments, such as communications, public relations, and printing/publications, can often provide professional tools like displays, literature, and flipcharts at more economical prices than outside agencies. In addition, utilizing the talents of in-house personnel can help build partnerships between the employment function and other departments.

Computers are another tool essential to a successful recruitment function. Computers, especially personal computers, have become the most powerful equipment at the disposal of recruiters, enabling measurement and control of the recruitment function. Automated employment tracking and control systems have proliferated during the last few years. Powerful software packages are available at affordable prices, costing from $1,000 to $10,000 depending on the range and volume of recruitment needs.

Successful computerization of the recruitment function also can depend on obtaining support from other in-house departments. Management information systems (MIS) departments do not want their corporate computerization plans disturbed by amateurs who purchase incompatible personal computers for their department's exclusive use. Yet, automation of the employment department often ranks low on the MIS agenda. Moreover, if the computer department does bring recruitment on-line, the existing mainframe system may not match recruiters' processing needs, cost concerns, and time requirements. Good relations between the recruitment and MIS departments help prevent these problems from hindering recruiters' efforts.

Staffing the Recruitment Function

In the past, HR professionals regarded a recruitment position as a brief but necessary step before promotion. However, as competition for employees increases and recruitment receives greater emphasis, HR employees are willing to spend significantly more time in this high-visibility role. These trends make it particularly important to identify the qualities of effective recruiters.

Communications Skills

A good recruiter must possess an image and appearance that reflects favorably on the organization; an outgoing nature; flexibility; willingness to take necessary risks; ability to think on one's feet; skill in setting priorities; self-motivation; and salesmanship. Communications and interpersonal skill underlie many of these attributes and contribute greatly to recruiters' success.

These skills also influence the overall effectiveness of the recruitment process. Within the organization, good interaction with other managers will foster a healthy flow of information and assure recruiters of input on employment decisions, backing for recruitment campaigns, and full cooperation in their efforts. Outside the organization, a recruiter's communication and interpersonal abilities can greatly influence the organization's reputation among individual applicants and employment agencies.

Finally, good communication can help recruiters say "no" when that answer is in the best interests of the company. Understaffed managers at times may pressure recruiters to do the impossible—make exceptions to the vacation policy for an entry-level employee; pay a new employee more than a current, equally qualified and similarly positioned employee; or fill a technical position within an impossibly short period. Recruiters who can communicate valid reasons for refusing impossible requests will earn their colleagues' respect.

Familiarity With the Organization

Given the impact that recruiters can have on an organization's reputation, familiarity with the company and its needs is essential. As one HR executive has noted, "It is not enough for [recruiters] to be able to select employees who have the technical ability to succeed. They have to be able to select qualified candidates who will fit into the organizational environment and value system."[2]

However, this aspect of recruitment often goes unnoticed in many organizations. Companies that have an in-house recruitment function often staff it with newly hired people and give them little training. Prospective employees expect an employment representative to provide information about the company's total HR function. They do not want to be referred to brochures, handbooks, and manuals.

Rather than placing newcomers in the recruitment function, organizations should look inside the company, especially in the HR department. Successful recruiters need more than mere knowledge of recruitment techniques; they also must be knowledgeable about compensation, benefits, affirmative action and equal employment opportunity standards, employee relations, and training and development.

If the HR department lacks a strong candidate, look elsewhere in the company for individuals who might make good recruiters. Employees with two to four years of experience in the organization's marketing, sales, communications, or other service-related positions could become successful recruiters. In general, close familiarity with the organization, its culture, and its people will give these individuals an advantage over outside candidates.

Business Sense

An understanding of business, including technical concepts like cost-effectiveness or value-added, has become critical to recruiters' success. Recruiters must possess the ability to track attrition and acceptance rates, calculate cost-benefit figures for different recruitment sources, factor in time and travel expenses, and come up with a balance sheet that demonstrates their value to the organization.

This emphasis on business sense and the bottom line is not unique to recruitment. Indeed, the entire HRM process has become subject to such scrutiny. As one observer has commented, "This concern over a cost-benefit relationship is an important concept in making sure that the HR function remains a vital and respected part of the organization. Top management will no longer accept the rationalization that we are in the people business and there is no way we can have impact or measure the cost-benefit relationship."[3]

External Recruitment Sources

Many of the traditional sources for external recruitment have changed little over the years. Employment advertising, career fairs, college campuses, employment agencies, and executive search firms have long dominated the recruitment scene. However, as the entry-worker labor pool shrinks, as college enrollments drop, and as technological changes require more highly skilled workers, recruiters must exercise innovative techniques to compete in these traditional labor markets.

University Relations

The projected decline in college enrollment—from the current level of 12.2 million to 11.5 million over the next decade—will bring a commensurate increase in the competition for the best and brightest on college campuses. To overcome this competition, recruiters will have to do more than simply forward company literature and arrive on campus for interview appointments. Successful college recruitment will require organizations to develop an ongoing university relations program.

The distinction between university relations and campus recruitment is subtle but important. As one observer put it, "University relations connotes more than just campus recruiting, which no longer is the only answer to the problem of getting the right people for your organization from campus. Competition and a growing selectivity by organizations have broadened the scope. More and more, activities directed at the campus become a two-way street, with a truly mutual cooperation necessary to solve all the problems involved in such a rapidly changing environment."[4]

The two-way street of university relations encompasses more than the relationship between a recruiter and the college's job placement coordinator. Recruiters should seek to develop strong ties between the organization's key department managers and related branches within the university. Since university relations is an ongoing concern, these functional ties should be maintained even in years when college recruitment will not be a major consideration.

Organizations that wish to remain competitive in the college recruitment area should consider undertaking the following activities:

- Identify functional areas within the company that are most likely to benefit from college recruiting.

- Find individuals within those functional areas who would make outstanding representatives on campus and provide recruitment training for these employees. Try to select representatives who are alumni of key universities where the organization wants to maintain a relationship.

- Locate professors on campus who lecture in disciplines related to the company's operations and work to develop professional relationships with these faculty members.

- Provide co-operative assignments and professional summer work for students, and offer consulting, seminars, or training and development opportunities for educators.

- Demonstrate an active interest in relevant campus activities.

- Concentrate on a select number of schools with which the organization can maintain a meaningful and ongoing relationship.

Outside Agencies

Two of the primary sources for third-party recruitment are executive search firms and employment agencies. The primary distinction between these external resources is the level of position for which they recruit. However, other key differences exist between executive search firms and employment agencies that organizations should consider when selecting a third-party recruiter. Table 1 summarizes a few of these differences which are discussed more fully in the following sections.

Executive Search Firms

Organizations typically retain executive search consulting firms to recruit for senior-level positions that command salaries over $50,000 and total compensation packages worth in excess of $100,000. Reasons for retaining a search consultant may include a need to maintain confidentiality from an incumbent or a competitor, a lack of local resources to recruit executive-level individuals, or insufficient time.

Despite the advantages, use of executive search consultants requires time and commitment from the hiring company. The organization must allow the search consultant to become a company insider, to develop knowledge and familiarity with the business and its key players. Although companies may not relish opening their corporate doors and exposing their "secrets" to an outsider, trust is vital to the success of the search.

Financial Arrangements

Using an executive search company can prove costly compared to other third-party sources. Total fees can range from 30 to 35 percent of the compensation package of the new hire. Executive search firms usually will receive a retainer, amounting to one-third the total fee, as soon as the search is commissioned. The remaining portion of the fee is usually paid in increments, with another one-third of the fee due 60 days into the assignment and a final third due upon completion. If an organization independently hires a candidate (on its own) prior to completion of the search, it still must pay all or some portion of the search firm's fee, unless other arrangements are made.

Table 1

Differences Between Executive Search Firms and Employment Agencies

Services	Executive Search Firms	Employment Agencies
Financial Arrangements	Fees based on 30 to 35 percent of candidate's salary and time needed to recruit, or a flat rate plus expenses.	Fees based on 20 to 35 percent of candidate's starting salary.
	Retainer fee required; payment due even if opening filled through other sources.	No retainer fee; fee due only if position filled by agency.
	Staff compensation may include salary, bonus, profit-sharing, and incentives for business generation.	Staff compensation usually depends on commissions for placements made.
Case Load	Personal consultant handles only three to five cases at once.	Agent works with many open job orders at one time.
	Firms usually handle openings at higher levels of organization.	Agencies typically assigned lower-level vacancies.
Relationship with Clients	Firms represent employers only.	Agencies represent employers and job-seekers.
	General management involved in decision to retain search firm.	HR department makes decision to use agency.
	Consultant thoroughly researches client organization and position requirements before search.	Agents spend less time on initial research and job specifications. Some assignments handled by phone with no personal contact.
	Firms conduct assignments on an exclusive basis.	Agencies compete with similar companies for placements.

Table 1 continued

Services	Executive Search Firms	Employment Agencies
Time Commitment	Consultant invests 40 to 50 hours per month on each search.	Limited investment of time on any one client, due to lack of guaranteed payment.
Referral Rates and Guarantees	Two to four highly qualified candidates recommended to each client.	Large number of applicants referred to increase odds of a placement.
	Recruitment and evaluation efforts target broad range of candidates, most of whom are not in job market.	Recruitment focuses mainly on candidates actively seeking new employment.
	Process- and results-oriented.	Placement-oriented.
	Reputable firms offer a professional guarantee and commitment to thorough, ethical practices.	Contingency fee arrangement eliminates any obligation to produce results.
Level of Client Involvement	Minimal HR and management time involvement required.	Considerable HR time required to screen, interview, and evaluate candidates.

Selecting an Executive Search Firm

The state of the recruitment art varies among executive search firms. While some observers contend that the executive search business has changed little over the decades, others feel that technology has made a major impact on the better firms. As one search firm executive stated, "Like other industries, the executive search business has joined the information age. Sophisticated computer systems enable us to extend the depth and reach of our candidate and company files, and provide us with the means to handle the sheer volume of our clients' needs. They also allow us to create the operational and structural controls necessary to produce better and more effective results."[5]

These technological innovations mean that as smaller executive search firms become computerized, organizations can expect more timely and cost-effective service. However, until computerization becomes more widespread within the industry, differences in technological capabilities should factor into decisions about which executive search firm to use.

Another factor that organizations should investigate before selecting a search firm is the consultant who will handle the company's recruitment activity. As the president of one executive search firm put it, "The right firm will have the 'right person' working on the assignment, utilizing a logical, rational process. By and large, this is a personal relationship business . . . clients primarily hire a person."[6]

Despite the important role of the search consultant, organizations should make sure that ". . . behind that person, there exists a process and the resources to assure successful completion."[7] The following questions can help HR managers to evaluate an executive search company's professional resources:

- Does the search firm maintain desired confidentiality?[8]
- Can it deliver qualified candidates quickly?
- Does it achieve a high percentage of completed assignments?
- Is the firm well-respected?
- Can it conduct an effective search in the geographic area designated or at the dollar level of the position under consideration?
- Does the firm keep clients informed of the status of their search assignments?
- Does it have sufficient time and resources to handle a specific assignment within a reasonable fee structure?
- Will the search firm understand your organization's needs and its unique functional or industry situations?
- Will the search consultant present an image that is favorable to and consistent with your organization?

Contingency Employment Agencies

Employment agencies are a viable source for candidates, especially when recruiters face a large number of open requisitions and little time in which to fill them. Employment agencies typically handle a number of job orders from many companies representing a broad cross-section of industries and disciplines. Given the plethora of companies contracting with a single employment agency, organizations can benefit from working with a small defined number—perhaps 5 to 20—employment agencies. Contracting with a far greater number of agencies may prove necessary when faced with a high recruitment demand, such as the opening of a new division or plant which may require hiring more than 100 professionals.

Like executive search firms, employment agencies do their best work for organizations with which they have solid relationships. To familiarize an employment agent with the organization's atmosphere and professional needs, the following actions may help:

- Describe the corporate environment and provide the agent with a tour if possible.
- Explain the organization's business and your particular area of responsibility.
- Thoroughly explain your recruiting requirements.
- Establish criteria for submission of résumés and telephone inquiries.

Financial Arrangements

Agency fees vary from 10 percent of the starting salary for clerical and support staff to 20 or 30 percent of the starting salary for professional, exempt-level hires. Organizations with long-term or high-volume recruitment needs may arrange an alternative fee structure, such as one percent of the starting salary per 1,000 candidates up to a maximum of 25 percent.

Unlike executive search firms, employment agencies receive payment only if one of their referrals results in a hire. In addition, most agencies offer prorated refunds when candidates prove unacceptable. A typical refund schedule would return 90 percent of the fee if a candidate stays less than 30 days, a 60 percent refund if a new hire lasts between 30 and 60 days, and a 30 percent refund if a candidate leaves after 60 to 90 days on the job.

Career Fairs

Whether local or national in scope, career fairs are valuable recruitment sources, especially for companies with large numbers of open requisitions (more than 50) across a variety of disciplines. The concept behind career fairs is simple: The sponsor advertises the fair in local newspapers to attract experienced professionals and sells booths to hiring companies. The number of hiring companies at the fair can range from several dozen to several hundred in the nation's highest employment areas.

Attendees generally bring a supply of résumés and visit the booths of those companies with challenging and appropriate openings in appealing geographic locations. The company's representatives include recruiters and line professionals, who briefly screen the individual's credentials for suitability. Promising applicants may be scheduled for immediate interview, or at worst, invited in later when the organization's line managers have reviewed résumés collected at the fair.

Some career fair sponsors take a more active role and collect candidates' résumés for participating companies to review prior to the fair. This procedure allows host organizations to prescreen candidates and select only the best prospects for interviews at the career fair.

Financial Arrangements

The cost of hosting a booth at a career fair can vary from $2,000 to $5,000 depending on the number of participating companies and volume of employment candidates. In addition, career fairs that offer advance résumé packets will charge higher fees, with the best rates going to the largest consumers.

Selecting a Career Fair

In choosing among different career fairs, organizations should identify sponsors that are experienced, reliable, and appropriate to their manpower needs. For example, sponsors that offer advance résumé packets can work particularly well when an organization has openings in specific geographical areas or anticipates that certain locales will provide higher-quality applicants.

Organizations should also set limits on the number of career fairs to attend. As the executive of one career fair organization noted, "If a source knows it's a major supplier, and that the client is truly bestowing on it a major portion of its business, the services supplied, the attention given, and the rapport created become that much greater."[9]

Recruitment Advertising

Organizations often view recruitment advertising in its narrowest context: an ad in the help-wanted section of the city newspaper. However, the current trend is toward a broader spectrum of advertising techniques which, in turn, has led to greater use of advertising agencies.

Advertising agencies offer a variety of services beyond ad design that can support recruitment activities. A good agency can help develop employee referral programs, toll-free telephone numbers, training advertisements, recruitment brochures, and direct mail campaigns. Technology will continue to improve the capabilities of ad agencies in such areas as telecommunications, computerized typesetting and graphics, response techniques, and tracking of results. Consequently, advertising agencies will likely become more important and expansive partners in successful recruitment efforts.

Selection of an appropriate ad agency will likewise become increasingly important. Figure 2 provides a sample checklist that organizations can use in selecting the most appropriate and cost-effective ad agency for its recruitment needs.

Alternative Recruitment Sources

Aside from these traditional sources, organizations can incorporate a number of creative sources in their recruitment efforts. A number of examples are summarized below.

Outplacement Firms

Recruiters should stay in touch with local outplacement firms that handle candidates highly qualified to meet the organization's needs. This source can prove especially cost-effective since no fee is involved.

Figure 2
Checklist for Selecting an Advertising Agency

	Grade Levels		
Poor	Fair	Good	Excellent

I. *Administrative*
- ☐ Steady growth and size of agency
- ☐ Financial stability of agency
- ☐ Diversification of clients
- ☐ Management's structure of agency
- ☐ Organizational structure of agency
- ☐ Hiring philosophy of agency
- ☐ Method of selecting account team for our account
- ☐ Experience within the company's markets
- ☐ Agency's business philosophy
- ☐ Size of account with agency
- ☐ Procedure and expense of handling account
    - ☐ Account Management
    - ☐ Creative
    - ☐ Media Placement
    - ☐ Research
    - ☐ Typesetting
    - ☐ Other
- ☐ Experience within related industry
- ☐ Quick service response due to locale

II. *Creative*
- ☐ Involvement of creative staff with company
- ☐ Creative ability to produce original ideas
- ☐ Creative ability that is based on company objectives
- ☐ Recognition of creative ability (awards)
- ☐ Ability of creative staff to produce on-time and to react timely to requests
- ☐ Creative staff's ability to control expenses
- ☐ Creative work that is concepted and produced to meet the needs of the clients' market

> **Figure 2** continued
>
> | | Grade Levels | | | |
> |---|---|---|---|---|
> | | Poor | Fair | Good | Excellent |
>
> III. *Media*
>   □ Number of staff in Media Department
>   □ Working relationship and knowledge of media within company's markets
>   □ Agency's ability to purchase cost effective media
>
> IV. *Research*
>   □ Ability to prepare recruiting strategies
>   □ Full-time market/research staff
>   □ Use & knowledge of outside marketing & research firms
>   □ Agency methods & facilities for research
>
> V. *General*
>   □ Campaigns which produced favorable results for other clients
>   □ Services beyond employment communications
>   □ Agency billing procedures
>   □ Interest and enthusiasm
>   □ Legal and accounting counsel
>
> *Source:* Reprinted with permission from Tim Gibbon, President, Austin Knight Advertising.

Former Employees

Recruiters should make a point of calling former employees who have left voluntarily or who were laid off and are now eligible for rehire. Not all voluntary terminees are happy in their new positions, and they may respond well to the idea of rejoining a former employer. Candidates will be particularly receptive to offers that involve bridging of benefits like vacations and pensions.

Rejected Offers

Hiring managers should maintain a tickler file of candidates who have rejected employment offers and call them periodically—

every 6 to 12 months. Such procedures may help rekindle the candidate's interest or lead to referrals for other prospects.

Retirees

Many major corporations have initiated programs to return their retirees to the workplace, often on a part-time basis. Compared with other recruitment sources, retirees comprise one of the most skilled and knowledgeable pools of talent.

Job Sharing

As young professionals begin to raise families, many consider part-time employment. Organizations should consider the possibility of filling one full-time requisition with two part-time workers.

Trade Shows

Employers should educate line managers to look for prospective candidates at trade shows. Trade shows provide a ready supply of qualified people, but managers need instruction on how to approach a prospect, detect interest, and collect appropriate information vital to a timely follow-up call from the employment department.

Co-op and Work Study Programs

Recruiters should encourage development or expansion of these programs within organizations. Students and companies receive mutual benefits from the experience, and companies can cultivate the best qualified students for full-time jobs.

Government Employment Agencies

Organizations should maintain constant contact with local government employment agencies. These programs can be a particularly good source for support staff, which are frequently the hardest positions to fill.

Internal Recruitment Sources

Employment may be the only business where the old saying "better the devil you know than the devil you don't know" is routinely ignored. More often than not, a company will recruit outside its ranks rather than first scrutinizing for a suitable inside candidate. Most companies provide job posting policies, and some organizations have even developed intricate succession plans. But when put to the test, relatively few companies thoroughly exhaust these internal sources before turning to the outside for fresh talent.

The Internal Recruitment Process

In part, underutilization of internal recruitment stems from the time-consuming procedures involved. Recruiters who face tight time constraints often view the internal employment process as a bureaucratic nightmare of paperwork and politics. An official appeal can generate volumes of in-house candidates for the recruiter to narrow to the qualified few. Obtaining permission from the current manager to interview an employee can pose problems, since most supervisors are about as reluctant to release a current employee as they are to take a cut in pay.

After selection, the real work begins, especially if the opening requires relocation of an employee. The employment manager must work out details of the relocation package with the employee, process the volume of paperwork required to transfer the employee to a new payroll, and set a starting date satisfactory to the current supervisor, the hiring manager, and the employee.

Simplifying internal recruitment requires organizations to make a commitment to the process. Internal recruitment policies should be so deeply ingrained that the employment professional would never consider looking outside without first exhausting internal resources. Companies that are truly committed to fostering internal advancement and opportunity have tamed the "paper chase" and made the rules of the game easy to follow.

Internal Recruitment Programs

The most common forms of internal recruitment are career opportunity and job posting programs. Figure 3 provides sample guidelines to follow in setting up such programs. Other, more recently developed, forms of internal recruitment include employee referral programs and in-house temporary pools. These programs are discussed below.

Employee Referral Programs

One of the most successful recruiting vehicles during the 1980s is the employee referral program. These programs typically offer a cash or merchandise bonus when a current employee refers a successful candidate to fill an opening. Employee referrals form an excellent recruitment source since current employees want to work with the best people available and usually will avoid the personal and professional embarrassment of referring a poorly qualified person.

With the increasing popularity of referral programs, companies have experimented with a variety of gimmicks to encourage employee participation. Interestingly, the rate of employee participation appears to remain unaffected by such efforts as higher cash bonuses, cars, or expense-paid trips. The message is that good employees will not refer potentially undesirable employees even if the rewards are outstanding.

However, organizations can institute a number of other procedures to encourage participation. The following guidelines can help assure effective operation of employee referral programs:

- Make the referral program an ongoing process. Use deadlines only for specific recruitment campaigns and publicize these deadlines when used.

- Referrals should include a résumé, a completed employment application, or a mini application for review by the HR manager responsible for the opening. Separate résumés or applications should be provided if the referred candidate might qualify for several openings.

- A completed referral program card should accompany each résumé or application. The HR department should maintain records of these cards and process them for payment as soon as a referred candidate begins employment.

- The referral bonus schedules should be based on the availability of candidates and not on differences in positions or candidates' qualifications.

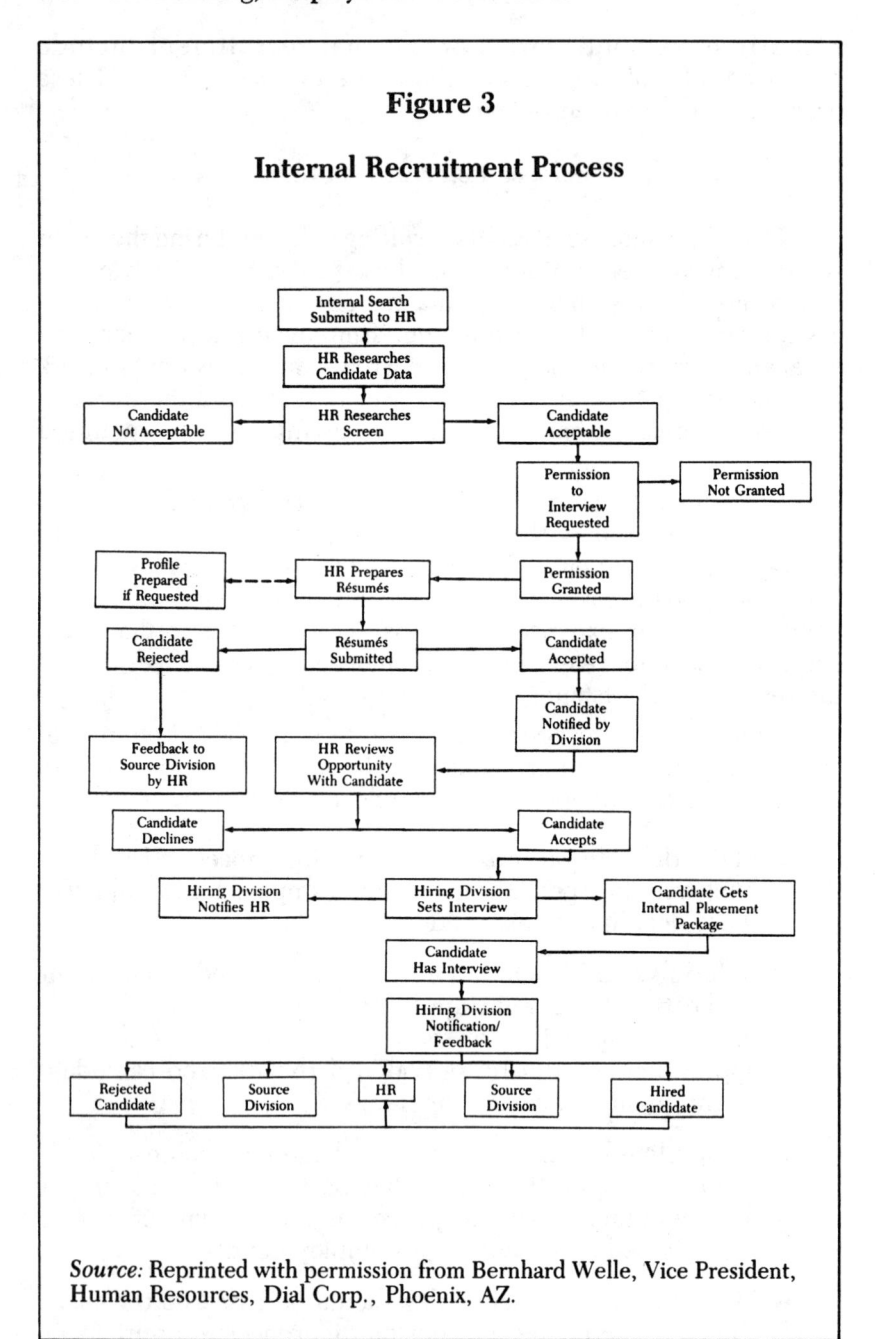

Figure 3

Internal Recruitment Process

Source: Reprinted with permission from Bernhard Welle, Vice President, Human Resources, Dial Corp., Phoenix, AZ.

External & Internal Recruitment   2-99

- Supervisors and managers should not be eligible for bonuses if the referral is for a position under their supervision. HR department employees also should not be eligible for participation in the referral program.
- Referrals for recent college graduates or entry-level positions should not qualify for bonuses, although such referral should still be encouraged.

In-House Temporary Pool

Temporary worker pools are an innovative development within the realm of internal recruitment. Companies have hired people with diverse skills (for example, laborer, word processing, clerical, accounting) to meet the day-to-day labor demands caused by illness, vacations, terminations, or resignations. The length of employment can range from hours to months, depending on the organization's needs.

Unlike workers supplied from temporary agencies, employees in an in-house temporary pool work directly for the hiring organization and may receive benefits, depending on the number of scheduled hours worked per week. Most companies instituting an in-house temporary pool have realized substantial savings over using temporary employment agencies since the commission paid to outside suppliers can amount to 50 percent or more of a temporary employee's hourly wages.

Conclusion

As noted at the outset of this chapter, employment is "big business" and business constantly seeks new ways to improve timeliness, cost effectiveness, and efficiency. Likewise, the employment function will continue to be measured by these yardsticks, and successful results will depend on enlightened management and control.

Employment professionals will be held accountable in quantifiable terms (for example, cost-per-hire, time to fill open requisitions, offer-to-interview, and acceptance-to-offer ratios). They will need this data readily at their disposal and, more importantly, be able to interpret the data to the satisfaction of management. In short, employment specialists must adopt a business attitude to replace their previous image: "I like to work with people."

Automation will aid in the process. However, the computer will only point to data, not manipulate or manage it. The successful employment professional will have a keen grasp of all elements in the recruitment process and their impact on each other. This knowledge will enable the individual to deal logically with many common problems (i.e., If we're not scheduling enough interviews, could the problem be with the quality of résumés being routed, with résumés not being returned after routing, or with corporate image?). Understanding the process will point to the problem and thus to possible solutions.

The employment professional must be in complete control of the process, not unlike the maestro leading a symphony orchestra. In both cases, it is critical to understand and evaluate each piece on an individual basis as well as in concert. Just as a talented and perceptive maestro identifies a need for the most subtle adjustment, the competent employment professional will recognize the discordant "note" and apply the appropriate skills to restore harmony within the framework of the recruitment process.

◆

Notes

1. Survey results appeared in *Perceptions*, the company newsletter of Costello, Erdlen & Co., and encompassed the opinions of 584 respondents representing 529 different companies.
2. Remarks made by Dallas Reynolds, vice president of personnel for State Farm Insurance Companies, appear in "Regaining the Competitive Edge," p. 124.
3. Ibid., p. 38.
4. Sweet, pp. 124–125.
5. Gerard R. Roche, chairman of the board, Heidrick and Struggles.
6. Donald T. Allerton, president, Allerton, Heinze and Associates.
7. Ibid.
8. Suggestions made by Roche.
9. Bill Aberman, president, Business People Inc.

Editor's Note: In addition to the References shown below, there are other significant sources of information and ideas on computer software applications for HR recruitment.

Books

Microcomputer Applications for Human Resources Management. VCR Consulting Group, Inc., 289 S. San Antonio Road, Los Altos, CA 94022, (415)948-1513.

Directories

Business Software Directory. Information Sources, Inc., 1807 Glenview Rd., Glenview, IL 60025, (312)724-9285. More than 7,000 listings. Also available in on-line data format: BRS, Datastar, and Esa-quist.

ICP Software Directory, Vol. 3: Management and Administration Systems: Vol. 7, Part I: Systems Software & General Business Application: and Vol. 7, Part II: Specialized Industry Application. International Computer Programs, Inc., 9100 Keystone Crossing, P.O. Box 40946, Indianapolis, IN 46240, (317)884-7461, (800)428-6179.

Microcomputers in Human Resource Management: A Directory of Software. Richard B. Frantzreb, Advanced Personnel Systems, P.O. Box 1438, Roseville, CA 95661, (916)781-2900.

The Software Catalog: Business Software, 2nd Edition. Elsevier Science Publishing Co., Inc., 52 Vanderbilt Ave., New York, NY 10017, (212)370-5520. Lists 7,600 business-related programs.

Journals

Computers and the Personnel Department: "A PERSONNEL JOURNAL" Reprint Series, Inc., 245 Fischer Ave., B-2, Costa Mesa, CA 92626, (714)751-1883.

HR/PC. David G. Mahal, publisher and editor-in-chief, DGM Associates, P.O. Box 455, Pacific Palisades, CA 90272, (213)459-4729.

Periodicals

Auerbach Application Software Report. Auerbach Publishers, Inc., 6560 N. Park Dr., Pennsauken, NJ 08109, (609)662-2070. A monthly software information service. Catalog available.

The HR Planning Newsletter. James Peters, Wargo & Co., Inc., 1685 Cole Blvd., Ste. 160, Golden, CO 80401.

Organizations

Clearinghouse for personnel administration software sponsored by the ASPA Foundation is being developed by the Institute of Management and Labor Relations at Rutgers University, New Brunswick, NJ 08093, (201)932-9022. Contact: Charles Fay.

Human Resource Planning Society, Box 2553, Grand Central Station, New York, NY 10163, (212)490-6387.

Human Resources System Professionals, Inc., P.O. Box 8040-A202, Walnut Creek, CA 94596, (415)945-8428.

◆

References

American Society for Personnel Administration. 1986. "Regaining the Competitive Edge." *Personnel Administrator* (July).

Costello, Erdlen & Co. 1986. *"Perceptions," The Newsletter for Human Resources Professionals* (Winter) 2, 1: 1, 4.

Sweet, D.H. 1973. *Modern Employment Function*. Reading, MA: Addison-Wesley.

2.4

Recruitment Sources

Philip Farish

A few decades ago, an employer could post a "Help Wanted" sign in his window and in no time, a number of fresh-faced applicants appeared, eager for the job. That kind of recruitment campaign still works, but only under limited circumstances. Employers today have a number of recruitment channels to choose from, as Table 1 demonstrates.

This chapter is designed to familiarize HR managers with some of the new media and methods available for recruitment. While many of these techniques also receive mention in Chapter 2.3, this chapter will adopt a somewhat different perspective. Chapter 2.3 contains a wealth of practical, hands-on information useful to experienced recruiters during the implementation phase of a recruitment program. This chapter instead concentrates on information needed by relative novices in the recruitment field. It provides a broad overview of various recruitment techniques and trends, and illustrates the discussion with real-life examples.

Internal Recruitment Sources

Internal recruiting channels are used to reach people already employed by the organization and outsiders who are tapped through an employee referral system. Company methods of filling job openings with current employees range from the informal and ad hoc methods to well-defined succession plans. Many jobs are filled by managers who already have chosen someone to take the place of a departed employee. A more formal arrangement is the job posting system, and for positions at the upper levels, a number of companies have succession plans. Job posting plans are usually managed by the

Table 1
Sources Which Respondents Use to Locate Candidates

		Office/ Clerical	Production/ Service	Professional/ Technical	Commissioned Sales	Managers/ Supervisors	All
Internal Sources	a. Promotion from within	94%	86%	88%	75%	95%	99%
	b. Employee referrals	87	83	78	76	64	91
	c. Walk-in applicants	86	87	64	52	46	91
Advertising	d. Newspapers	84	77	94	84	85	97
	e. Journals/magazines	6	7	54	33	50	64
	f. Radio/television	3	6	3	3	2	9
	g. Direct-mail	4	3	16	6	8	17
Employment Services	h. U.S. Employment Service (USES)	19	20	11	7	7	22
	i. State employment service	66	68	38	30	23	72
	j. Private employment agencies	28	11	58	44	60	72
	k. Search firms	1	Less than 1	36	26	63	67
	l. Employee leasing firm	16	10	6	2	Less than 1	20
	m. Computerized resume service	0	0	4	0	2	4
	n. Video interviewing service	0	Less than 1	1	0	1	2

Table 1 continued

		Office/ Clerical	Production/ Service	Professional/ Technical	Commissioned Sales	Managers/ Supervisors	All
Outside Referral Sources	o. Local high schools/ trade schools	60	54	16	5	2	68
	p. Technical/vocational institutes	48	51	47	5	8	77
	q. Colleges/universities	24	15	81	38	45	86
	r. Professional societies	4	1	5	19	37	55
	s. Unions	1	10	1	0	1	10
	t. Community agencies	33	32	20	16	10	39
Special Events	u. Career conferences/ job fairs	20	16	44	19	19	52
	v. Open house at your organization	10	8	17	8	7	22
Other		5	5	7	6	7	9
	Number of respondents	245	221	237	96	243	245

Source: Reprinted with permission from The Bureau of National Affairs, Inc., "Recruiting and Selection Procedures," in Personnel Policies Forum. Survey No. 146 (May) copyright © 1988, p. 7.

recruiter whereas the succession plan may be handled by a top management committee.

Job Posting

The practice of advertising open jobs internally before going to outside sources developed in the early days of affirmative action as a means of opening opportunities for women and minorities. It quickly became an established practice in many organizations.

The system usually encompasses positions up to the lower executive level, although a few organizations have included vice presidential openings on the list. The openings are published on bulletin boards or in lists available to all employees. Interested employees must reply within a specified number of days, and they may or may not have to obtain their supervisor's consent. Some job posting systems apply only to the plant or office in which the job is located, while other companies will relocate employees.

Organizations need to monitor job posting systems to assure smooth operations. For example, Transamerica Life Companies had been operating its job posting program for two years when problems began to develop. Employees in one line of business sometimes achieved grade or salary increases by transferring to a similar position in another group, even though the new post did not require different or additional skills. Transamerica dealt with this problem by reviewing the job grading and pay structure.

Other problems can arise from inefficient communication processes. Managers get impatient when the posting and selection process leaves vacancies unfilled for several weeks. Employee morale suffers if individuals who bid on a job find out through the grapevine, rather than through formal channels, that the job has gone to someone else.

A different type of internal recruitment occurs when a new venture is staffed entirely by people already in the company. When Gannett Company, Inc. inaugurated its national newspaper *USA Today*, it filled all 50 positions at the new office with experienced people from the chain's other 133 newspapers. Employees who worked on the start-up had the option of staying with *USA Today* once it was under way or returning to their former assignment.

A new form of in-house recruitment has emerged with the trend toward using contingency workers pooled from a company's own retirees. Retirees offer a number of advantages: familiarity with the organization and its way of doing things and, in some cases, familiarity with the job.

A survey for the Employment Management Association in 1986 showed that one-third of the members who responded used exempt and nonexempt retirees for part-time or temporary work assignments.[1] Almost one-half (45.2 percent) of the firms used retirees under some contractual arrangement, which included legal documents in about three-fifths of the cases. Almost one-tenth allowed retirees to share jobs with other employees. Most retirees continued to receive pension and insurance benefits when they came back to work. About 40 percent of the respondents paid the market rate for the work performed, while 26 percent paid employees what they had received at the time they retired.

The Travelers Corporation is a company that has established a pool of temporaries made up of its own retirees. It also supports a back-to-work program helping retirees from other firms, thereby creating a ready source of candidates for recruiters interested in this age group.

The actual sponsor of the program, which receives funds from the insurance company's foundation, is the Senior Job Bank, a 13-year-old nonprofit community service agency in Hartford, Connecticut. Its mission is to provide job counseling and placement help to individuals ages 55 and over who are seeking work. The bank runs a five-day, 15-hour post-retirement seminar three times a year. The program offers experts in retirement planning, employment, education, and volunteerism who discuss the many kinds of employment available to older people seeking full-time or part-time jobs.

Employee Referral Campaigns

Referral of job candidates by current employees has been and continues to be a major source of new hires at many levels, including professionals. A 1986 survey by the Administrative Management Society showed that 70 percent of the 292 responding members looked to current employees as a source of new candidates for office jobs.[2] In its simplest form, a campaign will describe the openings and, usually, offer a reward or bonus to the referring employee when the candidate suggested is hired. A prime requirement for all these campaigns is some type of recognition for employees who suggest a possible candidate.

Lockheed Missiles & Space Company's Referralot program is a good example of what it takes to keep a program productive. By the eighth month of its 1986 exercise, it had hired 260 new employees, 49 of whom were placed in upper-level science and engineering positions. In the seventh successful year of this program, Lockheed started afresh with a new theme and a new set of awards. The theme "Catch a Rising Star" draws on the company logo.

Cash awards ranged from $50 to $500, depending on the salary grade or the work classification of the new hire. A solar-powered calculator accompanied each referral award check. Four special award winners were chosen by lot each quarter from employees whose referrals were hired during the previous quarter. The 1986 special awards were two $1,000 U.S. Savings Bonds. In 1985, the special awards had been one tax-free $1,000 bond.

Another company that offered individual and special awards for referrals bolstered interest in the campaign by setting up an additional grand prize. A grand-prize drawing took place if the campaign produced more than a specified number of new hires.

Experience has also shown that effective award systems need not be elaborate. Some firms offer token gifts to referring employees and then hold drawings for several grand prizes, such as a new automobile, a computer, or a week or two of vacation at a desirable resort.

Procter & Gamble's sales division has a referral program that offers no tangible reward at all for attracting a new salesperson. Its success relies on employees' professional pride and fraternal feeling. Sales recruiting manager H.A. Phillips said that the campaign is based on the idea that "it takes one to know one."

Deutsch, Shea & Evans, an advertising agency that has developed a number of referral campaigns for clients, has some specific suggestions for implementing a program. During the first two to four months of a campaign, publicity should be heavy and continuous. The agency recommends using a campaign theme and promoting it in house magazine articles, envelope stuffers, and posters. A special letterhead with the campaign theme and logo should be used for transmitting information about the referral program within the organization. After the introductory period, poster designs should be changed about every six months, and articles about the program should appear about as often in the house magazine. According to the agency, a campaign can last from eighteen months to two-and-one-half years before a new one needs to be developed.

External Recruitment Sources

External recruitment channels range from public and private employment agencies to university and association placement programs to a variety of informal contacts. Twelve different external sources are reviewed in this section.

Employment Agencies

Employment agencies are one of the most widely available and used outside sources. They vary greatly in size and in quality of services. Recruiters who achieve the best results from this channel have generally cultivated a small group of firms and have thoroughly communicated the type and character of candidates needed, the fee structure they will honor, and the method of resolving disputes.

Types of Employment Agencies

Two developments are notable in the private placement industry. The first trend is structural: the recent formation of large chains of employment agencies, and the rise of specialized employment agencies. The second trend is professional: the development of a code of ethics for employment agencies.

Chains use regular salary surveys for selected management groups as a way of advertising their reach and capability. A chain usually maintains a common file of all candidates registered by its various outlets so that each unit has access to a large array of potential candidates.

At the other end of the service spectrum is the small agency that offers candidates for unusual situations. These highly specialized agencies are not common, but are likely to become more popular as the number of specialized working arrangements multiplies. One such agency dating from 1986 is the Pickwick Group. It handles only professionals and managers who are looking for part-time jobs in their fields of expertise. The bulk of registrants in the early days of the agency were middle-aged middle managers who had enough resources that they didn't have to work full time, and younger women who wanted to spend more time with their children without entirely leaving their careers.

Trend Toward Professionalism

The Employment Management Association has worked for years to resolve some of the disputes that seem to plague the recruiter-employment agency relationship. It has, at times, established hearing panels in certain metropolitan areas to deal with these cases. Its latest move has led to a code of ethics, developed in conjunction with the National Association of Personnel Consultants, the main organization to which employment agencies and contingency search firms belong.

The code attempts to spell out who is responsible for what in employment transactions. Many of its provisions are quite specific, such as this example:[3]

> Corporate recruiters retaining materials referred by a personnel consultant, including company employment applications, should realize that the use of these materials in contacting a job applicant obligates the employer to the payment of a fee, should placement follow from such contact.

Executive Search Firms

The executive search field has generated controversy from its very beginning after World War II, but it has become an established part of the recruiting scene. The major objection to this recruitment channel came from employers who disliked the efforts of consultants trying to lure away employees with offers of a better job elsewhere. That original objection has all but disappeared.

Characteristics of Executive Search Firms

Executive search is exactly what the term implies. The management consultant pursuing a search looks for a suitable candidate or candidates to fill the client's openings. Candidates sought generally hold senior management positions. Executive search activities differ from those of employment agencies in two main ways. (For a more detailed analysis of differences, see Chapter 2.3.) The search firm is paid for its time and expenses whether or not the client hires an offered candidate. Secondly, search firms are not subject to state regulations governing employment agencies.

Two trade groups help to regulate executive search activities and professional standards. The Association of Executive Search Consultants is made up only of consulting firms. The National Association of Corporate and Professional Recruiters includes management consultants and the corporate clients with whom they deal.

Some small regional firms occasionally offer a variant of the standard search pattern. The common form is to present a short list of likely candidates to prospective employers. By performing less checking and verification, these firms can offer names of potential hires at a much lower price than the standard executive search. Recruiters should thoroughly check firms offering these abbreviated services because no standards or watchdogs govern this type of activity.

Some employment agencies, known as contingency search firms, deal with higher-level management candidates who are the main staple of search firms. These companies sometimes work on a fee basis, as is the standard for a search firm, and at other times they follow the agency fee system. In the latter situation, the agency is not paid if there is no hire.

Out of the search firms has come another budding service for recruiters. Researchers who have gained experience in search consulting companies have started independent research services. They track likely candidates for managerial, professional, and technical jobs, develop résumés, and perform reference checking.

No trade association has appeared to give easy access to the firms in the field, but one directory aimed at job seekers has been published.[4] Many of the listings are solo practitioners, and no company is very large. However, executive search seems to be a sub-industry that will endure in the recruiting field despite turnover among the suppliers.

In-House Executive Search Functions

A recent and much debated development is the in-house executive search function. Critics call this recruitment activity everything from poaching to piracy. Along with the ethics of pirating the competition's star performers, some HR people express concern that highly knowledgeable insiders might inadvertently leak confidential information while talking to a competing firm. A third objection is that the company invites raids on its employees when it goes after another firm's executives.

However, the in-house function does have supporters. One of its proponents is Jack Bramlage, director of recruitment and placement for Mead Corp., and former president of the Employment Management Association. Bramlage holds that a company which spends over $150,000 a year in search fees can benefit from using an internal function for some or all of its executive search activities. He also argues that in-house personnel can accomplish the search more quickly since they know the needs of the unit seeking an executive and the politics and culture of the organization.

Bramlage also offers counterarguments to the piracy point. An employer's good executives and managers are going to be approached by search firms anyway. A company that does not use an inside search function may still face raids by other companies. The only internal search practice that would violate ethics occurs if the search person misrepresents himself or herself as belonging to an outside consulting firm rather than the actual hiring company.

An effective inside search function must be allowed to operate in the usual search pattern, according to Bramlage. If the organization limits search activities, such as prohibiting recruitment of people in firms whose executives serve on the company board, its internal search efforts may prove fruitless. Another situation that would militate against the use of an inside search function would arise when a company embarks on new ventures outside its usual scope of operation. An internal search under these circumstances would tip off competitors and other firms to new developments before the company was ready to reveal them.

Current Trends

Like any growing field, executive search activities may diversify in the future. James Kennedy, editor of *Executive Recruiter News*, discussed likely developments with 42 leaders in the executive search field.[5] Key conclusions included the following:

- External executive search firms will expand services to achieve greater understanding and involvement in client organizational and strategic planning.

- Research will become more sophisticated, more automated, and more demanding of intelligent direction and follow-on use.

- The large firms will get larger, and a considerable number of small firms will go under, but the market will always create places for high-quality small and mid-sized firms.

- Fixed fees will replace other methods of charging for search services.

- The most successful firms will have clearly defined off-limits policies to which clients will force them to adhere.

- International links will become increasingly essential.
- Average placement levels will continue to rise.
- Search will come close to becoming a true and respected profession.
- New markets will provide much of the growth.
- Many firms will have deeper relationships with fewer clients.

Outplacement Firms

Outplacement is the newest HR specialty to appear as a consulting field. Since these services are discussed in Chapter 2.8 in this volume, outplacement will only receive mention here. For recruiters, outplacement firms have become a new source of experienced candidates. Whereas employers once believed that the people receiving outplacement help were somehow incompetent in their jobs, the great downsizing wave of the 1980s and the resulting displacement of qualified employees demolished this idea.

College Recruiting

Colleges and universities are the traditional source of candidates for professional and managerial positions. Almost every higher education institution has a placement office staffed with people who, at the minimum, arrange interviews between students and recruiters from employer organizations. Many placement officers and recruiters belong to the College Placement Council, an organization which sets standards for the conduct of college recruitment operations.

Trends in College Relations

In recent years, recruiters have begun to look upon the actual recruiting as one part of an ongoing relations program that includes faculty members and student organizations. College relations efforts include making gifts and grants to the institution, providing summer employment and consulting projects for faculty, and inviting placement officers to visit company plants and offices. A number of special programs, operated in connection with placement offices and other campus agencies, have been developed to increase the number of women and minority students in engineering.

Organization Efforts. A notable trend among campus recruiters has been to pare the list of campuses visited and deepen the relationship with remaining colleges. Impetus for this trend occurred in the early 1970s when the rising price of crude oil made travel in the United States much more expensive. Methods used to manage these relations programs vary considerably, as the following examples demonstrate.

Mobil has changed its recruiting strategy so that it now deals with only 50 colleges and universities, instead of the 200 on its list a few years ago. In addition, Mobil has moved to using college teams. Each team focuses on a particular school and includes six to eight people from various Mobil units. Team members, many of whom are alumni of the particular school, help to plan the dozen or more campus activities each year, such as providing talent for student organization programs, conducting career information days, holding receptions, and sponsoring ceremonies at which recruiters present Mobil Foundation checks to support some campus activity. The recruitment team strategy has already helped to increase the number of graduates hired from targeted schools.

Lockheed Missiles & Space Company has been running its Key School program since 1973. A technical representative and an executive representative, usually alumni, handle relations with one school, setting up research projects and directing funds to relevant departments. Other measures for extending the connection include offering scholarships, using faculty as consultants, and providing summer jobs to faculty and students.

College Efforts. The demand for technically trained collegians and graduates of business courses remains high, but the market for individuals with liberal arts degrees is less strong. Accordingly, the College Placement Council has developed programs to help students make themselves more marketable. Many colleges and universities have put in courses which help students to develop practical career plans, and the council offers CPC a software package called Career Navigator that can organize the process. The association is also preparing print materials and videocassettes to help students and corporate recruiters do a better job of interviewing.

In addition, the College Placement Council hopes to establish a five-year follow-up study, tracking graduates each year to find out, on a national scale, what happens to them after their entry-level jobs. The study will be ongoing, dropping the earliest group after five years and adding a new cohort of that year's graduates.

A persistent issue between recruiters and placement offices concerns scheduling. Some recruiters try to increase the results of their campus trips by interviewing only those students who seem to be likely hires. Recruiters, rather than placement officers or students, control the interview schedule. The recruiters set certain requirements for admission to the schedule or they preview the résumés of interested students. Many placement officers resist prescreening since it burdens staff and raises the risk of discrimination charges. Other placement officers feel an ethical obligation to put students' interests first, and to increase their charges' access to organizations that interest them. Recruiters must check each school's practice.

College Recruitment Tools

An occasional innovation appears in the design of the college recruiting brochure, but for the most part, the content of these documents has remained the same for practically a generation. Students want to know about an employer's line of work, corporate philosophy, work locations, kinds of work performed, prerequisite degree fields, and career development possibilities. Brochures that offer an extra feature can help make an organization register more strongly with students. Atlantic Richfield at one time included a pull-out section made of worksheets the student could use to bring career expectations into focus. Baptist Medical Services of Birmingham, Alabama drew particular attention by including a flexible phonograph recording with part of its recruiting story, giving an extra dimension to its appeal.

Videocassettes are slowly becoming another medium for conveying information about an organization beyond the scope of a brochure. A 1986 survey by Bernard Hodes Advertising showed that 62 percent of 230 placement offices had a videotape library, usually in the placement office itself. A standard format for video presentations has yet to appear, but recruiting brochures likewise lack a set standard. While several companies have tried to make a business of supplying cassette players and videotape libraries to placement offices, this method of distribution has not taken hold as a significant service for the campus recruiter.

Nontraditional Sources

A number of innovative channels exist for locating college graduates with experience in a particular field. Alumni associations, Ph.D. programs, and cooperative-education programs are several particularly good sources.

Alumni Associations. The downsizing wave that began in the early 1980s, and which continues today at a lesser rate, has led many displaced managers back to their alumni associations. Curiously, this most logical source of information about degreed and experienced people has never been fully developed or exploited. Only a few alumni associations have established placement functions for members and other graduates of the school. No trade association or professional society exists for alumni association officers who handle placement. Those officers who are involved with a professional group usually belong to the College Placement Council, which places primary emphasis on serving new graduates.

In 1986, a survey by the newsletter *Recruiting Trends* showed that recruiters were hiring more people through alumni connections than they had during the previous year.[6] However, this trend may only be a temporary phenomenon reflecting the volume of downsizing activity in 1986 and 1987. In any case, lacking a central source of up-to-date information, recruiters have to check with each school to determine the availability of information about job-seeking alumni.

Stanford University's ProNet may herald a new trend. This service, begun by the California university's alumni association in 1987, keeps a data base of graduates. When inaugurated in November 1987, the system contained data on 4,000 alumni with degrees in engineering, business, and computer science. The addition of graduates in other fields was expected to expand the list to 10,000 names by the end of the first year of operation. The system, which contains only those graduates who want to be listed, was started because members had "a strong interest in some sort of an excellent search/placement service attached to their alma mater," according to Stanford Alumni Association director Mark Jordan.

Companies pay a subscription fee for a certain number of searches in the data base. Employers supply a profile of the type of person wanted, and receive the names of candidates who match the description and agree to have their names released.

Colleges and universities occasionally serve as sources for special groups of job candidates, but such services often receive little publicity. An example is MATCH (Metropolitan Area Transition Clearinghouse). This consortium of more than 80 colleges and universities within a 50-mile radius of New York City has a data base of qualified job seekers who are handicapped. Professional staff for the project screen applicants to ensure job readiness and also do follow-ups with employers to assure that placements are working out satisfactorily.

Ph.D. Programs. Another fairly exotic breed of candidates for managerial jobs—individuals with Ph.D.s—can be tracked through universities. Although a doctoral degree is the usual admission ticket to a university teaching career, only 30 percent of the annual crop of doctorates will ever end up in academic jobs, according to Richard Moore, executive director of Training Research Corporation.[7] Holders of Ph.D.s are often high performers in business jobs because of their skills in research and communication. General Motors CEO Roger Smith states, ". . . (T)hey have synthesized (in completing a doctoral dissertation) an enormous amount of information and carried out a full-scale, largely independent project, over a period of many months and even years, under the pressure of deadlines, conflicting demands on their time and energy and circumstances that can change quite unpredictably. All of this, it seems to me, bears a striking resemblance to the intellectual abilities, the perseverance and the resourcefulness of the successful manager."[8]

Graduates with Ph.D.s can be tracked through their major departments in most universities. Five schools offer special programs to help retrain Ph.D.s for business: New York University, the Wharton School of the University of Pennsylvania, Harvard University, the University of Texas-Austin, and the University of Virginia.

Many colleges and universities have added new services for adults, as the size of the most obvious student crop—teenagers—has begun to diminish. Recruiters can check with colleges and universities within their purview to determine if any help, beyond the regular placement function, is available.

Cooperative Education Programs. A special form of college recruiting takes place through institutions that offer cooperative education programs. Under this arrangement, a student alternates periods of study with periods of work. The work program is generally arranged between the employer's co-operative education manager and his or her counterpart on campus.

The program has advantages for the student and the employer. The student becomes accustomed to the world of work and learns to apply course studies to real-life situations. Employers enhance their opportunity to determine whether the student would work out as a long-term employee. In addition, co-op students generally have a lower turnover rate than those hired without previous work experience.

A few universities, notably Northeastern in Boston and Drexel Institute in Philadelphia, operate entirely on the co-op system. The great body of institutions offer co-op arrangements in a few departments and programs. The National Commission on Cooperative Education maintains a list of the colleges and universities that offer these programs. Employers also have a trade group—the Cooperative Education Association, Inc.—through which to gather information and share experiences and problems.

Internships. Internships are a growing recruiting channel. College students and women returning to the work force are the types of candidates usually reached. Internships generally last a prescribed duration, and the level of work assignment varies widely. They differ from co-op education in that they do not yield academic credit. A number of internships, in fact, are not paid except in the value of the training received.

One of the more elaborate internship programs is I.F. Interns, which prepares college students for the employee benefits field. Designed and administered by the International Foundation of Employee Benefit Plans, the program debuted in the Chicago-Milwaukee area and now is operating on the West Coast as well.

Recruitment Channels to Reach Unemployed Youth

The culture of poverty, the violence of the ghetto, and the lingering effects of racial segregation and discrimination have made it difficult for those out of the mainstream to obtain the kind of education to make them employable. Public school systems in large metropolitan areas have, for the most part, failed this task. The educational system is not entirely at fault, since school systems can not substitute for a stable family and community life that teaches people the behaviors needed to get and keep a job. Business has had to provide help in one way or another in order to get the entry-level workers needed.

Community service and prerecruiting efforts are built into the Academy of Finance program of American Express. The company works with high school administrators and teachers to develop curricula that introduce students to everything from basic accounting principles and computer skills to how a brokerage firm works. The program includes teacher training and gives the students internships so they learn first-hand about the financial world. Students selected by their schools for the academy receive paid summer internships. Ninety percent of the students who participated in the first few years of this program went on to college.

A program in Philadelphia, developed in conjunction with the Work in America Institute Inc. and the public school system, offers job-search training. Students practice interviewing, filling out application blanks, and performing other activities involved in seeking and applying for a job. Local businesses and business foundations have provided funds to train the teachers and to set up office-like workrooms to simulate the actual job-search environment.

The National Alliance of Business is the largest and one of the oldest organizations to address the employment problem of disadvantaged youths. It works with the Private Industry Councils that operate in connection with the state labor departments to develop areawide special job training.

Along with these newer programs, recruiters can receive assistance through two organizations which originated efforts to bring blacks into the economic and social mainstream: the National Urban League and the National Association for the Advancement of Colored People.

Recruitment Advertising

Recruitment advertising has become every bit as colorful and imaginative as consumer advertising. While classified notices still dominate recruitment advertising, employers now spend millions of dollars on display ads in newspapers, magazines, and trade journals and on preparation of radio and TV ads. Although two monthly measures of the volume of advertising are published,[9] neither source compiles regular figures or the total spent on recruiting ads. The number of magazines that serve primarily as vehicles for recruiting ads has increased, and a growing number of advertising agencies now specialize in recruiting accounts. All aspects considered, advertising is one of the livelier and more challenging elements of the recruiting operation.

Newspapers and Magazines

Competition among ad outlets takes place mainly within the print media rather than between print and broadcast. Affirmative action generated a number of publications, mostly magazines, designed to carry recruiting messages to people in one or another of the protected classes. Although growth of this medium has slowed, new publications do appear occasionally.[10]

Newspapers have worked hard to maintain their share of the recruitment advertising budget. The Newspaper Advertising Bureau has a vice president whose main concern is to produce material that will help advertisers prepare effective ads. The Association of Newspaper Classified Advertising Managers is working to standardize column widths, which would reduce employers' costs by allowing a classified ad to appear in a number of newspapers without resetting. The American Newspaper Publishers Association and the Newspaper Advertising Bureau are collaborating on a Future of Advertising project designed to enhance understanding of advertisers' wants and needs.

Some newspapers in large metropolitan areas have introduced zoned classifieds so that recruiters can target their ads for districts where possible candidates might reside. Other economical placements are available. For example, when a single paper dominates one community but surrounding communities have other papers from different publishers, the publishers sometimes cooperate to offer a discount for using the whole group. Recruiters should check regularly with the media people in the advertising agencies or their own advertising departments, since many of these deals are short-term affairs; they come and they go.

Both the general trade press and magazines aimed at a specific group of job candidates offer special deals. Incentives can range from a free ad in an issue with a relevant feature story to studies of reader response to specific ads. As with newspapers, ad agencies and advertising departments are a primary source of current information on magazines.

Direct Mail

Direct mail or direct response advertising is a medium that recruiters have yet to use widely, although some employers have been obtaining good results from it. The key to successful direct mail is access to lists that give the home addresses of people in a desired field. While lists that give business addresses are easier to obtain, many people consider it unethical to solicit competitors' employees at work.

The most common direct mail campaign involves a single employer, but postcard mailings with appeals from a number of companies do occur. The limited availability of statistics on any aspect of direct mail recruiting has hampered objective conclusions about the effectiveness of this method.

Other Media

Broadcast media are generally more expensive to use than print, but under certain circumstances, radio and television appeals may be worth the price. Situations favoring use at broadcast media arise when print advertising is ineffective, when a large number of prospects live in a limited geographic area, when the recruiter has multiple job openings, and when a large response is needed quickly.[11]

Less commonplace techniques can also help get the message seen or heard by prospective candidates, wherever they may be. Billboards near plants or along the tracks of commuter railroads carry messages of near-by employers. Fast-food outlets post handbills throughout neighborhoods in which a new store is opening. A suburban company passes out fliers to homeward bound crowds converging on a Chicago rail terminal. Employers in resort towns post notices in hotels and lodgings. Technical companies advertise on electronic bulletin boards which people can access through their home computers. The list of additional possibilities is bounded only by the imagination.

While most advertising agencies have the same array of talents to offer for preparing and placing ads, a number of agencies try to distinguish themselves by offering regular newsletters and special research studies.

Advertising Themes

Fads in ads are common. At one time, employers of engineers extolled the recreational attractions of their locations, so many sandy beaches or sunny slopes appeared in recruitment materials. A more recent *Personnel Journal* survey of ads and campaigns found the following advertising trends:

- Widespread use of employees in ads
- An emphasis on intangible benefits offered by the particular employer, such as room for creativity, alternative development paths, independence, and the like
- Point-of-purchase advertising techniques, including returnable coupons and mini-resumes
- Greater reliance on entertainment, i.e., witty headlines and amusing illustrations that have nothing to do with the job

Other examples of notable ads and campaigns appear in a booklet showing award-winning designs in the "Advertising Excellence" competition, sponsored annually by the Employment Management Association.

Cost Control

Most recruiters have to work with limited budgets. One employment and staffing director offers a number of pointers for managing a recruitment advertising budget:[12]

- Track the experience with ads in terms of the media used and compare against the results obtained through other sources of candidates.
- Know as far in advance what staffing needs will arise. Keep markets and competitors in mind, also. Check turnover and attrition rates for various groups. Stay abreast of trends or changes in the company.
- Have an identifiable ad image, such as a standard logo, border, or graphic design. Change the identifier every 12 to 18 months so it does not go stale.
- Have complete job specifications. Keep a list of past ads and analyze why they did or did not work. Ad agency and media people can help perform these analyses.
- Stay up with trade publications and future editorial specials. Such issues are frequently passed along to others and produce additional readership for your ad. This technique reinforces the importance of anticipating future needs.
- Back up print advertising for job fairs and open houses with fliers, direct mail, and local radio campaigns.

Government Sources

The old and still controversial program now called the Job Service continues to bring the federal and state governments into the employment field. This government competitor to the employment agency system has regularly encountered attacks, for impinging on private enterprise, and in the mid-1980s, another federal agency fueled the debate. The General Accounting Office (GAO), the Congressional watchdog group, scored the Job Service for failing to cooperate with private agencies. GAO's report said that government employment services should recognize services available from private agencies and refer people to these agencies provided they did not charge fees.[13] Despite this criticism and the efforts of federal budget-cutters, the Job Service system seems likely to survive.

Joint public and private-sector efforts to help dislocated and the hard-to-employ individuals are functioning more effectively than they have in the past. A number of successes have emerged through the Job Training Partnership Act (JTPA), which replaced the old Comprehensive Employment and Training Act. The likely key to JTPA's success is the vigorous involvement of the private sector, which helps to focus training on actual openings rather than hypothetical work opportunities.

One effective JTPA program trains displaced engineers and drafters for jobs in computer-aided drafting design. The Private Industry Council serving the San Gabriel, California, foothill area coordinates efforts to develop and implement the program. California State University of Los Angeles and Santa Fe Braun Company, an international engineering firm, conducted the first project, which produced 13 graduates. Cal State took responsibility for program coordination and job placement, using JTPA funds to develop the program, and Santa Fe Braun provided equipment and training.

Such private-public efforts seem likely to expand. For example, the National Alliance of Business and the National Association of Private Industry Councils agreed, in late 1986, to cooperate on strengthening services to the 600 Private Industry Councils across the country.

Career Fairs

The job fair, or career conference, is a post-World War II addition to the standard recruiting channels. In its current form, it was probably developed by Ernest Lendman. When large numbers of commissioned officers returned to the job market after the war, Lendman began arranging recruiting weekends at which he would gather a group of Navy officers and invite recruiters to interview them. This format, in which a sponsor provided an orderly meeting ground for candidates and recruiters, took firm hold and a number of entrepreneurs came into the business. In almost all cases, job fair candidates have a specific character: women and minorities, experienced managers, scientists and engineers, and recently, new graduates from small colleges that are not visited by recruiters from large organizations.

The open house is a local equivalent of the career conference that is used in densely populated areas. A company seeking new employees in a specific field will hold a "recruiting party" to which people in that specialty will be invited through large newspaper ads.

Like job fairs, open houses often feature exhibits or appropriate presentations. A great advantage for the candidate is that an open house provides an opportunity to talk with company managers and possible colleagues and to learn about the opening without making a formal application.

A variant is the open house by special invitation. This event is announced in an ad that describes the kinds of openings available and includes a blank mini-résumé to complete and return or a telephone number to call for a brief qualifying interview. Interesting candidates receive a direct invitation to attend.

Open houses are held for a variety of jobs and fields from secretary to sales to science, and it's a rare weekend without one or two ads for these events in the Sunday editions of major metropolitan newspapers.

Affirmative Action Organizations

The outreach required under affirmative action plans has led to a number of special recruitment efforts that have proved productive. Inroads, Inc. and the National Action Council on Minorities in Engineering are two organizations dedicated to increasing the number of minority students entering fields in which minorities are proportionately underrepresented. The Society of Women Engineers includes groups of members who attract young women to that profession. The National Association of Minority Engineering

Program Administrators aids students in adjusting to the rigors of college life. Many organizations and resources exist to help reach handicapped people.[14] A less conspicuous "protected" group, Vietnam era veterans, receives assistance through federal policies requiring government contractors to list openings suited to veterans with local Job Service offices.

Associations and Professional Societies

Almost all professional societies and many trade associations have some sort of placement program. A number of these organizations now publish help-wanted and situations-wanted publications on a regular basis. Job market conditions affect these programs, but the trend seems to be toward providing more help for members. The demand for placement programs has paralleled the increasing mobility of professionals, managers, and technical people which resulted from downsizing, mergers, acquisitions, and other developments resulting from the turbulence of the economy.

Freestanding Computer-Based Name Banks

Skills banks form an obvious source of computerized recruitment information because of the ease of access and rapid sorting capabilities offered by computers. Membership organizations and individual companies maintain computer-based name banks, but freestanding computer banks have not succeeded too well. Although the idea seems like it should work, somehow it does not, given the mortality rate of firms offering name banks. No research has been published to explain the situation, and it remains unclear whether any of these services can serve as a reliable source of candidates for long-range and continuous recruiting efforts.

Despite these difficulties, certain companies offering this kind of information service may offer productive recruitment services. Many innovative service industries and sub-industries go through a trial-and-error period before finding their particular niche in the marketplace. The computer-based name bank will probably find a place among the standard array of recruiting channels, but until this process is completed, recruiters should be aware of the unstable condition of this mini-industry.

Temporary Agencies

Temporary agencies are growing in size and importance, and recruiters no doubt will draw on these sources more often and for more reasons. One notable development in the labor market during the 1980s has been the increasing number of contingency workers, that is, experienced people with no permanent attachment to a single organization. As this labor market expands, temporary agencies will become a more popular recruitment channel.

A number of factors account for the growing use of contingency workers.[15] One force driving this development pertains to the rationalization of corporate structures under the pressure from global competition. The large bundle of expected employee benefits is a second reason that employers show a greater interest in temporaries. A third factor is the growing number of people who do not have to work full time to satisfy their income needs.

The downsizing wave of the 1980s also has contributed greatly to the growth of temporary agencies. While many experienced management people cast into the market have found full-time jobs, not everyone has been so fortunate. The temporary agency has become the channel through which some individuals have located work. As the need for downsizing diminishes, so will the cohort of people who had not anticipated working as temporaries.

For the indefinite future, companies are expected to hold down the size of their work forces at all levels and to use contingent workers for peak periods and special projects. Agencies supplying temporaries are responding to this change by broadening the types of workers offered. Temporary agencies have long been a primary source of clerical workers and casual labor. In defense industries and among utility companies, job shops have become a source of technicians and engineers. Agencies serving business have added managers and professionals to their rosters. In fact, one new company has appeared that specializes in a single field; chemistry, and other specialized agencies will no doubt appear in the future.

The "Future Possibles"

Many recruiters keep a file of interesting applicants who have not accepted offers, along with data on employees who have left the company in good standing. These people can serve as future candidates or sources of information about potential candidates.

Recruitment Sources 2-127

Special Inducements

Special inducements have become increasingly popular recruitment tools. Two methods used to hire prospective employees are discussed below.

Relocation Aid

The ever-upward attitude of a bull-market society has had an effect on recruitment budgets. Managers and professionals who change jobs now expect to receive a larger salary and protection against any financial loss resulting from a move to another area. A whole new relocation industry has appeared as a result.

Examples of sources offering relocation assistance abound. Companies, many of them allied to banks and insurance firms, help employers with the residence left behind by relocated employees. A national association, the Employee Relocation Council, gathers information and publishes regular surveys of relocation practices and the amounts of money involved. Some relocation firms and one publishing company—Runzheimer International—produce additional data so that recruiters can reasonably estimate the costs of bringing new hires aboard.

Services for the family of a new hire are also increasing, stimulated in part by the emergence of the dual career family. Many managers and professionals, men and women alike, are reluctant to relocate unless the spouse will be able to find suitable employment in a new location. One way that recruiters are dealing with the situation is by trading information informally. One example of this is found in Ohio. Starting in 1979, Armco, National Cash Register, and Mead employment managers began meeting regularly to pass around information about trailing spouses who were seeking suitable slots. By 1987, the group had expanded to include 38 companies. This type of network is not unusual in most metropolitan areas.

School Match is a unique service which enables recruiters to provide detailed information on school systems, public and private, in the area to which a job candidate or new hire would be moving.[16]

Sign-On Bonuses

Another recruiting inducement, separate from any relocation aid, is the sign-on bonus. The practice seems to have migrated into business and industry from professional sports. Originally used for executives and professionals, signing bonuses have spread to other ranks as well. In 1987, a Boston bank gave $1,000 to successful applicants for secretarial jobs, and a New York City hospital offered a like amount to nurses. An unusual twist to this practice came from the Kemper Group, which offered senior-level insurance professionals a "self-referral" award.

A 1986 survey by Peat Marwick showed that sign-on bonuses were more common among young, rather than older established, firms.[17] This report also found that the great preponderance of firms offering such bonuses belonged to the computer and peripherals industry.

Conclusion

The increasing types of services available to recruiters, the difficulties in attracting certain kinds of candidates, and the ever-rising costs of recruiting and selecting employees require a comprehensive approach to recruitment. Given the turbulence of the economy, the recurring shortages of certain kinds of candidates and continuing changes in social values, recruiting efforts must be re-examined and revised regularly. Recruiting has become one of the most challenging assignments in the HRM field, and this trend will likely continue for an indefinite period.

Employment management is one of the most important assignments an HR manager will have during his or her career. A few people will specialize in the subject throughout their working lives. Most managers, however, will become HRM generalists, and recruitment can provide excellent training. The recruiter has to stay aware of what is happening in the world at large: the demographic changes, the alterations in social values, the state of educational systems, and the findings of behavioral scientists about human behavior and aspirations.

All these factors have to be examined with the organization's needs in mind. Each set of organizational circumstances differs, and the range of recruitment needs is broad. Recruitment is fairly simple for a small manufacturing firm in a well-populated rural area. But large high-tech firms with global markets face far different recruitment challenges.

Besides understanding these cultural factors, recruiters must handle budget limitations, especially with the current emphasis on measuring the effectiveness of HR operations. Some recruitment costs, such as agency fees and advertising rates, are fairly constant. However, recruitment now can involve high school and college relations campaigns, the results of which are not easy to quantify. In the 1980s, for example, companies had to recognize that a noticeable percentage of job candidates were functional illiterates and they began to offer remedial classes for new hires. Other companies have established joint programs with high schools to help upgrade educational facilities and provide additional social training for students. At the other end of the spectrum is the relationship between an organization and college campuses. Students' job expectations and demands change from one college generation to the next, so recruiters must maintain a constant dialogue with student and faculty.

All factors considered, recruiting is a valuable assignment. It requires alertness to tangible and intangible aspects of business management. It broadens the imagination through the necessity of understanding the job requirements of many kinds of people. It requires a thorough understanding of the organization and it demands communication skills in order to interpret the organization to diverse audiences.

◆

Notes

1. Employment Management Association.
2. Administrative Management Society.
3. Miller.
4. Kennedy.
5. Tarrant.
6. Farish.
7. Moore.
8. Groneman and Lear.
9. The Help-Wanted Advertising Index is prepared by the Conference Board, a New York City-based research organization, and the High Technology Recruiting Index is developed by Deutsch, Shea & Evans, an advertising agency. Both indices measure advertising volume and appear regularly in the business press.
10. The annual Deutsch, Shea & Evans Human Resources Manual is a primary source for the list of these publications.
11. Hodes, p. 167.
12. Robert Podgorski, Northrop Corporation, Defense Systems Division.
13. U.S. General Accounting Office.
14. See Rabby for a useful guide to these organizations.
15. This discussion of contingency workers is drawn from analyses conducted by Audrey Freedman, a labor economist at The Conference Board.
16. Information on School Match can be obtained by writing the organization at 5027 Pine Creek Drive, Westerville, OH 43081.
17. Peat Marwick.

2-130 HR Planning, Employment & Placement

Editor's Note: In addition to the References shown below, there are other significant sources of information and ideas on recruitment sources.

Organizations

American Management Association, 135 W. 50th St., New York, NY 10020.

American Society for Personnel Administration, 606 N. Washington St., Alexandria, VA 22314.

Association for International Practical Training, Inc., 217 American City Building, Columbia, MD 21044.

Association of Executive Search Consultants, Inc., 151 Railroad Ave., Greenwich, CT 06830.

Association of Human Resource Systems Professionals, Inc., P.O. Box 8040-A202, Walnut Creek, CA 94596.

Association of Outplacement Consulting Firms, Inc., 2 Sunrise Place, Armonk, NY 10105.

Association of Retarded Persons, P.O. Box 6109, Arlington, TX 76006.

College Placement Council, 62 Highland Ave., Bethlehem, PA 18017.

Cooperative Education Association, Inc., 665 15th St., NW, Washington, DC 20005.

Council on Professionals in Science and Technology, 1500 Massachusetts Ave., NW, Washington, DC 20005.

Employee Relocation Council, 1627 K St., NW, Washington, DC 20006.

Employment Management Association, P.O. Box 2598, Raleigh, NC 27602.

Human Resource Planning Society, Box 2553, Grand Central Station, New York, NY 10163.

Inroads, Inc., 1221 Locust St., St. Louis, MO 63103.

International Foundation of Employee Benefit Plans, 18700 W. Bluemound Rd., Brookfield, WI 53008-0069.

Mainstream, Inc., 1200 15th St., NW, Washington, DC 20005.

National Action Council for Minorities in Engineering, 3 W. 35th St., New York, NY 10001.

National Alliance of Business, 1015 15th St., NW, Washington, DC 20005.

National Association for Health Care Recruitment, P.O. Box 93851, Cleveland, OH 44101-5581.

National Association for the Advancement of Colored People, 186 Remsen St., Brooklyn, NY 11201.

National Association of Corporate and Professional Recruiters, 197 Cedarwood Rd., Stamford, CT 06903.

National Association of Minority Engineering Program Administrators, c/o Nate Thomas, 3200 S. Wabash, Box One, Chicago, IL 60616.

National Association of Personnel Consultants, 1432 Duke St., Alexandria, VA 22314.

National Commission for Cooperative Education, 360 Huntington Ave., Boston, MA 02115.

National Society for Internships and Experiential Education, 122 St. Mary's St., Raleigh, NC 27605.

National Urban League, 500 E. 62nd St., New York, NY 10021.

Newspaper Advertising Bureau, 1180 Ave. of the Americas, New York, NY 10036.

Publications

Black Resource Guide. Washington, DC: R. Benjamin Johnson. Lists of organizations, businesses, civil rights groups, social organizations, media, and other facets of the black community.

Bowes, Lee. 1987. *No One Need Apply: Getting and Keeping the Best Workers.* Boston: Harvard University Press. Practical advice for smaller organizations.

Bureau of National Affairs, Inc. 1988. *Recruiting and Selection Procedures.* Personnel Policy Forum Survey No. 146. Washington, DC: The Bureau of National Affairs, Inc.

Calvert, Robert, Jr. *Affirmative Action.* Garrett Park, MD: Garrett Park Press. Ideas for reaching people in protected groups.

Cole, K.W., ed. 1987. *Minority Organizations.* 3rd ed. Garrett Park, MD: Garrett Park Press. Organizations that serve Alaska natives, American Indians, blacks, Hispanics, and Asian Americans. Data given include job placement activities.

College Recruiting Report. Crete, IL: Abbott, Langer & Assoc. Salary offers to college graduates during the past recruiting season. Includes data on associate degrees.

CPC Salary Survey. Bethlehem, PA: College Placement Council. Early season and end-of-season reports on offers to new graduates in a variety of fields.

CPC National Directory. Bethlehem, PA: College Placement Council. A who's who in career planning and college placement.

Directory of Executive Recruiters. Fitzwilliam, NH: Consultants News. Extensive listing with geographic, industry, and management specialty indexes.

Directory of Outplacement Firms. Fitzwilliam, NH: Consultants News. Profiles firms and provides a geographic index.

Directory of Special Programs for Minority Group Members. Garrett Park, MD: Garrett Park Press. Institutions and programs that prepare minority group members for employment.

DSE Human Resources Manual. New York: Deutsch, Shea & Evans. Contains lists of media directed to particular audiences and checklists for recruiting activities, such as open houses.

2-132 HR Planning, Employment & Placement

Employee Relocation Policies. White Plains, NY: Merrill Lynch Relocation Management. Current practices by companies.

Employment Marketplace. St. Louis: Employment Marketplace. Lists services for recruiters.

Engineering/Technology Degrees. Washington, DC: American Ass'n of Eng'g Societies. Number of degrees by school, minority degrees, and curriculum breakdown.

Engineering/Technology Enrollments. Washington, DC: American Ass'n of Eng'g Societies. Includes engineers, technicians, and technologists and breakdowns for women, minorities, and foreign nationals.

Frantzreb, Richard, ed. *Microcomputers in Human Resource Management.* Roseville, CA: Advanced Personnel Systems. Software directory.

Hiring Costs and Strategies: The AMA Report. 1986. New York: American Management Ass'n. One-time survey showing that costs can vary from less than $1,000 to over $100,000 to fill a manager's job.

Human Resources Effectiveness Survey. Saratoga, CA: Saratoga Institute. Measures of effectiveness of HR activities, including cost-per-hire, time to fill jobs and similar measures of recruiting activity.

International Directory of Executive Recruiters. Fitzwilliam, NH: Consultants News. Search firms outside the United States.

Journal of Career Planning and Placement. Bethlehem, PA: College Placement Council. Articles of interest to college placement directors.

Knowles, Asa & Assoc. *Handbook of Cooperative Education.* San Francisco: Jossey-Bass. A compendium of information by specialists.

Lordeman, Ann et al. 1987. *Making JTPA Work for Older Persons.* Washington, DC: National Ass'n of State Units on Aging. Catalog of successful programs.

Northwestern-Lindquist Report. Evanston, IL: Northwestern University Placement Office. Starting salaries offered to new college graduates; data supplied by recruiters in large companies.

Prescreening, Preselection and Prerecruiting. Bethlehem, PA: CPC Foundation. Discussion of controversial issues in college recruiting.

Principles and Practices of College Recruiting. Bethlehem, PA: College Placement Council. Standards of practice.

Professional Women and Minorities. Washington, DC: Comm. on Professionals in Science and Technology. A comprehensive source that gives numbers of professional women and minorities by professional fields.

Recruiter's Handbook. Chicago: Enterprise Publications. List of sources of information and services for recruiters.

Recruiting Trends. East Lansing, MI: Michigan State University Placement Office. Salary offers to new graduates by employers and other data about recruiting practices.

Recruiting Trends: The Monthly Newsletter for the Recruiting Executive. Chicago, IL: Enterprise Publications. Practical information for recruiters on recruiting practices, services, and sources of information.

Recruitment Advertising Guide. Cleveland, OH: Nationwide Advertising Service. Lists newspaper and magazine circulation data, rates, and mechanical requirements.

Recruitment Directory. New York: Bernard Hodes Advertising. Employment analysis of the 50 top markets in the United States, includes city profiles showing media, hotels, and transportation.

Recruitment Today. Costa Mesa, CA: AC Croft. A magazine for the recruiter and employment manager in private and public-sector organizations.

Reports on Relocation. Northbrook, IL: Runzheimer International. Twelve-page reports featuring mini-surveys, mortgage data, relocation industry trends, and viewpoints.

Stanton, Erwin S. 1977. *Successful Personnel Recruiting and Selection.* New York: American Management Ass'n. Detailed overview of the process.

Survey of Employee Relocation Policies. Washington, DC: Employee Relocation Council. Current practices of organization members.

Sweet, Donald H. 1973. *Modern Recruitment Function.* Reading, MA: Addison-Wesley.

Yoxall, George et al. *The Campus Connection.* New York: Brecker & Merryman. Basic points of an effective college relations and recruiting program.

♦

References

Administrative Management Society. 1986. "The Hiring Score." News release issued in September.

Employment Management Association. 1986. "Utilizing Retired Employees." *EMA Reporter* (October) 12, 8: 1.

Farish, P. 1986. "Changes in Recruiting Channels." *Recruiting Trends* (May): 1.

Groneman, C., and R. Lear. 1985. *Corporate Ph.D.*, New York: Facts on File.

Hodes, B. 1982. *The Principles and Practice of Recruitment Advertising.* New York: Frederick Fell Publishers Inc.

Kennedy, J. 1987. *The Future of Executive Search.* Executive Recruiter News: Fitzwilliam, NH.

Miller, E.R. 1987. "EMA Approves Code of Ethics for Recruiters." *EMA Reporter* (November) 13, 9: 1.

Moore, R.W. 1987. "Hiring Ph.D.s." *HR Reporter* (August) 4, 8: 5.

Peat Marwick. 1987. "Signing Incentives—Fad, Fancy or Strategic Tool?" Compensation Briefs (March).

Rabby, R. 1983. *Locating, Recruiting and Hiring the Handicapped.* Babylon, NY: Pilot Books.

Tarrant, J. 1986. *Stalking the Head Hunter.* New York: Bantam Books.

U.S. General Accounting Office. 1986. "Employment Service: More Jobseekers Should Be Referred to Private Employment Agencies." GAO/HRD-86-61. March.

2.5

Merit-Based Selection: Measuring the Person for the Job

Milton D. Hakel

Selection: Its objective is to pick the best person for the job. Talent comes in both sexes and all sizes and shapes, ages, and races. As the slogan "Sometimes the best man for the job is a woman" points out, selecting the best person for the job is neither a simple nor an easy task.

This chapter is about selection. It begins with a brief review of American values, as shown in laws concerning employee selection, to help define "best" in the phrase "best person for the job." It then reviews job analysis and job description, the "for the job" part of the slogan.

The major part of the chapter is devoted to a general discussion of methods for measuring the merit of prospective employees, from interviews and tests to genetic screening and polygraphs. Further information of particular techniques is discussed in Chapter 2.6. Selection is complicated because the best candidate as shown by one method may not be the best candidate when another method is used. This chapter will cover the strengths and weaknesses of each method and summarize criteria employers should consider in choosing methods for measuring prospective employees. The final sections will discuss how to combine all the preemployment information and select a candidate. The chapter concludes with suggestions for keeping up with research and development work on employee selection procedures. In any profession there will be differences of opinion about the merits of various procedures, and the research literature is the best place to keep track of new developments.

National Values and Legal Requirements

The dominant values of American life that shape much of the controversy over employee selection procedures date to this country's earliest days. The Declaration of Independence neatly digests these values into a single statement: "We hold these truths to be self-evident, that all men are created equal; that they are endowed by their creator with certain unalienable rights; that among these are life, liberty, and the pursuit of happiness."

Legal protection of these values also has existed from this country's start. The Fifth Amendment to the United States Constitution states "No person shall be deprived of life, liberty, or property without due process of law," and the Fourteenth Amendment extends this limitation on federal power to cover states and their subdivisions. In addition, the Fourteenth Amendment provides that no state shall deny to any person within its jurisdiction the equal protection of the laws. Due process and equal protection provide the basis for the commonly accepted idea that all persons similarly situated be treated alike, both in the privileges conferred and in the liabilities imposed.

In 1964, equality, life, liberty, and the pursuit of happiness were given a new interpretation that specifically applies to employment. Title VII of the Civil Rights Act prohibits discrimination in employment, making it illegal for an employer with more than 15 employees to refuse to hire, to discharge, or otherwise to discriminate against any individual, with respect to compensation, terms, conditions, or privileges of employment because of an individual's race, color, religion, sex, or national origin. The legislative history of Title VII[1] and subsequent judicial decisions[2] make it abundantly clear that merit should be the basis for making selection decisions. What is not clear, however, is the operational means by which merit should be measured. Who requires "equal protection"? Who is "similarly situated"?

In the 1971 case of *Griggs v. Duke Power*, the Supreme Court ruled that the Civil Rights Act prohibits not only overt discrimination, but also seemingly neutral practices that operate in a discriminatory fashion.[3] The *consequences* of employment decisions, not simply intentional discrimination, can determine the legality of a particular practice. However, the Court conditioned this statement, noting "The touchstone is business necessity. If an employment practice which operates to exclude Negroes cannot be shown to be related to job performance, the practice is prohibited."[4] Thus, employment practices that have disparate impact can still be legal provided the standards are necessary for the conduct of businesses and have a manifest relationship to the particular employment situation.

In *Griggs*, the Supreme Court also addressed the issue of selection tools. While noting that tests and measuring devices are not to be disparaged and are useful, the Court cautioned that such devices should measure the person in relation to the job and not the person in the abstract.

Establishing Job-Relatedness

The message in *Griggs* is clear: Employment managers must use methods that are job-related. Job-relatedness provides the starting point for specifying how different applicants might be "similarly situated." This section reviews how job analysis and job description provide the job-related basis for employee selection.

Job Try-Outs

Job try-outs are the clearest case of job-related selection. When the content of the selection procedure is the job itself, nothing could be more job related. However, tryouts are extremely expensive (since the applicant becomes a paid employee, at least temporarily) and may prove infeasible for other reasons, such as safety. In addition, the "measurements" made during tryouts tend to be subjective and no better than those made in interviews and performance appraisals. Nevertheless, a clear relationship does exist between the tasks and duties of the job and the content of the selection procedure—they are identical. No job analysis is needed.

For other selection procedures, the links between job content and selection procedures need to be made as clear as possible. The need for this linkage makes job analysis essential. As discussed in Chapter 2.2, job analysis can integrate the strategic and tactical objectives of organizations and the work that employees do. When employee selection is the purpose, job analyses can also help to link what the person does on the job to selection procedures and standards. This task is not simple, but there are several ways to do it.

Job Content Linkages

Content-oriented test development is one approach for linking selection procedures to job content. Content validation for typing tests and other tests or simulations of key job duties is based on expert judgments that effective performance on the test requires the same behaviors needed to perform effectively on the job. Along with tests of specific skills, this approach also is used to justify tests of job knowledge and more general skills and abilities. The key is to establish a one-to-one correspondence between the items of the selection test and important tasks and duties performed on the job.

Job analysis will help identify the critical components of job performance. Table 1 presents a short list of measures of successful work performance, sometimes known as "criterion constructs." One or more of these factors will likely prove important to success on the job.

Employee Characteristic Linkages

Another construct-oriented approach that links selection procedures to job content uses job analysis to identify the abilities and traits employees need to perform their jobs effectively. If job analysis shows that high amounts of particular abilities or traits are needed to perform the job, and research shows that the selection procedure measures those same abilities or traits, then the selection procedure is job related. For example, job analysis might show that manual dexterity, finger dexterity, and wrist-finger speed are essential abilities for workers who assemble electronic components. The problem then becomes finding appropriate measures of these constructs.

Although the rationale for this approach is more complex than for the previous one, it probably better represents the way employment managers think about jobs and selection. Table 2 shows a listing of over 50 constructs, abilities, and traits that research psychologists and personnel researchers have studied in connection with employee selection. While the list is not complete, it does illustrate the range of knowledge, skills, abilities, and other personal characteristics that have received serious study.

Table 1
Criterion Constructs[1]

Performance during Training
Job Knowledge
Technical Skill and Proficiency
Leadership
Support for Peers
Demonstrating Commitment
Performance under Adverse Conditions
Avoidance of Disciplinary Problems
Attendance
Punctuality
Tenure
Productivity
Promotion

[1]Note: This list is not exhaustive.

Future Developments

Researchers are now working to summarize studies that correlate the predictor constructs (ability, motivation, and personality factors) from Table 2 with the criterion constructs (job performance factors) in Table 1. The next edition of this handbook will likely include a matrix that estimates how well each ability or trait predicts each job performance factor and how these findings vary across various job families. For now, HR management must rely on information supplied by test publishers, job analysis results, and the published research that establishes a connection between a test and a particular job. The following discussion summarizes some of this research linking preemployment measurement methods to predicted job performance.

Methods for Measuring Merit

No measurement method does a complete job, and each method has its strengths and weaknesses. Nevertheless, employers must attempt to measure a candidate's merit, and the following methods are commonly used.

Table 2

Predictor Constructs[1]

Cognitive Skills

Verbal:	Verbal Comprehension
	Reading Comprehension
	Ideational Fluency
	Analogical Reasoning
	Omnibus Intelligence/Aptitude
	Word Fluency
Analytical:	Word Problems
	Inductive Reasoning: Concept Formation
	Deductive Logic
	Investigative Interests
	Figural Reasoning
	Verbal and Figural Closure
Quantitative:	Numerical Computation
	Use of Formulas in Number Problems
Attentional:	Perceptual Speed and Accuracy
	Processing Efficiency
	Selective Attention
	Time Sharing
	Rote Memory
	Following Directions

Spatial

- Two-dimensional Mental Rotation
- Three-dimensional Mental Rotation
- Spatial Visualization
- Field Dependence
- Place Memory (Visual Memory)
- Spatial Scanning
- Mechanical Comprehension

Motor Skills

- Control Precision (Accuracy of psychomotor responses)
- Rate Control (Pacing of psychomotor responses)
- Arm-hand Steadiness
- Aiming
- Multilimb Coordination
- Speed of Arm Movement
- Manual Dexterity
- Finger Dexterity
- Wrist-Finger Speed

> **Table 2** continued
>
> Personality Variables
> ──
>
> >   Sociability
> >   Social Interests
> >   Realistic Interests (Preference for tangible activities)
> >   Artistic Interests
> >   Enterprising Interests
> >   Physical Condition
> >   Energy Level
> >   Dominance
> >   Self-esteem
> >   Traditional Values
> >   Conscientiousness
> >   Non-delinquency
> >   Conventional Interests
> >   Locus of Control
> >   Work Orientation
> >   Cooperativeness
> >   Emotional Stability
>
> [1]Note: This list is not exhaustive, but it illustrates the range and diversity of ability, motivational, and personality characteristics that have been studied as predictors of job performance. It is adapted from research done for the U.S. Army's Project A (Eaton, et al., 1984).

Tests

Tests are as old as civilization. Plato's *Republic* advocated the use of a series of selection tests for staffing positions, and as far back as 700 A.D., the Chinese had implemented a system of written examinations for selecting civil servants and clerks.

Today, tests are still the employer's best bet. Despite recurrent debate in the professional media, tests are as good as or better than other techniques for assessing applicants and forecasting job performance.[5] The technology for measuring individual differences in cognitive, perceptual, and psychomotor performance is well developed and well validated. Hundreds of tests have been published, and more are introduced each year. Employers who discount the value of these measures need to take another look at tests.

Performance Tests

Performance tests constitute a very promising category of selection tools. Performance tests resemble job try-outs, but use standardized measures to observe and evaluate examinee performance. This standardization provides a direct comparison of different applicants' behaviors.

Unlike cognitive tests, performance tests assess the candidate's ability to do, rather than knowledge or the ability to learn. This distinction is illustrated by the performance testing program of Miami Beach, which covered some 21 different performance tests.[6] If the city wanted to assess a candidate's developed skills, then the test consisted of actual work samples. For jobs where the testing objective was to assess an applicant's aptitude to develop a skill, simulations were used. For example, in the performance exam for concession attendants, applicants first were taught how to use a cash register, then tested at the actual job site on their ability to count the cash on hand, make change, fill out a revenue report, react to an irate customer, and make several announcements, such as paging someone to the control desk. Interrater agreement was consistently high, and adverse impact was absent. The tests obviously related to the job, and perhaps most importantly, examinee attitudes were very favorable. For years, researchers and psychologists have denigrated the importance of face validity in testing programs, but applicant (and therefore public) acceptance of testing is the key issue.

The greatest advantage of performance tests is their obvious job-relatedness. Unfortunately, this type of test costs much more to administer than ordinary paper-and-pencil tests because of the need to train test administrators, provide special testing facilities, and test applicants individually.

Cognitive and Personality Tests

In general, conventionally administered paper-and-pencil ability and personality tests have several shortcomings: excessive administration time; poor differentiation among people of exceptional ability; limited capacity for measuring some types of abilities, such as target identification and tracking; cumbersome and error-prone scoring; and high vulnerability to theft and compromise. Administering tests by computer overcomes some of the problems associated with written tests. Several vendors now offer software versions of many tests, and as personal computers spread through employment offices around the country, an increasing number of computerized selection tests will become available.

For the most part, these computerized programs simply change the mode of administration from paper and pencil to computer screen and keyboard. However, some programs incorporate adaptive testing, in which the computer selects the next item based upon the examinee's response to the previous item. If the examinee's previous response was correct, the next item will be slightly more difficult. If the previous response was incorrect, the next item will be slightly easier. In this way, computers can create tests that are both briefer and have the right feel for the examinee—neither too easy nor too difficult. Individually tailored tests may promote greater public acceptance of testing, and research shows that comparable reliability and validity can be attained with tests that are only 40 percent of the length of standard scales.[7]

Computerized Test Interpretation

Computers also can assist in the interpretation of scores and the integration of results from multiple tests. Computerized test interpretation can maintain the advantages of expert interpretation while offering increased efficiency, standardization, accuracy, and permanence. Such a computerized interpretation system has been developed and validated for personnel tests given to Sears managers and executives.[8]

Future Developments

Looking to the future, some very interesting research on cognitive abilities might increase test validity. This research has expanded the concept of intelligence from the classroom focus on abilities, such as verbal fluency and quantitative ability, to include "real world" skills, which others might describe as "practical intelligence," "street smarts," or even "savvy."[9] If job analysis shows that "practical intelligence" is needed, then this is research to watch.

Another development to watch concerns validity generalization and meta-analytic procedures.[10] Meta-analysis is a quantitative procedure for distilling the results of many studies into a conclusion that is more trustworthy than the results of any single study. Thousands of validation studies have been carried out over the past seven decades; meta-analysis offers the procedure for combining those results. Although the procedures are still new, professional standards recognize the usefulness of meta-analysis,[11] and the findings of several published meta-analytic studies show convincingly that validity generalizes across similar situations.[12]

When supplemented by appropriate job analysis information, meta-analysis can justify using a test in a situation for which local criterion-related validation research is not feasible. For example, a clear finding from meta-analytic research is that brief paper-and-pencil tests of cognitive ability validly predict job performance, as measured by success in training and by supervisor's ratings. If an organization's job analysis shows that its jobs involve reading comprehension or numerical skills, then the job analysis can be combined with meta-analysis results to form the basis for a job-related testing program.

Limitations on Testing

Meta-analytic research shows that the validity of tests is as good or as better than that of any alternative selection procedure. However, tests are not infallible predictors of job performance, and they have other limitations. They are unpopular. They have been the focus of much litigation. Their use may result in disparate impact.

On the surface, selection based on standardized test scores seems to satisfy the concept of fairness. Tests are color blind, and all test takers are treated alike, without regard to race, sex, religion, or other irrelevant considerations. The problem, however, is that test scores, by their specificity, narrowness, and appearance of precision, may inhibit the introduction of other considerations relevant to the employment decision. Test scores typically reflect only one or a few dimensions of individual differences. The "whole person" is not measured by a single test score, and yet the "whole person" is hired for the job. What tests lack are reliable and accurate measures of other employee characteristics that job analysis shows to be important.

In a recent report, the Committee on Ability Testing of the National Academy of Sciences noted, "The diminished prospects of the average American give the debate about testing an especially sharp edge. Because they are visible instruments of the process of allocating economic opportunity, tests are seen as creating winners and losers. What is not as readily appreciated, perhaps, is the inevitability of making choices: whether by tests or some other mechanism, selection must take place."[13] By supplementing tests with other assessment procedures, employers may get a broader and more comprehensive picture of the "whole person."

Interviews

Interviewing is ubiquitous. Organizations use interviews for just about every type of job opening and rarely select someone without conducting one or more interviews with the candidate. Unfortunately, the reliability and validity of interviews fall short of the standards set by other measurement methods, such as tests, assessment centers, and biographical data. Nevertheless, organizations continue to use interviews, despite the availability of more reliable and more valid measures.

Researchers have conducted hundreds of studies during the past two decades to investigate the factors that influence interviewing decisions. Interviewing is a complex and difficult cognitive and social task. Managing a smooth social exchange while instantaneously processing information about an applicant makes interviewing uniquely difficult among all managerial tasks. Research has shown that first impressions, stereotypes, and various biases—such as the "similar to me" effect and the halo effect—influence interviewers' judgments.[14]

Structured Interviews

The most important practical finding among hundreds of studies is that structured interviews are more reliable and more valid than unstructured or *laissez-faire* interviews. Structured interviews follow interview guides, outlines, or programs that are usually customized for the specific job or job family. Many variations are possible in the format and content, but all structured interviews share the same essential elements: The same questions are used to interview all candidates for a particular job, and the questions come from the results of the job analysis.

From the standpoint of reliability, use of an interview guide gives every candidate a chance to offer responses to the same questions. Thus, when choosing from several candidates, the interviewer has comparable information about them. In contrast, the *laissez-faire* style of interviewing results in haphazard sampling of information about applicants. When an organization has more than one interviewer, the advantages of comparable sampling become even more apparent.

Situational Interviews

The situational interview appears to be a very promising approach. One recent study gathered critical incidents as part of a job analysis and turned the incidents into interview questions.[15] Job applicants were asked to indicate how they would behave in 10 or more given situations, and their answers were rated independently by two or more interviewers using behaviorally anchored scales. For example, during the interview the following question asked: "Your spouse and two teenaged children are sick in bed with a cold. There are no relatives or friends available to look in on them. Your shift starts in three hours. What would you do in this situation?" Applicants' responses were rated on a 5-point scale consisting of the following benchmarks: 1—"I'd stay home because my spouse and family come first"; 3—"I'd phone my supervisor and explain my situation"; and 5—"Since they only have colds, I'd come to work."

Follow-up research on this type of interview shows that it has acceptable reliability and validity, and that people who received higher ratings for their answers were later rated as better performers by their peers and their supervisors.[16]

Future Developments

One development to watch concerns computerized interview procedures and aids. Although highly rated by proponents, more research is needed to evaluate whether these programs perform effectively.

Biographical Information

Since the 1950s, biographical information (or biodata) has become widely used as a part of employee selection. Biodata is a general term encompassing a broad range of information, from the objective and verifiable (for example, age), to unverifiable self-reports about life and work history (for example, favorite hobbies). The information is usually collected from applications or special information forms that contain multiple-choice or short-answer questions, so scoring is objective.

A review of 58 studies that used biographical information as a predictor consistently found objective biodata items, such as age, marital status, and number of dependents to be valid predictors, especially of tenure.[17] However, fair employment practices limit the use of these biodata items since age discrimination and sex discrimination (marital status and number of dependents) are illegal. Nevertheless, valid and legal biodata measures do exist. For example, the Life Insurance Marketing and Research Association has used more diverse biodata (such as work and activity preferences) successfully for several decades in selecting life insurance agents.[18] The association's aptitude battery is a feasible and cost-effective approach to personnel selection that deserves to be emulated.

Personality and Interest Inventories

The use of personality and interest tests in selection has recently received renewed interest. This interest comes partly from the realization that ability tests do not measure the whole person, and partly from developments in measurement technology and validation research. For example, a measure of "service orientation" has been developed to use in selection for jobs where a helpful, thoughtful, considerate, and cooperative disposition is an important part of nontechnical performance.[19] The service orientation score correlates well with overall job performance. As another example, research conducted for the Army shows that a vocational interest inventory can predict several aspects of enlistees' job performance, particularly their adjustment to military discipline.[20]

Personality and interest inventories typically receive limited use in employee selection because applicants may object to inventories as an invasion of privacy, and employers may be concerned about faking. New tests are in the works and research is underway to resolve these problems. The applicability of personality and interest inventories should continue to be monitored in the future.

Polygraph

The polygraph, popularly known as the lie detector, is a portable machine that measures and records pulse rate, relative blood pressure, rate and depth of respiration, and galvanic skin response. Commercial banks and retailers are the most common users of the polygraph, employing it for preemployment screening, periodic surveys of employee honesty, and investigation of specific thefts or other irregularities.[21] However, these uses involve very different circumstances, so research conducted on the accuracy of the polygraph may have limited generalizability.[22] Many states have laws that either restrict the use of polygraphs or require licensing of polygraph operators. Similar federal legislation, proposed in each session of the U.S. Congress for the past decade, finally passed in the summer of 1988.

While the use of the polygraph in investigations of wrongdoing receives some support, preemployment screening and periodic screening of employees remains unpopular. Moreover, use of the polygraph in these applications is highly likely to misidentify the "innocent" as "guilty." Even if, as its proponents claim, the polygraph were 90 to 95 percent accurate, many applicants and employees will be erroneously accused of attempting deception. Thus, employers tempted to use polygraphs need to consider morale and public relations costs, along with error rates. These costs, together with potential legal costs, may outweigh the gains made in identifying and deterring dishonesty.

Honesty Tests

Compared to other psychological tests, the use of honesty tests in employment screening has experienced the fastest growth. These paper-and-pencil tests, developed as alternatives to polygraph screening, commonly include items such as the following: What percentage of people take more than $1 a week from their employer? Should a person be fired if caught stealing $5? Have you ever thought about taking company merchandise without actually paying for it? How easy would it be for a dishonest person to steal from an employer? What percentage of employee thieves are ever caught? Do you know for certain that some of your friends steal from their employers? Does an employer who pays people poorly have it coming to him when his employees steal? Compared to other people, how honest are you?

Many of the scales are quite transparent, but nevertheless, they seem to work well. The scales are scored by comparing the applicants' responses to scoring keys that identify the "correct" answers; that is, answers that differentiate among more and less honest respondents.

Limitations on Honesty Tests

Validation research reveals a mixed but generally positive picture.[23] However, the research designs that have been used so far contain many faults, and more research is certainly needed. A particular difficulty in using honesty tests concerns where to set the "passing" score. If the cutoff score is set low, about 25 percent of applicants are likely to fail the test and be rejected. If a high cutoff score is used, as many as 75 percent will fail, and recruitment costs will increase as a result.

Like polygraph exams, the cutoff score on honesty tests may eliminate many people who are actually "innocent." In addition, many applicants feel that extensive questioning about their attitudes toward theft and their previous theft behavior is offensive and an invasion of privacy. Finally, more research is needed on the "fakability" of honesty tests. If desirable answers are transparent, then these tests will reward dishonest candidates who choose the obvious answer. Rather than detecting dishonest applicants, an employer might end up selecting the better liars.

In the years ahead, developments in validation research and the legal arena could affect honesty testing. State and perhaps federal law may constrain the use of such tests for employment decisions.

Recommendations and Reference Checking

Despite legal constraints imposed by the Fair Credit Reporting Act and the Family Educational Rights and Privacy Act, opinions of previous employers and others about applicants have long been valued in selection. Employers expect that former colleagues who have closely and frequently observed an applicant performing a similar job can provide highly useful information. While this expectation is reasonable, in practice past employers rarely make even mildly negative statements about an applicant. Research indicates that letters of recommendation suffer from poor response rates by previous employers, leniency error, and low reliability.[24] In addition, recommendations have relatively low validity, partly as a result of the preceding three problems.

However, letters of recommendation may be useful in the rare instance where negative information is reported. A negative recommendation should never be the only cause for rejection, but it should signal a need for further information. Furnishing a negative recommendation or denying employment on the basis of a negative recommendation may expose an employer to a suit for damages (lost wages), due to an erroneous reference report.

In summary, the use of letters of recommendation in pre-employment screening has little empirical support, even though most application forms still request the names and addresses of persons who could furnish recommendations. Personnel screeners should cease asking for recommendation letters unless researchers can improve the accuracy and usefulness of this selection tool.

Reference checking—verifying the dates and nature of employment, the content of educational courses, and the possession of degrees and certifications—is a preemployment activity distinct from evaluating the contents of letters of recommendation. Reference checking should be done, and failure to pass a reference check should be treated as a much more serious matter than getting an unfavorable letter of recommendation.

Assessment Centers

Assessment centers are often used by supervisors and managers. Six to twelve candidates may attend an assessment center during a session, which typically consists of one and one-half to two-and-one-half days of group and individual exercises, role playing, simulations, and tests. Common assessment techniques include leaderless group discussions, business games, and interviews. Observations of candidate behavior are recorded by a team of specially trained assessors. The team then meets for a day or more to pool observations and to evaluate each candidate's performance on a set of job-related dimensions. Given the numbers of candidates, the special training needed for assessors, and the costs of developing assessment exercises, assessment centers are probably the most expensive selection technique.

Assessment centers are rarely used solely for selection (or promotion) because of the time and cost involved. The centers are best used for extensive training, when candidates can benefit from extensive feedback or when the duties of the current job differ greatly from those of the promotional job. Since entry-level supervisory and management jobs frequently involve new and different responsibilities, assessment centers tend to be used for such positions.

Assessment center ratings have high validity, particularly when used to predict who will receive promotions.[25] Because the results have demonstrated validity, job-relatedness, and face validity, assessment centers are often the technique of choice in equal employment opportunity cases—AT&T's consent decree is the biggest case in point.

Peer Evaluations

Peer evaluations are often viewed as untapped tools for use in selection decisions. Who can better evaluate the strengths and weaknesses of an applicant than his or her peers? In some circumstances, particularly in military organizations and training classes, peers have extensive opportunities to observe the behavior of job candidates.

While research shows good validity for peer evaluations,[26] this method still presents many practical and technical problems. Peer evaluations will likely prove infeasible for entry-level selection since employers normally have no way to obtain peer judgments about applicants' potential. In using peer evaluations for promotion, HR managers encounter problems that relate to a lack of standardization and the need to include a correction for the size of the peer group. Finally, peer evaluations tend to be unpopular among the people called on to produce them. Co-workers view peer evaluations as tattling or reporting one's friends in violation of a group norm to maintain solidarity. Thus, despite favorable findings of validation research, peer evaluations are likely to remain a rarely used approach to pre-selection screening.

Accomplishment Record

The accomplishment record is an interesting new technique that appears to yield results different from traditional psychological measures, but correlated with job performance. This technique asks applicants to provide written descriptions of accomplishments in highly relevant, behavioral job dimensions.[27] For example, attorneys might describe work done researching and investigating, using knowledge, planning and organizing, writing, making oral presentations, and demonstrating assertive advocacy. The job dimensions surveyed come from job analysis and the questionnaire allows up to one page of description on each dimension. Applicants are instructed to review their accomplishments which reflect the particular skill, and write general statements of what they accomplished, exactly how they accomplished it, and who could verify their record. Scoring uses a set of rating scales anchored by accomplishments elicited from applicants or employees in a pilot study and has high reliability. The accomplishment record appears promising, and it deserves further use and research.

Professional Assessments

Consulting psychologists are often called upon to evaluate job candidates in situations where criterion-related validation research may not be technically feasible (for example, selection of top executives for a corporation). A professional assessment may require a half-day to a full day of a candidate's time and usually includes an interview, several paper-and-pencil tests of abilities, interests, and personality, and also biographical data forms. Scores on the various tests are combined with information from the interviews in a narrative report describing the candidate's strengths and weakness. The average cost for a four-hour to one-day assessment is $600.[28]

The various methods used in a professional assessment have higher validities when used separately—that is, the validity of each cognitive test is much higher than the validity of professional assessments.[29] The same finding is true for biographical information. Professional assessment (expert judgment) validities approximate those achieved for interviewing and personality inventories.[30] In addition, professional assessments are relatively costly and time consuming. While scattered evidence indicates that professional assessments can predict performance in sales and managerial occupations,[31] this method as a whole has received little investigation, and more research is needed.

Handwriting Analysis

Handwriting analysis is marketed as a means of assessing individual characteristics, such as those listed in Table 1, by judging the graphic form of the person's handwriting (for example, slantedness, pressure). There is, as yet, no credible evidence that handwriting analysis accurately predicts employee job performance. The best-designed study on this topic found significant but borderline reliability and no evidence of validity.[32]

Genetic Screening

Genetic screening offers a new technology that may become a standard preemployment activity for jobs involving potential exposure to toxic chemicals. Since individuals with certain genetic conditions are hypersusceptible to toxins in the work environment, screening for those genetic conditions could allow employers to improve occupational health and safety through selective placement of these workers. In recent years, the technology of genetic engineering has made many advances, some of which will surely lead to industrial applications of genetic screening.

A review of genetic screening has found strict criteria for effective preemployment testing set forth in professional standards and legal requirements.[33] Genetic screening is covered under the federal Occupational Safety and Health Act, the Rehabilitation Act, and Title VII of the Civil Rights Act, as well as state worker's compensation, privacy, and right-to-know laws. The greatest legal ambiguities revolve around requiremnts of the Civil Rights Act. One uncertainty concerns whether susceptibility to occupational disease would constitute a job-related characteristic, thereby justifying rejection on the basis of business necessity. In addition, the validity data on genetic screening that employers would need to refute charges of disparate treatment and disparate impact are not available. This issue is particularly important since many genetic syndromes are distributed unequally among different ethnic populations. As research continues, genetic screening is clearly a topic to watch for further developments.

Medical, Physical, and Drug Screening

One final category of preemployment measurements that deserves attention is medical screening. For years, applicants for certain jobs have been required to pass physical examinations, a practice usually justified on the basis of health and safety concerns. Some employers recently have expanded medical screening to include drug testing (e.g., for police and firefighter applicants) and testing for exposure to the AIDS virus (for example, for military inductees). Preemployment medical screens are almost always used on an exclusionary or knock-out basis.

In recent years, physical standards for employment and the possibility that physical standards will produce adverse impact have generated considerable interest. Despite this interest, the research base on validation of physical standards is relatively small and could benefit from further research.[34]

Drug testing is, and will continue to be, controversial because it involves the conflict among individual rights, employers' rights, and societal values. Moreover, drug tests fail to distinguish between legally prescribed drugs and illicitly used drugs, fail to identify performance impairments due to drug/alcohol abuse (as opposed to use), and, like polygraph exams, may result in too many false positives (erroneous identifications of drug users). Employers who use drug screening as a preemployment procedure need to keep abreast of technical and legal developments continually.

Choosing Measurement Methods

The preceding section provided general descriptions of various selection tools. Along with this information, employers must consider which method might best predict performance in a specific job or job family. The first step in choosing any method for measuring merit is to gather information about the job. With that information, employers can then begin selecting an appropriate set of measures.

Several criteria can help employers in selecting among measurement methods. As discussed in the preceding section, useful methods should be reliable, valid, and acceptable to examinees, and provide high value for the cost and time spent on them.

The interrelationship among these criteria are complex, and employers will need to make difficult judgments about the trade-offs among them. For instance, reducing the time devoted to measurement will usually mean sacrificing a degree of reliability, and probably validity—shorter tests tend to be less precise and less accurate than longer ones. In a similar vein, cost and validity do not have a one-to-one relationship. Cognitive ability tests tend to be quite inexpensive, and assessment centers tend to be quite expensive, but both are quite valid. Other techniques in the mid-range on cost tend to have lower validities.

All the factors need to be taken into account when installing or maintaining a selection program. Study the references listed at the end of this chapter. Consult texts on personnel management.[35] Write to test publishers and other suppliers for copies of manuals and specimen sets of tests. The manual will specify the time needed for measurement and also should include information about reliability and validation research. With regard to judging face validity, look at the measure yourself, or have a panel of subject matter experts review it. Evaluate several different alternatives and then choose the ones that are optimal for you.

HR managers can easily compute dollar estimates of the gains from improved selection. Utility analysis provides a rigorous mathematical way of interrelating information about applicants' abilities, costs, test validities, and the value of performance.[36] These estimates can be extremely helpful in identifying the benefits of valid selection relative to the costs.

Combining Preemployment Information

Once employers identify a set of measures, the remaining task is to select a procedure for combining those measures to reach decisions. Almost every employment decision involves a sequential series of steps; indeed, few applicants are fully evaluated on *every* preemployment measure. Rather, a large initial pool of applicants will be reduced in successive stages to a smaller, more manageable pool before more costly or more intensive evaluations are made.

The appropriate sequence of these stages will differ depending on the organization and its needs. Once again, this decision involves complex trade-offs among cost, time, reliability, validity, and examinee acceptance. When all else is equal, employers should first use the most valid techniques. But everything else is not always equal, so employers also should consider first using less expensive, less time-consuming, more face-valid measures. Here again, HR managers need to evaluate the alternatives and choose one of them.

Averaging and Multiple Hurdles

At each stage of the selection process, employers also must choose whether to use the multiple hurdles approach or an averaging procedure to select among the applicants. The so-called compensatory model uses averaging to create a weighted composite score. This model gets its name because high scores on one measure might help to offset or compensate for low scores on another. If the selection process uses several different measures, all equally important to the job so that strength on any one measure might offset weakness on any other, then averaging is the way to go. In selecting management trainees, for example, such measures as college grades, interpersonal skills, and work experience might all deserve equal weight.

On the other hand, if performance on one measure is so important to a job that no amount of other skills or attributes could counterbalance its absence, then a multiple hurdles approach is needed. This approach requires applicants to pass the first hurdle to be eligible for evaluation on subsequent measures. For example, if an applicant for the company's physician post does not possess a license to practice medicine, collecting any other preemployment information would prove pointless.

Once again, job analysis plus the research literature can help HR managers in choosing between the averaging (compensatory) and multiple hurdles approaches.

Concluding Comments

Given the rapidity of job turnover these days, HR managers should document the steps taken and the rationale used in creating and implementing a merit-based selection program. In addition, record-keeping procedures should be set up in a way that will facilitate later research and statistical analyses. Filing government reports and conducting validation research are impossible without adequate records.

Along with keeping current records in order, HR managers should keep up with selection research and development. The list of references at the end of this volume suggest many places to look, but *Personnel Psychology* and the *Journal of Applied Psychology* are the best places to look for research reports on selection issues.

♦

Notes

1. The debate leading to adoption of the Tower Amendment permitting use of employment tests is particularly relevant.
2. For a good review of significant decisions on merit-based selection, see Arvey.
3. 401 U.S. 424, 3 FEP Cases 175 (1971).
4. See majority opinion in *Griggs*, 3 FEP Cases at 178.
5. Hunter and Hunter; Reilly and Chao; Schmitt et al.
6. Cascio and Phillips.
7. Sands and Gade.
8. Vale, Keller, and Bentz. See also discussion in Quaintance, Chapter 2.7 of this volume.
9. Wagner and Sternberg.
10. Hunter, Schmidt, and Jackson.
11. American Psychological Association, 1985; Society for Industrial Organizational Psychology, 1987.
12. Schmitt et al.
13. Widgor and Garner, p. 203.
14. For comprehensive reviews of the research literature on interviewing, see Hakel; Arvey and Campion.

15. Latham, Saari, Pursell, and Campion.
16. Latham and Saari.
17. Reilly and Chao.
18. Owens and Schoenfeldt; Owens.
19. Hogan, Hogan, and Busch.
20. Eaton et al.
21. Belt and Holden.
22. Sackett and Decker.
23. Sackett and Harris.
24. Reilly and Chao.
25. Schmitt et al.
26. Reilly and Chao; Hunter and Hunter.
27. Hough.
28. Ryan and Sackett.
29. Reilly and Chao.
30. Ibid.
31. Hunter and Hunter; Reilly and Chao; Schmitt et al.
32. Rafaeli and Klimoski.
33. Olian.
34. Campion.
35. See, e.g., Cascio (1987a).
36. See, e.g., Cascio (1987b) and Boudreau, *ASPA/BNA Handbook*, Volume 1, Chapter 1.4.

♦

References

American Psychological Association. 1985. *Standards for Educational and Psychological Testing.* Washington, DC: Author.

Arvey, R.D. 1970. *Fairness in Selecting Employees.* Reading, MA: Addison-Wesley.

Arvey, R.D. and J.E. Campion. 1982. "The Employment Interview: A Summary and Review of Recent Literature." *Personnel Psychology* 35: 281–322.

Belt, J.A. and P.B. Holden.. 1978. "Polygraph Usage among Major U.S. Corporations." *Personnel Journal* 57: 80–86.

Campion, M.A. 1983. "Personnel Selection for Physically Demanding Jobs: Review and Recommendations." *Personnel Psychology* 36: 527–550.

Cascio, W.F. 1987a. *Applied Psychology in Personnel Management.* 3rd ed. Englewood Cliffs, NJ: Prentice Hall.

———. 1987b. *Costing Human Resources: The Financial Impact of Behavior in Organizations.* 2nd ed. Boston: PWS-Kent Publishing Co.

Cascio, W.F. and N.F. Phillips. 1979. "Performance Testing: A Rose Among Thorns?" *Personnel Psychology* 32: 751–766.

Eaton, N.K. et al. 1984. *Improving the Selection, Classification, and Utilization of Army Enlisted Personnel: Annual Report, 1984 Fiscal Year.* Technical Report 660. Alexandria, VA: U.S. Army Research Institute for the Behavioral and Social Sciences.

Hakel, M.D. 1982. "Employment Interviewing." In *Personnel Management.* Edited by K. Rowland and G. Ferris. Boston: Allyn and Bacon.

Hogan, J., R. Hogan, and C.M. Busch. 1984. "How to Measure Service Orientation." *Journal of Applied Psychology* 69: 167–173.

Hough, L.M. 1984. "Development and Evaluation of the 'Accomplishment Record' Method of Selecting and Promoting Professionals." *Journal of Applied Psychology* 69: 135–146.

Hunter, J.E. and R.F. Hunter. 1984. "Validity and Utility of Alternative Predictors of Job Performance." *Psychological Bulletin* 96: 72–98.

Hunter, J.E., F.L. Schmidt, and G.R. Jackson. 1982. *Meta-analysis: Cumulating Research Findings Across Studies.* Beverly Hills, CA: Sage Publications.

Latham, G.P. and L.M. Saari. 1984. "Do People Do What They Say? Further Studies on the Situational Interview." *Journal of Applied Psychology* 69: 569–573.

Latham, G.P., L.M. Saari, E.D. Pursell, and M.A. Campion. 1980. "The Situational Interview." *Journal of Applied Psychology* 65: 422–427.

Olian, J.D. 1984. "Genetic Screening for Employment Purposes." *Personnel Psychology* 37: 423–438.

Owens, W. 1984. "A Generalized Classification of Persons—A Box within a Box." Paper delivered at the annual meeting of the American Psychological Association, Toronto, Ontario, August.

Owens, W., and L. Schoenfeldt. 1979. "Toward a Classification of Persons." *Journal of Applied Psychology* 65: 569–607.

Rafaeli, A. and R.J. Klimoski. 1983. "Predicting Sales Success through Handwriting Analysis: An Evaluation of the Effects of Training and Writing Sample Content." *Journal of Applied Psychology* 68: 212–217.

Reilly, R.R. and G.T. Chao. 1982. "Validity and Fairness of Some Alternative Employee Selection Procedures." *Personnel Psychology* 35: 1–62.

Ryan, A.M. and P.R. Sackett. 1987. "A Survey of Individual Assessment Practices by I/O Psychologists." *Personnel Psychology* 40: 455–488.

Sackett, P.R. and P.J. Decker. 1979. "Detection of Deception in the Employment Context: A Review and Critical Analysis." *Personnel Psychology* 32: 487–506.

Sackett, P.R. and M.M. Harris. 1984. "Honesty Testing for Personnel Selection: A Review and Critique." *Personnel Psychology* 37: 221–246.

Sands, W.A. and P.A. Gade. 1983. "An Application of Computerized Adaptive Testing in U.S. Army Recruiting." *Journal of Computer-Based Instruction* 10: 87–89.

Schmitt, N. et al. 1984. "Metaanalyses of Validity Studies Published between 1964 and 1982 and the Investigation of Study Characteristics." *Personnel Psychology* 37: 407–422.

Society for Industrial and Organizational Psychology. 1987. *Principles for the Validation and Use of Personnel Selection Procedures: Third Edition.* College Park, MD: Author.

Vale, C.D., L.S. Keller, and V.J. Bentz. 1986. "Development and Validation of a Computerized Interpretation System for Personnel Tests." *Personnel Psychology* 39: 525–544.

Wagner, R.K. and R.J. Sternberg. 1985. "Practical Intelligence in Real-World Pursuits: The Role of Tacit Knowledge." *Journal of Personality and Social Psychology* 49: 436–458.

Wigdor, A.K. and W.R. Garner. 1982. *Ability Testing: Uses, Consequences, and Controversies, Part I.* Washington, DC: National Academy Press.

2.6

Tools for Staffing Decisions: What Can They Do? What Do They Cost?

Rick Jacobs
Joseph E. Baratta

This chapter reviews the various techniques used by organizations to select employees. Six different selection procedures are described in terms of application, effectiveness, cost estimates, and legal implications. Procedures covered include interviews, tests, work samples, assessment centers, experience, and realistic job previews. The information contained in this chapter should familiarize readers with a wide range of qualitatively different selection techniques as well as variations within a given technique.

While selection of new employees forms the focus of the chapter, many of the techniques discussed and findings cited apply to other personnel decisions, such as promotion and termination. Personnel practitioners daily face a host of decisions regarding their work force. Several techniques discussed in these pages may help personnel professionals to make higher-quality decisions about applicants in the context of transfer or promotion. In addition, the information offered may stimulate new programs that will enhance current organizational decision making about employee placement. In using this chapter, readers should distinguish between data that pertain to more general personnel decisions and data that only apply to selection of prospective employees.

Interviews

Most people define an employment interview as a face-to-face interaction between a job applicant and a representative of the organization. This section will evaluate the success of the interview as a tool for identifying the most capable applicants for a position. The discussion will investigate factors that inhibit and enhance the accuracy of interviews as indicators of future performance. Finally, the analysis will examine the personnel requirements and other cost factors involved in the interview technique.

When to Use

The employment interview is the most popular and dominant technique for selecting employees, and its popularity dates back decades. Nearly 40 years ago, surveys documented widespread use of employment interviews, finding that nearly all employers rely on interviews to select employees.[1] Other research indicated that applicants had to endure numerous interviews in attempting to secure a job.[2] More recent reviews also show universal acceptance of the interview in the selection process.[3] Given the pervasive nature of the employment interview, HR managers should examine this selection technique and evaluate its effectiveness as a forecaster of future job performance.

Effectiveness

Consistent with its omnipresence, the employment interview has generated plentiful and diverse research. As psychological studies expanded into such areas as memory, multiple-cue decision making, and performance appraisal, the type of research conducted on employment interviews shifted. Early studies focused on the product or outcome of interviews, and many of these studies documented relatively poor reliability and validity for the interview technique. Later research approached the interview from a new perspective, adopting a process orientation rather than a product orientation. Process-driven research offers practitioners information on specific factors that may affect the validity of the interview and ways to improve the interview process.[4]

From all this research, three important variables in the interview process have emerged: the interviewer, the interview format, and the applicant. The following discussion briefly reviews important research results in each of these areas.

Interviewers

One important issue concerns variables that the interviewer brings to the interview and the effect these differences may have on the process and product. Key factors identified through research include the amount of stress on the interviewer, stereotyped attitudes toward candidates, and interviewers' level of training and experience.

Stress. Interviewers who are under stress during an interview generally perform more poorly. Negative reactions to stress can include lowered levels of rapport, lack of systematic collection of information, and improper evaluation of information gathered. These consequences of stress can profoundly impact the accuracy of assessments made during the interview.

Reducing the stress level of interviewers requires understanding the underlying causes. First, the interviewer may be uncomfortable in his or her role. Not everyone enjoys conducting an interview with a stranger and making evaluations based on this information. A second cause of stress in the interview results from organizational pressures to find candidates. Interviewers desperate to find a qualified candidate will experience stress if they anticipate the consequences of failing to identify talented applicants. This type of stress, while different in origin from the stress of role discomfort, can have similarly disastrous effects on the accuracy of evaluations.

Stereotyping. Interviewers also can bring impressions to the interview regarding the desired candidate. This factor is often referred to as the interviewer's stereotype. The relationship between stereotypes and interview accuracy is complex and can vary from positive to negative.

The interviewer's cognitive description of the "suitable candidate," regardless of the strength or explicitness of these perceptions, sets a standard for evaluating applicants. If based on knowledges, skills, and abilities relevant to the job, the stereotype can enhance evaluations. However, the interviewer stereotype may contain little or no job-relevant information. In this circumstance, the evaluative context of the stereotype will inhibit interviewer accuracy. To be effective in determining qualified candidates, interview stereotyping must be based on job requirements and not on preconceived notions of an ideal candidate.

Interviewer-Interviewee Similarities. Another powerful factor identified in research is the impact of candidate-interviewer similarity. In one sense, this variable resembles stereotyping: Interviewers believe that they could do well in the job opening, and they develop a job stereotype that candidates who are similar to them will do well. However, interviewers often attend to shared characteristics that bear little relationship to job performance. Research indicates that candidates who are similar to interviewers in terms of physical appearance, background, and preferences receive higher evaluations than applicants viewed as dissimilar on these dimensions. As a result, the relationship between candidate-interviewer similarities and interview accuracy often is negative.

Interviewer Skills. An interviewer also brings to the interview a certain level of training and experience. The important issue here concerns the degree to which experience facilitates the interview process and the accuracy of evaluations resulting from information gathered.

Although research in this area is inconsistent, it seems reasonable to assume that well-planned rater training can improve the quality of the interview. This assumption certainly holds true when the training includes systematic methods for collecting information and models for evaluating the information. The training also should caution interviewers on problems that can occur during the interview as a result of stereotyping or interviewer-candidate similarities.

While interviewer training may consistently improve the quality of interviews, the relationship between experience and accuracy is not as straightforward. For instance, research shows that quotas have a negative effect on inexperienced interviewers and little or no effect on experienced interviewers. However, in many other circumstances, experience is unrelated to the quality of interviews. For many interviewers, experience simply means that the interviewers have conducted many interviews. Some experienced interviewers might never have learned to conduct good interviews and simply perpetuate their poor skills over time.

In conclusion, trained interviewers likely will perform more effectively than untrained interviewers, and experience may enhance the capabilities of trained interviewers. However, experience without any formal training does not always improve interview quality.

Interview Format

A second important area of interview research has examined the way in which interviews are conducted. Many of these factors are under the control of the interviewing organization and can affect the accuracy of the interview. This section will highlight those factors that organizations should attempt to control so as to maximize the effectiveness of the interview.

Structured vs. Unstructured Interviews. One of the most consistent research findings in the interview literature concerns the relationship between the amount of structure imposed on the interview and the subsequent quality of the interview. In general, more structure is better. In a structured interview, the interviewer follows a list of activities and asks a series of predetermined questions. While structured interviews may reduce spontaneity, they ensure collection of similar information from all candidates. Unstructured interviews or interviews with minimal structure have the distinct disadvantage of gathering qualitatively different information. When the interviewer later must evaluate candidates interviewed, he or she may face the proverbial task of "comparing apples to oranges." While structured interviews cannot guarantee the quality of conclusions drawn from the data, they make it possible to compare data across candidates.

In addition, unstructured interviews are far more susceptible to premature decision making. Without a predetermined set of questions, the interviewer may reach an early, and potentially inaccurate, conclusion about a candidate, which will influence the types of questions that are asked later in the interview. While any interviewer can fall prey to this problem, the structured interview puts some requirements on the latter portion of the interview. All of these problems result in the potential reduction of the accuracy of conclusions drawn from the interview.

Type of Questions. Another finding relevant to interview format concerns the information gathered. Research shows that interviewers are more accurate in making specific ratings than global evaluations. Organizations that request interviewers to provide targeted evaluations of each candidate's level of skills and abilities will increase the effectiveness of the interview process. To accomplish this result, organizations must define specific job performance requirements and develop evaluative tools for interviewers to use in judging each candidate. The time spent in determining this information will pay off in enhanced levels of interviewing accuracy.

Multiple Interviewers. Interview evaluations will also improve if more than one representative of the organization is involved in the interview process. Organizations can have several interviewers administer independent sessions and develop separate evaluations of each candidate. While this method will add to the amount of information used in the final evaluation, it does not solve the problems that can arise when interviewers must perform a variety of tasks in a limited amount of time.

A second option is to involve two or more interviewers in the same interview, but assign each interviewer a different role and make each one responsible for a separate outcome. For instance, an organization could make one interviewer responsible for asking a series of predetermined interview questions, and assign two others to evaluate the candidate on rating scales specifically designed for the interview. In addition, one of the evaluators could be responsible for "selling" the job to applicants. In this way, the various interviewer roles are divided among several individuals who can perform the separate interview activities with far greater focus and accuracy.

Applicants

To complete the picture of the interview process, a final consideration is what the applicant brings to the interaction. Consistent findings indicate that such factors as competency, verbal fluency, age, sex, and attractiveness of the applicant can influence the outcome of an interview.

Competency. A basic question about the interview process is whether it can identify the more competent individuals from those who are less qualified. Laboratory experiments and field studies have consistently found that both experienced and inexperienced interviewers prefer more qualified applicants to less qualified applicants. This finding may seem obvious, but making distinctions between applicants can become difficult when candidates are close to one another in qualifications. Nonetheless, the interview process does distinguish between gross levels of competency.

Verbal Fluency. A second finding related to applicant characteristics concerns the relationship between an applicant's verbal fluency and subsequent ratings of suitability for the job. Verbal fluency depends on an applicant's ability to express thoughts and ideas, as well as to carry on an interactive conversation. Interviewers consistently give more favorable evaluations to applicants who demonstrate better verbal fluency.

Two important points need to be made about this finding. First, since many jobs require some degree of verbal fluency, including this factor in an evaluation may serve an appropriate goal. However, for jobs in which verbal fluency contributes little to job performance, including this factor will result in erroneous evaluations. Accurate evaluations will hinge on an interviewer's ability to determine the appropriate weight that verbal fluency should play in the overall evaluation.

Sex. Another issue receiving a good deal of attention in the research literature is the sex of the applicant. While a number of studies have indicated that applicants who are the same sex as the interviewer may have a slight edge, the congruence between the applicant's sex and the sex of the incumbent appears to play a dominant role. In other words, when a woman applies for a job that, in the past, has been held predominantly by men, or when a man applies for a traditionally "female" position, the ratings are systematically lower. This finding suggests that accuracy of ratings may be compromised by a sex-related bias. Since sex is a rather poor predictor of subsequent performance for most jobs, interviewers should guard against the influence this bias might have on ratings.

Attractiveness and Age. Two remaining applicant factors that show consistent relationships to overall suitability ratings are attractiveness and age. Studies have indicated that younger, more attractive applicants fare better in interviews. A key question is whether either factor has a significant influence on subsequent job performance, and the answer for most jobs is no. To maximize the accuracy of interview ratings, interviewers must recognize the potential problems caused by elevating ratings due to the younger age or increased attractiveness of the applicant.

Other Factors

While the above set of findings focuses attention on factors related to the interviewer, the applicant, and the interview format, several other variables seem to fit somewhere between these categories. These features of the interview process include the contrast effect and the primacy and recency effects.

Contrast Effect. The contrast effect occurs when the interviewer makes judgments about a specific applicant based on a comparison to the previous applicant. This effect can be very positive or very negative to a particular applicant, depending on the evaluation of the prior applicant. As an example, an applicant who follows a relatively poor applicant might receive higher ratings because of the comparison to the preceding applicant. The result is an inaccurate evaluation, but the total process of interviewing, and not just the interviewer, causes the problem.

Primacy and Recency Effects. Two problems that are similar in origin to the contrast effect may also reduce the accuracy of interviewer ratings. First, research consistently shows that interviewers seem to attach greater importance to negative information than to positive information. As a result, an interview that touches on negative information may produce overly negative evaluation.

A second problem is that negative or positive information takes on different meanings depending on when it is elicited in the interview. One line of research holds that positive or negative information has a larger impact on the final evaluation if it occurs early in the interview. This finding is referred to as primacy effect. Other studies reach the opposite conclusion, finding that information elicited later in the interview has a more profound impact. This effect is called recency. Regardless of which effect occurs most consistently, these findings indicate that the dynamics of the actual interview situation can have a direct impact on the accuracy of evaluations.

Reliability and Validity

The previous sections have shown how various factors combine to influence the outcome of the interview. While research data show that employment interviews can be reliable, the data also suggest that reliability is not guaranteed and that many factors can reduce the consistency of information and evaluation. Given these findings, organizations should seek to limit potential inhibitors of consistency in order to establish reliable interview results.

The validity of the employment interview is probably the most important concern to the personnel practitioner. Validity refers to the accuracy of the interview ratings as predictors of future job performance. To be a useful tool, an interview must generate information that will allow organizations to sort applicants in terms of how they will perform on the job. This issue is closely related to reliability. Many of the empirical studies and review papers published in the 1950s and 1960s painted a picture of questionable validity for the interview. This case clearly will occur with interviews of reduced reliability. Where reliability of the interview is high, validities are less problematic.

A final consideration is whether the interviews give information about applicants that is not supplied by other methods of collecting applicant data. For many years, employers assumed that an interview was the only process by which an organization could identify such factors as ability to communicate, appearance, and sociability, and that these factors were directly related to job performance. Both these assumptions have come under scrutiny in more recent years.

Cost Estimates

The employment interview is a costly selection procedure. Many of the costs are obvious, and arise regardless of the complexity of the interview process. Other costs are more covert and vary according to a number of factors. These factors fall into four general categories: time to prepare interview materials, time to conduct interviews, time to conclude post-interview decision making, and applicant expenses. Finally, organizations should estimate the relative cost of conducting interviews; that is, total expenses weighed against the resulting benefits.

Preparation Time

As discussed above, the quality of interviews depends on the degree to which the organization prepares interviewers for the task. Preparation includes such factors as training interviewers and defining job requirements. Each of these activities requires time commitments from current employees and from in-house personnel professionals or external consultants. The exact costs of such activities are difficult to measure and depend on the level of the job opening. However, developing a well-outlined interview and training interviewers to use the system can quickly exceed $10,000 in direct costs.

Interviewing Time

A second cost results from the actual time spent interviewing candidates. Many organizations estimate this cost by simply multiplying the rate of pay for interviewers by the number of hours spent interviewing. Unfortunately, a large percentage of companies use sequential interviews and repeatedly interview many applicants, often in several different locations. For example, one real-life company conducted interviews for recent college graduates using campus interviews, corporate headquarters interviews, and site interviews.[5] Successful candidates participated in an average of seven interviews, and the organization attempted to have at least three candidates go through the entire process for each job. With about 150 jobs, the organization needed to send interviewers to different locations, and the price of interviewing totalled more than $100,000. This cost estimate included the hourly rate of pay for interviewers, travel expenses, and communications to arrange the logistics of conducting the multi-site program.

Decision-Making Costs

A third cost relates to the actual selection of candidates. In many organizations, a single individual handles organizing information and reaching a conclusion about an applicant's suitability. The costs for this selection activity amount to the hourly rate of pay for that individual times the number of hours spent making decisions about the candidates.

A second model used by many organizations is a selection committee. In this model, selection costs grow as the number of decision makers increases, and these expenses can have a sizeable impact on the total cost of interviews. For example, a selection project conducted by the authors used a committee approach to interview about 450 candidates for 140 manufacturing positions and to make final decisions about candidates. Two and one-half days of meetings involved 12 supervisors, 2 personnel representatives, the plant manager, the legal counsel, and 2 industrial psychologists. While an exact total is difficult to calculate, a conservative cost estimate for this activity would amount to more than $15,000.

Candidate Expenses

A final cost factor that affects the employment interview is direct candidate expenses. Organizations that invite candidates to interviews frequently pay all expenses incurred by the individuals. These expenses can include travel to the interview, lodging, meals, and additional entertainment for the candidates, as well as the costs of providing meals and entertainment for the host. For two days' worth of interviews, the grand total could quickly amount to $1,000 per candidate. The more elaborate the activities and the more candidates invited, the more costly the interview becomes.

Relative Costs

A key question to ask when analyzing variables that influence interview costs is what the organization gets for its expenses. The answer can range from very little (for an interview process lacking validity) to a sizeable return on investment. Organizations that utilize valid employment interviews can accurately forecast future performance. When the implications of performance have large dollar-based consequences, a valid interview can become the organization's means of "buying" the benefits of high performance.

Legal Implications

The legal status of the interview is related to the question of validity: Does this procedure make accurate inferences about future performance? Several factors that influence the legality of interviewing procedures include the job-relatedness of evaluation criteria, the consistency of ratings among interviewers, the outcome on work-force composition, and type of questions used.

Job-Relatedness

If the interview measures job-related variables, then it is a valid and legal selection tool. However, organizations will have difficulty defending the use of interviews to select candidates for a job that requires little verbal interaction and sociability, but lots of eye-hand coordination and wrist-finger speed.

Consistency Among Interviewers

The legality of interviews also depends on the way in which interviewers interpret their role and use the data they collect. Most organizations spend little time evaluating differences between employment interviewers. Some interviewers may perform the job in the manner prescribed by the organization, while others may follow a different and unspecified mandate. If an applicant's probability of employment varies according to which interviewer he or she sees, the organization is not fulfilling its mission of fair employment. As an example, an applicant lacking in attractiveness or considered to be of the wrong sex for the job may be rejected by one interviewer and accepted by another. When variations of this type occur regularly, it indicates an organizational problem that may result in unfair and unlawful employment decision making.

Impact on Work-Force Composition

A third legal issue concerns the long-term impact of the interview. Many organizations treat the employment interview as a "non-test" situation, and therefore do not evaluate it in light of the 1978 Uniform Guidelines on Employee Selection Procedures. In fact, the interview is just as much a test as any paper-and-pencil device a personnel department might administer. In this context, organizations should review the outcomes of employment interviews to ensure that any systematic differences between identifiable subgroups, such as minorities and women, are clearly related to job performance. For example, an organization's review of employment interview records might reveal that a far larger percentage of women are found as unacceptable for a particular job than a comparison group of males. In the absence of additional information suggesting that men can outperform women on the job, this outcome will present a potential legal dilemma.

Type of Questions

A final legal consideration is the nature of the questions asked during the interview. Interview questions should establish a link between what an applicant is capable of doing and what the job requires. Interviewers should be sensitive to the kinds of questions that commonly arise during an interview but have little bearing on future job performance. Questions concerning the applicant's marital status, number of dependents, day-care arrangements, or spouse's salary should be excluded from a fair interview. Other questions to avoid include queries regarding circumstances of military discharge, arrests, and citizenship.

Cognitive Abilities Tests

Cognitive abilities tests include measures of general intellectual capacity, as well as tests designed to assess specific components of thinking, such as memory, inductive reasoning, and spatial relations. Other tests that tap thinking abilities examine a candidate's knowledge of the job, such as promotion tests.

Organizations that use cognitive abilities tests must show, either empirically or logically, that the test activities and the duties and responsibilities of the job overlap. In promotion decisions, and in many similar situations, tests of job knowledge are appropriate and helpful in making selections among candidates.

Effectiveness

For many years, researchers have questioned the effectiveness of various tests in predicting success on the job. Recent studies have provided a rather detailed set of data to address this issue.[6]

The findings indicate that cognitive tests do predict success on the job in a variety of occupational groups, for a variety of measures of job success, using a wide variety of tests. According to research data, about 10 percent of job success is related to skills tapped by cognitive abilities testing.[7]

While this predictive validity may seem somewhat low, several characteristics make it a very favorable number. First, validity is only one of several factors that influence the ultimate usefulness or utility of a selection device. Other factors include the number of applicants, the difficulty of the job, and the dollar-based difference between various levels of job performance. At high levels of these factors, cognitive tests with moderate correlations to job success can prove quite useful in most selection situations.

Cost Estimates

Testing of cognitive abilities, whether general measures, specific abilities tests, or knowledge-based examinations, can be very cost-effective. As outlined above, when combined with selectivity, job difficulty, and the potential for dollar-based value, a valid selection test may save an organization a great deal of money. However, this result represents the benefit side of the equation, and overlooks the direct costs of using tests as selection tools. The following discussion examines the costs associated with each stage of developing a testing program and identifies the organizational resources required to support a testing program.

Preliminary Expenses

The first stage of any testing program involves identifying potential selection tests. This step may be done in house, or it may require contracting with a consulting organization. Consulting fees for outside experts to simply review job analysis information and recommend a set of tests can total several thousand dollars. A smaller cost might be attached to the time required by in-house personnel to perform the same tasks.

Once the tests have been selected, they must be purchased. Cognitive tests can cost as little as 25 to 50 cents per test and $10 to $15 for the test manual and scoring guide or as much as $25 per candidate tested depending on the method used to score the test. Some tests may be scored by clerical personnel and routinely interpreted by a member of the personnel department based on a cursory review of the test manual. Other tests require little in the way of scoring expertise, but do depend on the interpretation of someone experienced with the test. Finally, some tests are sold with the understanding that scoring and interpretation will be done by the test publisher. As the expertise needed to score and interpret a test increases, the cost of the testing program escalates dramatically.

Administration Expenses

Another factor affecting testing costs is the method of administration. Many cognitive tests can be given to groups and therefore cost little to administer. Individually-administered tests may result in more information about each candidate, but they come with a very high price tag. Every hour spent testing each candidate costs an hour of a testing specialist's time. In addition to requiring more time to administer, individual testing demands greater expertise, further escalating the expense of a testing program.

Outcome Analysis Costs

A final cost consideration is tied to legal issues. Any organization using a test should document the appropriateness of that test as a selection device and how well it conforms to legal guidelines governing selection activities. Regardless of the form this evidence takes, it always requires sizable amounts of organizational resources to accumulate the necessary documentation. The usual form for this documentation is a validity report summarizing the relationship between the test and the job. Developing a validity report often requires a series of activities that may involve candidates, incumbents, supervisors, and both in-house and outside testing specialists. When an organization adds up all these time expenses, it may find that a simple study of 100 current employees can cost in excess of $50,000.

Cost-Benefit Analysis

Two different studies have addressed the relative cost-effectiveness of selection based on cognitive testing. The first study examined the value of using a programmer aptitude test for the selection of computer programmers.[8] The dollar-based estimation of savings from improved selection of programmers, above and beyond the cost of testing, was staggering. The study concluded that in one year alone, the federal government could save several millions of dollars by using the programmer aptitude test for selection of new computer programmers. While the exact magnitude of these savings has generated debate, even the most conservative estimates show a tremendous return on investment for testing in this context.

Another approach to the cost-benefit issue is to evaluate the dollar value of performance differences between an average performer and those employees selected using a testing program. The first step in such an evaluation is to estimate the dollar-based consequences between average performance (50th percentile) and high performance (85th percentile). The study of computer programmers discussed above estimated that a $10,000 difference existed between these two levels of performance.

Next, the validity and costs of testing should enter the equation. For example, one recent study varied the costs of testing and the validity coefficients, and obtained estimates of the dollar-based consequences between 50th and 85th percentile job performance necessary for the testing program to "break even." For example, a cognitive test which costs $50 per candidate and has a validity coefficient of .20 would have to produce performance improvements worth $893 to break even.[9] When the cost of testing doubles, the break-even value grows to $1786. When validity improves by .30, the corresponding job values are $595 for average performance and $1190 for high performance.

These dollar-based values for jobs should be placed in a context. Data collected on a variety of jobs show that most jobs have corresponding dollar-based values far in excess of $1,800.[10] For example, the job of first-line supervisor in three different organizations can range from a low of $4,674 to a high of $12,857. In a similar fashion, the job of purchasing manager was estimated at $44,286 in one plant and $50,500 in a second plant. As mentioned above, the value of a computer programmer is estimated at over $10,000.

These figures, when coupled with an average selection ratio of 20 percent and research on validity, clearly indicate that selection programs using cognitive tests have the potential to produce positive results.

Legal Implications

Many of the legal implications for testing apply to all forms of tests, whether cognitive, personality, or physical measures. This section will review the general legal implications of using tests and the specific problems associated with cognitive tests. In each of the succeeding sections on legal implications, the discussion will examine only those issues that apply to the specific type of test being discussed.

Job-Relatedness

Federal guidelines, professional standards, and case law generally recognize that testing can serve an important role in personnel practices. Laws governing the use of selection tests require little other than adherence to sound testing practices. Organizations should make certain that the material covered in the test reflects what is required on the job. If this precaution is taken, then the problems of unfair discrimination and invalid selection standards will not occur.

However, job-relatedness is not an all-or-nothing proposition. given that no test can represent perfectly the entire range of job requirements, HR managers must decide how much representativeness is enough to warrant use of a given test. Unfortunately, the lack of standards regarding how to define and measure job-relatedness complicates this issue. At this point, organizations simply must attempt to ensure the test used measures as much of the job as possible.

Adverse Impact

While job-relatedness should underlie employment interviews or any other selection device, it is discussed in detail here because tests are some of the most easily scrutinized and commonplace types of selection devices. Cognitive tests, more than any other selection procedure, result in a directly interpretable figure. This number can be compared to normative data or, more important, it can be used to compare various subgroups within a sample of job candidates.

This direct measurement of an attribute or set of attributes also makes tests the most easily identified liability when selection practices result in adverse impact. However, adverse impact is not illegal, and lack of adverse impact does not guarantee that a test is job-related or useful in predicting job performance. In using cognitive tests, the best defense is data that supports the job-relatedness of the test or test battery.

Personality and Interest Inventories

Personality and interest inventories assess candidates' preferences, behavioral predispositions, and characteristic responses to situations. The logic underlying these instruments assumes that candidates who possess certain interests and characteristics will better fit the job. To complete this process successfully, employers must have some notion of the "appropriate" pattern of interests or personality characteristics for the job. In contrast to cognitive tests, which profile a job in terms of required abilities or knowledges, these tests describe a job in terms of desired personal attributes, such as interests or personality characteristics.

One strategy used to develop this job profile is to survey current incumbents on the instruments of interest and look at their responses to the scales. By sorting incumbents into two or three groups according to level of job performance and investigating differences in scale scores, employers can develop a test profile that distinguishes between different performance groups. If a high performing group scores higher on a set of traits than average or poor performing employees, then the organization could look for new employees who also score high in the same areas.

When to Use

In contrast to cognitive tests, the use of personality tests and interest inventories in selection is far less pervasive. Organizations often restrict use of these tools to upper-level positions or jobs where some clearly relevant characteristic can be identified. For example, some companies administer personality tests to sales personnel, on the belief that someone who is outgoing, sociable, and assertive might be better equipped to perform the job. Similar job content analyses support the use of personality tests for such jobs as stock broker, insurance counselor, and social service worker. In addition, many experienced interviewers describe their role as one that seeks to identify individuals with a particular personality profile or interest pattern. In effect, these interviewers are performing personality assessments without the benefit of paper-and-pencil tests.

Personality and interest inventories also are used as screening devices for jobs such as police officers, government workers dealing with security issues, or nuclear power plant operators. Organizations that use personality tests in this way are not seeking to identify high performers and select the most qualified individual; rather, they are looking to block employment of any individuals who might show deviant tendencies, based on their current personality profiles. Since this screening function removes candidates from the selection process and prevents tracking of future performance, little data is available regarding the forecasting efficiency of personality tests under these circumstances.

Effectiveness

As a general selection tool, personality tests do not offer as high a level of prediction as cognitive tests. One study reported an average correlation for personality tests as predictors of job success of .15.[11] Of the entire set of potential predictors investigated in this study, personality tests showed the lowest levels of forecasting efficiency regardless of the method used to measure job success.[12]

Job-Specific Predictiveness

These low levels of prediction indicate that personality tests do not greatly facilitate the forecasting of future job performance. However, the above-cited study included a variety of occupational categories, ranging from professional and managerial personnel through clerical and sales staff to skilled and unskilled laborers. As stated before, the most common use of personality tests and interest inventories seems to be in selection decisions involving managerial, sales, or service personnel. In these situations, personality tests may have higher predictive power.

For example, one recent report describes how a battery of cognitive tests, personality measures, and interest inventories can combine to show substantial predictive power.[13] Looking at different definitions of overall job performance, position level attained, managerial effectiveness, and salary level, the study examined the correlations between these criteria and the battery of predictors. While the results do not deviate greatly from the first study, they do show slightly greater correlations for several of the personality scales and the management attitudes measure.

Another recent study attempted to predict supervisory ratings of sales personnel in a large northeastern utility company.[14] In addition to traditional selection tools like cognitive tests and interviews, the assessment battery included a sales interest inventory and a personality measure as parts of the assessment package. The study found that the sales interest inventory served as the best indicator of job performance, followed by two of the four personality scales. The correlations for these three scales with a supervisory rating criterion of overall performance ranged from .32 to .54, while the correlations of cognitive tests with the same criteria ranged from .00 to .25. Although this study represents a rather limited example, it does highlight the potential of interest inventories and personality tests for forecasting job performance.

Cost Estimates

Personality tests and interest inventories are relatively low-cost selection tools. While these devices cost little to develop and administer, organizations should weigh these expenses against the benefits produced from use of these tools.

Development Costs

Numerous personality tests and interest inventories are widely available for reasonable prices, often less than one dollar per candidate. Unless the user needs to measure a rather rare interest or unusual personality factor, an assessment device probably exists to meet any employer's specific requirements. This fact precludes the need to spend a great deal of time and money on the development of an instrument.

Administration Expenses

Since most of these assessment devices can be given to groups, administration costs can be kept low. Scoring and interpretation services range from simple clerical expenses to complex configural scoring requiring the expertise of a professional. For the most part, organizations can incorporate personality tests and interest inventories into their selection programs for reasonably low costs.

Cost-Benefit Analysis

Given the relatively low predictive validities of personality tests and interest inventories, these devices may produce minimal benefits relative to their costs in many situations. However, personality tests may offer substantial predictability of performance in specific types of jobs. This potential and the relatively low costs associated with personality testing may make organizations take a closer look at these assessment devices.

Legal Implications

Legal support for personality characteristics or interest inventories as critical predictors of job performance is shakier than it is for tests of cognitive or physical abilities. First, cognitive and physical abilities are more rigorously defined than are interests or personality variables and can be more concretely linked to aspects of a job. Another issue concerns the degree to which personality measures or interest inventories can be faked. While candidates can't easily disguise cognitive factors like verbal comprehension, inductive reasoning or dynamic strength, they could try to look a little more sociable, a little less aggressive, or a little more interested in sales activities when filling out a survey. Finally, the lack of well-documented research showing consistent relationships between specific personality tests or interest inventories and job performance makes it impossible to argue for the use of such tests in one setting based on research done in another. Such procedures, referred to as validity generalization, are pervasive in the area of cognitive testing.

Without specific documentation of a direct relationship between personality test scores and actual job performance, the potential for misuse of these tests exceeds the potential for benefits. Unlike cognitive tests, which offer some validity regardless of the occupational category, the efficacy for personality and interest inventories is far less pervasive. At best, personality tests or surveys of specific interests may only prove valid for a few jobs in a very limited set of occupations. As a result, anyone looking to incorporate such assessment devices into selection programs should undertake a complete validation study to back up use of these tools.

Physical Abilities Tests

Physical abilities tests can assess movements of the entire body, of the arms or legs, or just of the fingers. They may involve the use of equipment, or they may simply tap an individual's ability to perform a specific task without additional apparatus. For example, many of the tasks firefighters perform can be directly incorporated into a test of physical abilities. During a call, firefighters often must carry equipment up and down stairs or place a ladder in a specific position. Each of these job tasks can be used to test candidates on their abilities. Other physical tests may require a slight modification of the actual job task to allow for safe and adequate testing.

When to Use

All physical abilities tests are predicated on actual job behaviors. As a result, these tests can be as diverse as the jobs involved and the equipment and settings in which the work is performed. Along with firefighters, many other jobs require physical abilities to meet performance demands. Utility workers must climb poles, lift heavy objects, and reposition cables while precariously positioned at the top of a pole. Other jobs, such as city sanitation workers, require the repeated lifting of heavy objects over long periods of time.

Effectiveness

Physical testing is only appropriate for jobs that have specific physical requirements. Therefore, these tests apply to a smaller number of jobs than those for which cognitive testing might be used. Nevertheless, information supports the validity of physical tests for particular job categories.

One analysis that investigated 22 validation studies of physical testing found an average correlation across these studies of .32.[15]

Not surprisingly, 21 of the 22 studies were limited to the occupational categories of skilled and unskilled labor—positions that have greater physical requirements than clerical, professional, or managerial posts. The same analysis also revealed that physical abilities testing has its greatest predictive impact when work samples are used as a criterion for job performance ($r = .42$), and is least effective when turnover is used to measure success ($r = .15$).

Differences Between Tests

The predictive power of a physical test also depends on the type of exercises used to assess candidates' abilities. Unfortunately, employers have often restricted physical abilities tests to easily measured and administered physical exercises rather than actual job tasks. For example, police and fire departments, as well as utility companies, often reason that since the job is physically demanding, strenuous exercises like push-ups, pull-ups, climbing walls and running distances will adequately test the necessary physical characteristics of the job. While these types of physical measures may have some bearing on subsequent job performance, the relationships tend to be very small.

One recent study did find that a physically demanding work sample test which required no specific job knowledge could do a very good job of predicting supervisory performance ratings of job incumbents. This study, conducted for firefighter positions, obtained correlations large enough to support the use of the test for hiring entry-level firefighters. However, several factors enhanced the appropriateness of a physical test for selection in this context. First, the job itself demanded a high level of physical abilities. Next, the test devised was systematically related to job activities, both empirically and logically. When these factors are present, a physical abilities test will be useful in estimating future job performance.

Cost Estimates

Physical abilities tests are expensive. Several factors unique to physical measures make these tests quite costly to develop and administer.

Development Costs

The costs associated with physical testing will escalate if the organization has to develop special apparatus for the assessment process. Employers typically want to test candidates using either the same equipment found on the job, or a reasonable approximation of that equipment. The expense of this equipment stands in marked contrast to the costs of pencils and papers used in cognitive testing.

Another cost consideration is the expense of pilot testing the physical test on current employees. In addition, the organization may need to develop baseline measures of acceptable performance on the physical tests, which would require another set of incumbents to go through the testing process after the pilot program.

Administration Costs

Physical abilities tests are costly. Since a test administrator must focus attention on one candidate at a time, physical tests often require individual administration. Even when physical tests are run sequentially so that groups of candidates are taken through the testing process, actual performance of the activities takes place one at a time. This time-consuming process impacts directly on the costs associated with test administrators, and it proves particularly costly when the number of applicants is quite high. Another administration-related cost is the need for a suitable test location. Many physical tests require large amounts of space, which employers may have to rent from another organization or agency.

Cost-Benefit Analysis

These expenses may be offset by the benefits of physical testing, at least for a small number of physically demanding jobs. With validity coefficients in the .30 to .50 range, physical abilities tests may enhance the accuracy of selection programs. In many cases, selecting the wrong employee can have very serious personal and organizational consequences and costs. For example, any job that requires great amounts of lifting has the potential for back injuries, even when the incumbents are physically capable. A work-related injury may mean a lifelong disability for the employee and a rather sizeable disability payment for the organization. These costly consequences might be avoided if selections were made using a predictive physical abilities test. Despite the high costs of the exams, the potential for saving corporate dollars and workers' health may offset the expenditure.

Legal Implications

Most physical tests pose immediate and profound legal jeopardy. First, the physical abilities measured by most tests are unequally distributed between the sexes. Men can outperform women in almost every type of physical ability measure. For example, one recently developed physical abilities test showed that the 10th percentile score for men corresponded to the 80th percentile score for women.[16] These results highlight concern that most physical abilities tests will show adverse impact against women. Employers who use physical abilities tests must be prepared to document the job-relatedness of these tests.

One recent study on physical abilities tests found that the combination of adverse impact against women and the resulting need for high predictive validity has made courts far more skeptical of physical abilities tests that do not directly represent job behaviors.[17] Research conducted over the past several years revealed that courts have repeatedly rejected the use of basic physical measures (push-ups, pull-ups, etc.) because most jobs do not require these activities and they are not clearly related to job behaviors. Based on these findings, the authors argued that the use of simple physical stature measures (height and weight) are also unlikely to survive most legal challenges.

In short, any employer seeking to institute physical abilities tests should make sure that the job warrants such tests and that the tests utilize solid work samples or high-fidelity simulations. In the absence of support for both these points, chances are that physical testing will not withstand outside legal challenges.

Work Samples

Work samples represent another form of assessment devices that can assist in personnel selection. Organizations typically use work samples as selection tools whenever a candidate should possess some job-relevant knowledge prior to obtaining a particular job.

Work samples provide an opportunity to appraise candidates on specific, and possibly complex, tasks in a standardized environment. As subsets of actual job behaviors, these tests are highly job-related and should predict job performance with increasing accuracy as the amount of the job sampled increases.[18] When compared to traditional tools like interviews and written tests, work samples represent a more direct relationship between the predictor (test score) and the criterion (job performance). Along with providing better predictive power, the job-relatedness of work samples actually may enhance candidates' compliance with performing the tasks.[19] This finding represents a clear legal advantage over certain paper-and-pencil tests that may elicit candidate questions regarding the relevance of the testing process.

When to Use

This criterion of job-specific knowledge holds true for many entry-level jobs. For example, a work sample for secretarial positions could include a typing test and for a dictation exam, while candidates for a mechanic's job might be asked to assemble portions of an engine or repair other mechanical or electrical devices. In both of these examples, the selection test assumes a knowledge base and assesses not only what candidates know, but also what they can do when applying that knowledge.[20]

Another use of work samples occurs in the context of promotion decisions. Here candidates clearly possess job-relevant knowledge, and the decision rests on candidates' suitability to assume a position of greater importance. For example, one large utility corporation segments many of the skilled trade positions into classes, such as steamfitter 3rd-class or electrical mechanic 2nd class. Incumbents seeking promotion to the next class must take a qualifying exam consisting of tasks that make up the higher-level job. Candidates who pass the qualifying exam are considered ready for the promotion since they have successfully performed the tasks of the higher-level job.

Work samples may assume a variety of formats. The trade example presented above tests psychomotor activities, while other work samples focus attention on candidates' cognitive activities. One example of a cognitive work sample is the "in-basket" test used to assess managerial competence. Tasks suitable for an in-basket test include making personnel assignments, writing a memo describing how a decision was reached, or developing a procedure for interviewing job candidates.

Specific Research Findings—Effectiveness

One of the most important questions regarding work samples concerns their effectiveness in estimating future performance. One study tackled this issue by reviewing the results of more than 60 work samples.[21] The review encompassed work samples requiring the manipulation of equipment or machinery, and verbal work samples that focus on written or oral job skills. The results of this investigation found solid predictive validity for both types of work samples. Verbal work samples had predictive validities between .40 and .50 in 20 percent of the studies and exceeding .50 in an additional 21 percent of the studies. Motor work samples showed even more impressive predictiveness with 27 percent of the studies reporting validities between .40 and .50 and 43 percent documenting validities above .50.

A similar, more recent, review examined the results of another 60 work samples and corroborated findings from the earlier review.[22] The second study broke work samples into four categories: psychomotor, individual situational decision making, job-related information, and group discussions/decision making. Once again, all types of work samples consistently demonstrated high levels of predictive validity, with psychomotor work samples showing the highest predictiveness. Further support comes from a meta-analytic report finding an average correlation of .39 for work samples as predictors of job effectiveness measures,[23] and a study of entry-level hiring that found an average predictive validity for work samples of .54.[24]

These studies and empirical findings clearly point to the high potential for accurate prediction of job performance based on the results of work samples. Work samples appear to provide a definite benefit from a cost-benefit perspective. As stated earlier, the superior predictive power of work samples over traditional cognitive or physical tests no doubt results from the similarity between tasks found on the assessment device and activities inherent to the job.

Cost Estimates

Work samples are costly in terms of developmental time. They require a detailed understanding of job tasks and the ability to translate those job tasks into an observable event that can be quantified and scored. Some work samples must be developed from scratch, while others are commercially available and lend themselves to direct application in several settings. Some work samples require the use of existing equipment; some require the development of tools that closely approximate the equipment in use; and others require no equipment beyond a paper and pencil. The types of work samples are potentially as diverse as the jobs they seek to forecast.

The utility industry is one setting in which work sample testing has been successfully employed to select and promote individuals for both trade and managerial positions. For the job of a nuclear plant operator, selection decisions utilize traditional knowledge tests supplemented by "hands-on" testing that assesses candidates' ability to make equipment adjustments and document operating procedures. For steamfitters in power plants, work sample tests assess candidates' ability to make bends in pipes and to weld pieces of pipe together in configurations identical to those found on the job. Finally, in the area of management selection, in-basket tests have been used successfully to forecast management candidates' ability to meet the demands of future jobs.

While the costs of these applications vary depending on the characteristics of the work sample, the expenses clearly exceed paper and pencil testing. However, as documented above, the outcome is also likely to be substantial with respect to the accuracy of predicting future performance.

Legal Implications

Work samples appear to have strong legal support since they provide high predictive efficiency and may substantially reduce or eliminate adverse impact on minority groups. Research conducted at AT&T supports the use of work samples as fair predictors for minority and majority candidates,[25] and two other studies have confirmed the superiority of work samples to paper-and-pencil tests in terms of predictive validity and reduced amounts of adverse impact.[26] These findings, and others like them, provide strong support for the use of work samples as selection tools.

Despite the positive effects of work sample testing on employment decision making, work samples do have a fairly important limitation. Most work samples presuppose a level of knowledge or skill that may not be warranted in practice. For example, a work sample might assume familiarity with knowledges and procedures for which new hires will receive on-the-job training. When this situation arises, the work sample lacks validity since many of the skills and knowledges it assesses are not expected to be part of a candidate's repetoire prior to employment. In practice, work sample testing is best limited to situations in which an organization is making promotions or seeking new but experienced employees. With respect to entry-level hiring, employers should carefully evaluate work samples to assure they do not presume knowledges or skills that the candidate will acquire while on the job.

Assessment Centers

Assessment centers employ an integrated series of measurements designed to identify a wide range of candidates' strengths and weaknesses. An assessment center battery will usually include several types of interviews, work samples or simulations, and written tests, including cognitive abilities, personality, and interest inventories. In addition to multiple measurement devices, assessment centers also use multiple assessors to develop a complete picture of each candidate.

When to Use

Like work samples, assessment centers are more commonly used for promotion decisions rather than for the selection of new employees. However, some organizations have developed and implemented assessment centers for the selection of middle-level managers, both from inside and outside the organization.

This wide range of assessment center techniques can provide far more detailed information about candidates than the data from any single measurement device. In fact, organizations often adopt the assessment center approach not only to decide among candidates, but also to provide individual feedback so each candidate can better understand his or her current strengths and weaknesses.

Effectiveness

The logic behind the assessment center assumes that more information should result in more accurate prediction. While each assessment procedure does not always contribute new information, each type of predictor does add some unique perspective on the candidate's suitability for the job. This assumption raises two issues about the effectiveness of assessment centers. The first issue relates to the absolute magnitude of predictability from assessment center ratings. The second issue concerns the comparative value of assessment centers when weighed against the effectiveness of other measures that cost less to develop.

Predictive Validity

With respect to the first question, various summaries from assessment center research provide some answers. One such summary examined the overall effectiveness of assessment center approaches for estimating various job performance measures such as performance ratings, ratings of potential, indices of progress through the organization, and indices of salary.[27] In 25 of the 30 studies which used ratings of performance or potential, the overall assessment center score significantly predicted the criterion measure. For studies looking at progress in the organization, significant results were reported for 38 of 57 studies.

Another approach is to evaluate the overall effectiveness of assessment center predictions by looking at the average correlation between predictor and criterion. One analysis of 21 studies reported a value of .41 for the correlation between assessment center results and a variety of criterion measures.[28] Other studies have examined the effectiveness of assessment centers in forecasting different types of criteria. Assessment center scores were equally predictive of wages (.44) or performance ratings (.43), and less predictive of achievement (.31). These results indicate that the overall judgments made using assessment centers have a significant relationship to a variety of performance indicators and are similar in predictiveness to work samples.

Comparative Validity

When the gains made by involving multiple assessment devices and multiple raters are compared to the results of a cognitive test or work sample, the small increases in predictability seem not to warrant the additional effort. In terms of pure prediction, this conclusion is probably warranted. However, one of the strong suits of the assessment center approach is its ability to provide a wide range of information not only about candidates' performance on various tests, but also about their communication skills and other specific areas of performance. From this perspective, the assessment center can prove valuable as both a selection device and a diagnostic process that provides constructive suggestions for future training.

Cost Estimates

Because assessment centers incorporate numerous evaluation procedures, they are extremely costly. In addition to the costs of buying, administering, and scoring standardized cognitive and personality tests, organizations must pay for the development, administration, and scoring of work samples and situational interviews. With all of this activity, the costs are necessarily high. In addition, many assessment centers conduct multi-day evaluations, thereby increasing time costs for assessment center staff and for candidates and expenditures on food and lodging.

Administration Costs

Most organizations lack the in-house staff needed to develop and implement an assessment center and must rely on consulting firms. These assessment center specialists can develop several different programs and tailor a total assessment package to meet the unique characteristics of the contracting organization. While such services cost far less than the expense of developing and using an in-house assessment center, they still are quite expensive, often costing at least $1,000 per candidate.

Cost-Benefit Analysis

A critical question about assessment centers is whether their value warrants the expenditure of funds. From the perspective of forecasting future performance, the answer is unclear. Assessment centers can improve predictive efficiency, but the cost will be high. In addition, some critics have charged that assessment center research fails to control factors that inflate levels of predictability. According to critics, candidates who participate in assessment centers receive higher ratings, increased promotion opportunities, and greater salary increases as a result of participating in the assessment center. This form of criterion contamination may affect many assessment center studies and artificially enhance estimates of predictive power for this process.

An alternative way to examine the value of assessment centers is to assess their utility as a diagnostic and training device. Rather than simply looking at the degree of prediction, this approach includes the training potential and goal-setting resulting from feedback and evaluates these outcomes relative to the overall cost of the assessment center. Looking at the total cost-benefit picture, assessment centers are clearly heavy on the cost side, predictive of future performance but perhaps lacking the incremental validity of work samples and other predictors, and potentially valuable in a host of non-selection activities.

Legal Implications

The use of assessment centers in selection seems to have solid legal support. Interestingly, when the Equal Employment Opportunity Commission reorganized its middle-level management positions in 1977, it used an assessment center approach to identify the most talented candidates for three key positions in each of several offices. The watchdog organization for fair employment practices, by virtue of using this methodology, gave a clear signal that the assessment center represents a state-of-the-art means of selecting employees.

Additional support comes from several research programs conducted by AT&T on the results of their assessment centers. These studies consistently found equal predictive validity for blacks and whites based on assessment center results. This finding is encouraging since it suggests that the procedure is fair for both groups.

Experience and Past Performance

For many positions, candidates must possess a minimum level of experience before they can be considered qualified. Employers and applicants alike accept two or three years of experience in the same job area or a related field as a reasonable criterion for many jobs. However, this requirement is not always reasonable and may need some justification. The underlying assumption is that through the process of performing a job for some specified period of time, an employee becomes competent. This rule may in fact hold true for certain jobs and individuals, but exceptions do occur. When employers look at experience as a predictor, they should be sensitive to the assumed relationship between length of experience and competence. To use experience successfully as a predictor, employers should assure the measure incorporates both longevity and quality of performance.

When to Use

Decisions involving promotions or lateral transfers from within offer a distinct advantage relative to evaluating outsiders. With internal candidates, an organization can not only define the length of tenure on a job, but also assess the quality of past job performance and the degree of preparation provided by the past job. When assessing outsiders, an organization can readily obtain information regarding years of service or seniority, but may find it difficult to collect details regarding levels of performance and specific duties. In these circumstances, organizations tend to rely on seniority to describe experience, thus only measuring a small portion of the important information.

The argument for using seniority to predict future performance is one of exposure: the longer someone is around a job, the greater the opportunity to benefit from the experiences of being around the job. In many selection models, seniority does help evaluate at least a portion of the information embodied in past job performance. However, in the absence of information about job requirements and the quality of past performance, seniority may tell us very little about future job performance.

Effectiveness

Studies often show good correspondence (.30 and above) between performance on a lower-level job and performance on the next job. While these findings seem to support the use of performance appraisal devices, a number of factors can influence the relationship between past and future job performance. The first issue concerns the degree to which the lower-level job has responsibilities similar to those of the higher-level job. When the correspondence between job duties is high, the empirical relationships between past and future performance can reach .45 and above. Second, as the quality of the evaluation data improves, by using either well-defined assessment devices and/or trained and knowledgeable raters, the ability to forecast future performance likewise increases. Finally, in situations where raters feel free to give accurate assessments of performance, the correlations between the two measures of performance should increase.

Rater Variables

The last point brings up an important qualifier regarding the use of performance data as a predictor. In many settings, it is very difficult, if not impossible, to gather quality performance ratings. When the situation involves in-house candidates and raters, the rater may not want to hurt the ratee's chances for promotion. In this context, the rating is inaccurate due to upwardly distorting the description of performance. A similar situation arises when several supervisors are rating their own subordinates. Raters often state that since supervisor 1 gave all his subordinates very high marks, they should do the same for their people. This kind of thinking results in performance ratings that offer very little in terms of predicting future performance. Finally, ratings of job performance may reflect differences among raters rather than ratees. When certain raters are tough while others are easy, resulting evaluations for a group of ratees cannot be directly equated. The ratees of tough raters will look worse than the ratees of easy raters, even though their performance shows the opposite findings. All of these problems suggest that organizations must understand the appraisal system proposed for use as a predictor prior to making a decision regarding its use. The data presented above indicates that if the performance appraisal system is of high quality, it should make a rather good selection tool.

Cost Estimates

While most organizations routinely collect performance data for most jobs, use of this data to predict performance in higher-level jobs is far less pervasive. However, the data do exist and do have the potential for use in a selection model. Collecting performance data on in-house data will entail minimal clerical costs, but assessing outside applicants may prove more expensive. For external candidates, organizations must contact the former employer and ask a series of questions concerning job responsibilities and levels of performance. Sometimes these questions are answered in letters of recommendation, while other times the information must be obtained via telephone or personal interviews with past employers. As the time spent gathering data grows and as the level of the person collecting the information increases, costs begin to escalate.

Despite the potential time costs involved in collecting performance information, the benefits resulting from performance data seem to outweigh the costs. With correlations between past and future performance in the range of .30 to .45, the time spent developing a picture of past performance can far outweigh the personnel and telephone costs associated with assessment.

Legal Implications

Seniority as a predictor has great potential for legal problems. First, employers lack sufficient empirical support showing that years on the job relate to job performance. In the absence of empirical support, the relevant issue centers on adverse impact. For jobs that have designed affirmative action programs or other hiring practices to encourage minorities and women, inclusion of seniority as a predictor will place these groups at a distinct disadvantage. Seniority requirements will simply perpetuate the situation that the employer attempted to correct with special hiring programs, but at the next level within the organization.

With respect to the use of performance data as a predictor, legal issues relate to the quality of the performance appraisal instrument: the better the instrument, the lower the probability of difficulties. Still, an organization that uses such tools should document the overlap between duties and responsibilities at the lower-level job and those at the new position. The organization must also address potential challenges regarding the quality of the appraisal system. It must ensure that raters use a well-developed instrument, receive appropriate training on use of that instrument, and conduct ratings in a fair manner. If an organization can demonstrate congruency between job requirements and assure appropriate use of a valid instrument, performance data should serve as a legitimate predictor of performance.

Realistic Job Previews

Regardless of the selection tool used, organizations will always run the risk of hiring individuals who, after exposure to the job, might decide that the position is unacceptable. This type of selection error results from the candidate's lack of information about the organization and the job prior to accepting the offer. A technique that attempts to minimize this problem is the realistic job preview.

When to Use

Realistic job previews come in many forms, from brochures describing the company and the positions available, to videotapes of the working environment, to job visits. The specific form of the preview matters less than its underlying philosophy. Organizations that use realistic job previews share the belief that selection is a mutual choice process involving the employer as well as the candidate. While most selection tools are designed to enhance the organization's choice, job previews are intended to help the candidate make a more informed decision about the job. The preview should present candidates with relevant information concerning actual job requirements and circumstances surrounding the job. Unlike recruiting programs that focus on only the positive aspects of employment, realistic job previews attempt to give a balanced perspective on the work to be performed and the context of that work.

Effectiveness

In theory, realistic job previews should reduce turnover and, more generally, improve organizational commitment. Turnover should drop since a job preview can set appropriate expectations about the job, create an air of honesty about the organization, and encourage self-selection, thereby identifying a work force that wants to stay with the organization. Greater commitment comes from the lack of coercion in reaching the decision to join and the positive evaluation of the organization as an honest broker of information.

Several analysts have advanced ideas about conditions that may enhance or negate the effectiveness of realistic job previews. For example, previews may have limited effectiveness when the unemployment rate is high or when other conditions cause a high selection ratio. Under these conditions, job openings will generate a large number of applicants and competition for positions may lead many applicants to discount or ignore the job preview. Conditions that might enhance the ability of a job preview to reduce turnover occur when candidates have high a priori expectations about the job and when applicants have more than one job offer.

The research literature is replete with examples of job previews put into practice in a variety of settings from bank tellers to production workers to managers. Unfortunately, the nature of job previews and the need to evaluate them over rather long periods of time using relatively small samples makes it difficult to design rigorous empirical studies. While many studies on job previews fail to show statistically significant results, much of the research has shown small reductions (3 to 9 percent) in turnover for groups given job previews when compared to groups that do not receive the information. Despite these modest findings, a strong theoretical base and preliminary empirical support make realistic job previews procedures to consider for organizations engaged in selection.

Cost Estimates

The cost of a realistic job preview is difficult to pinpoint. No research seems to address this topic, and in practice, the wide variety of previews means that the costs associated with each type are very different. Verbal statements for use by recruiters and interviewers seem relatively inexpensive to develop and implement, while brochures cost slightly more to develop. An organization might spend $2,000 to $3,000 designing and printing a brochure that could be distributed to several thousand job applicants. Videotapes and the equipment to produce and display the tape are even more expensive but the cost is still tolerable, given the number of potential candidates who might be exposed to the information. In general, the cost of using previews seems reasonable, regardless of how they are developed and implemented.

As to the benefits of previews, cost figures may be more directly accessible. Studies have shown that turnover can cost between $400 and $4,700.[29] If job previews reduce turnover for one or more of the higher cost positions, they will prove cost-effective, regardless of the type of preview used. While the data are sketchy, realistic job previews seem to represent a relatively low cost method for reducing turnover and they may provide positive dollar benefits.

Legal Implications

Provided a job preview is indeed realistic, use of this technique as a selection tool clearly meets the legal criterion of job-relatedness. The only real legal threat to the use of previews arises if organizations selectively present previews to one group and not another. In this situation, one group might be discouraged from taking the job because of information given to its members and not to members of other groups. Employers can easily avoid this problem by offering previews to all applicants for a specific position. In practice, realistic job previews seem to pose no legal threats.

Summary

Several conclusions can be reached regarding the use of selection procedures discussed in this chapter. The employment interview has been and will continue to be the most frequently encountered form of selection activity. Interviews can prove quite effective in identifying qualified individuals if an organization spends the time and resources to define characteristics of candidates that lead to successful job performance. Employers also must be prepared to train interviewers and monitor their performance. When interviews are done properly, high cost of interviews is offset by identifying more qualified individuals. Without these safeguards, organizations could spend a great deal of money on interviews and gain very little in the way of useful information about the candidates. Since the interview, like other selection procedures, has serious legal consequences, its use should be monitored to ensure fairness to all applicants.

Selection tests are as varied as the candidates who take them. Cognitive tests, the most popular type of test, seem to identify talented candidates across a wide range of jobs. The cost-benefit ratio associated with cognitive tests seems to favor the benefit side, and the potential for legal problems depends more on the organization's ability to support use of these tests rather than something inherent in the technique. In contrast, personality tests face far more restrictions in terms of effectiveness and defensibility. Finally, physical abilities tests serve as good predictors for a small number of jobs that are loaded with physical requirements. While physical abilities tests are somewhat more expensive than other types of tests, they do seem to forecast job performance well. In using physical abilities tests, organizations must anticipate adverse impact against women and make sure that the test is strongly linked to the job.

Work samples constitute a very good way of identifying the most qualified candidates for a wide range of jobs. While work samples can be very expensive, the return in accurate selection seems to support use of this technique across numerous job categories. Work samples also seem to be one of the most defensible forms of selection testing. Assessment centers utilize a set of procedures that combine various individual assessment techniques. They entail high costs and provide questionable benefits when compared to use of cognitive tests coupled with work samples. However, the cost-benefit ratio improves when assessment centers are viewed as both a selection tool and a training event.

Performance appraisals from previous jobs provide a relatively low-cost method for developing accurate selection decisions. While many pitfalls can affect the value of this information, empirical studies show support for the idea that behavior is consistent and that performance at one job should offer insight into performance on another job. Organizations can do very well by developing a system for appraising performance and integrating that system with their selection procedures.

Finally, realistic job previews form a relatively low-cost method for reducing turnover via the selection process. By accurately informing candidates about the job and the organization, appropriate expectations can be set that lead to increased tenure. While the data are somewhat mixed regarding effectiveness, realistic job previews do seem to merit serious consideration for many jobs.

Modern personnel practitioners clearly face many different choices when deciding on selection tools. Many of these tools have a high potential for seriously improving the quality of employment decision making. Practitioners should consider many of these techniques whenever their organizations are fortunate enough to have more applicants than vacancies. As this ratio grows, so does the potential value of the selection process. It is up to us to realize the full measure of that potential.

◆

Notes

1. Scott, Clothier, and Spriegal.
2. Uhrbrock.
3. Ulrich and Trumbo; Guion; Landy.
4. For a discussion of variables associated with the employment interview data, see Schmitt and Coyle. For information on experimental studies on interviewing in the general context of decision-making procedures, see Dunnette and Borman. For a tentative model of the interview process, see Arvey and Campion.
5. This example is drawn from research conducted by the authors several years ago.
6. Schmitt, Gooding, Noe, and Kirsch.

7. Ibid. The average correlation between job success and general cognitive ability measures, when examined across a variety of occupational groups and using different measures of job success, is .25. For special aptitude tests, the correlation with job success is slightly higher (.27). When ratings of job performance are used to measure success, general cognitive tests have an average correlation of .22, and special aptitude tests have an average correlation of .16. When job behaviors or work samples are used to rate success, the average validity coefficient for general ability tests is .43, and for special aptitude tests, the correlation is .28. When speed of promotion is the criterion for success, the average correlation for general cognitive tests is .28.
8. Schmidt, Hunter, McKenzie, and Muldrow.
9. This estimate is obtained from unpublished study conducted by the authors using a break-even analysis.
10. Figures for the dollar-based value of jobs derive from unpublished research conducted by the authors.
11. Schmitt, Gooding, Noe, and Kirsch.
12. Personality tests have a .12 correlation with predictions of turnover, a .15 correlation with measures of achievement, and a .13 correlation with status change.
13. Sparks.
14. This example is an unpublished study conducted by the authors.
15. Schmitt, Noe, Gooding, and Kirsch.
16. These findings concern a physical abilities test developed by the authors.
17. Hogan and Quigley.
18. Asher; Asher and Sciarrino.
19. Gordon and Kleinman.
20. Cascio and Phillips.
21. Asher and Sciarrino.
22. Robertson and Kandola.
23. Schmitt, Gooding, Noe, and Kirsch.
24. Hunter and Hunter.
25. Gael and Grant; Gael, Grant, and Ritchie (1975a and 1975b); Grant and Bray.
26. Field, Bayley and Bayley; Howard.
27. Thorton and Byham.
28. Schmitt, Noe, Gooding, and Kirsch.
29. McEvoy and Cascio.

Editor's Note: In addition to the References shown below, there are other significant sources of information and ideas on testing tools.

Books

Ghiselli, E.E. 1966. *The Validity of Occupational Aptitude Tests.* New York: John Wiley & Sons.

Articles

Ghiselli, E.E. 1973. "The Validity of Aptitude Tests in Personnel Selection." *Personnel Psychology* 26: 461–477.

Guion, R.M. and R.F. Gottier. 1965. "Validity of Personality Measures in Personnel Selection." *Personnel Psychology* 67: 239–244.

Schmidt, F.L. and J. Hunter. 1981. "Employment Testing: Old Theories and New Research Findings." *American Psychologist* 36: 1128–1137.

References

Arvey, R.D. and J.E. Campion. 1982. "The Employment Interview: A Summary and Review of Recent Literature." *Personnel Psychology* 35: 281–322.

Asher, J.J. 1972. "The Biographical Item: Can It Be Improved?" *Personnel Psychology* 25: 251–269.

Asher, J.J. and J.A. Sciarrino. 1974. "Realistic Work Samples: A Review." *Personnel Psychology* 27: 519–534.

Cascio, W.F. and N.F. Phillips. 1979. "Performance Testing: A Rose among Thorns." *Personnel Psychology* 32: 751–765.

Dunnette, M. and W. Borman. 1979. "Personnel Selection and Classification." *Annual Review of Psychology* 30: 477–525.

Field, H., G. Bayley, and S. Bayley. 1977. "Employment Test Validation for Minority and Nonminority Production Workers." *Personnel Psychology* 30: 37–46.

Gael, S. and D.L. Grant. 1972. "Employment Test Validation for Minority and Nonminority Telephone Company Service Representatives." *Journal of Applied Psychology* 56: 135–139.

Gael, S., D.L. Grant, and R.J. Ritchie. 1975a. "Employment Test Validation for Minority and Nonminority Telephone Operators." *Journal of Applied Psychology* 60: 411–419.

_____. 1975b. Employment Test Validation for Minority and Nonminority Clerks with Work Sample Criteria." *Journal of Applied Psychology* 60: 420–426.

Gordon, M.E., and L.S. Kleinman. 1976. "The Prediction of Trainability Using a Work Sample Test of Aptitude: A Direct Comparison." *Personnel Psychology* 29: 243–253.

Grant, D.L. and D.W. Bray. 1970. "Validation of Employment Tests for Telephone Company Installation and Repair Occupations." *Journal of Applied Psychology* 54: 7–14.

Guion, R.M. and R.F. Gottier. 1965. "Validity of Personality Measures in Personnel Selection." *Personnel Psychology* 67: 239–244.

Hogan, J. and A. Quigley. 1986. "Physical Standards for Employment and the Courts." *American Psychologist* 41: 1193–1217.

Howard, A., 1983. "Work Samples and Simulations in Competency Evaluations." *Professional Psychology: Research and Practice* 14: 780–790.

Hunter, J.E. and R.F. Hunter. 1984. "Validity and Utility of Alternative Predictors of Job Performance." *Psychological Bulletin* 96: 72–98.

Landy, F.J. 1985. *The Psychology of Work Behavior*. Chicago: The Dorsey Press.

McEvoy, G.M. and W.F. Cascio. 1985. "Strategies for Reducing Employee Turnover: A Meta-Analysis." *Journal of Applied Psychology* 70: 342–353.

Robertson, I.T. and R.S. Kandola. 1974. "Work Sample Tests: Validity, Adverse Impact and Applicant Reaction." *Journal of Occupational Psychology* 55: 171–183.

Schmidt, F.L., J.E. Hunter, R.C. McKenzie, and J.W. Muldrow. 1979. "Impact of Valid Selection Procedures on Work Force Productivity." *Journal of Applied Psychology* 64: 609–626.

Schmitt, N. and B.W. Coyle. 1976. "Applicant Decisions in the Employment Interview." *Journal of Applied Psychology* 61: 184–192.

Schmitt, N., R.Z. Gooding, R.A. Noe, and M. Kirsh. 1984. "Metaanalysis of Validity Studies Published between 1964 and 1982 and the Investigation of Study Characteristics." *Personnel Psychology* 37: 407–422.

Scott, W.D., R.C. Clothier, and W.R. Spriegel. 1949. *Personnel Management: Principles, Practices and Point of View*. 4th ed. New York: McGraw Hill.

Sparks, C.P. 1982. "Job Analysis." In G.R. Ferris (Ed.), *Personnel Management: New Perspectives*. Boston: Allyn & Bacon.

Thornton, George C. and William C. Byham. 1982. *Assessment Centers and Managerial Performance*. New York: Academic Press.

Uhrbrock, R.S. 1948. "The Personnel Interview." *Personnel Psychology* 1: 273–302.

Ulrich, L. and D. Trumbo. 1965. "The Selection Interview Since 1949." *Psychological Bulletin* 63: 100–116.

◆

2.7

Internal Placement and Career Management

Marilyn K. Quaintance

Top management now recognizes that the survival and growth of an organization depends upon effective strategic planning that can respond to external and internal events. This realization has also generated an increasing recognition of the need for strategic HR planning to ensure the accomplishment of the organization's mission and goals and to preserve its culture.[1] The growing belief that the keys to the organization's competitive edge are its people and the HRM programs that maximize their utilization has brought heightened prestige and responsibility for HR managers as they are integrated into the strategic planning process.

Two of the most important programs for maximizing an organization's human resources concern the career opportunities afforded individuals through internal placement and career management. These opportunities have a major impact on the employees' overall quality of life,[2] as well as upon their job attitudes.[3] This chapter examines research and real world applications to identify factors that influence the effectiveness of internal placement and career management programs, and to formulate recommendations for successful program development.

Internal Placement Programs

The strategic plan of any organization may seek to accomplish its objectives through the efficient use of current human resources. In some cases, this goal is critical, such as when a company imposes a moratorium on hiring until the financial picture brightens. The HR manager's challenge is to design an internal placement and promotion program that will assign individuals to available jobs in order to maximize organizational effectiveness. Effective placement has advantages for the organization and for the employee in terms of greater work proficiency, stability, and work satisfaction.[4]

Research Findings

While other types of HRM programs have received a great deal of attention in the theoretical and applied literature, the research on internal placement initiatives is far less complete. In particular, the consequences of internal placement strategies for either the individual employee or the organization have received little attention.

The research results that are available on internal placement have focused on the processes involved in internal placement, types of internal placement strategies, statistical formulas to assist employers in their placement decisions, and conditions that affect placement decisions. The following discussion summarizes some of these research findings.

The Internal Placement Process

The dearth of research on internal placement is surprising, given that internal placement decisions involve a variety of career moves that can have a crucial effect on both employees and the organization. In any organization, four broad types of internal moves are possible:[5]

- Promotions—to positions of greater responsibility, authority, pay, benefits, and/or privileges
- Demotions—to positions of less pay, status, privileges, or opportunities
- Lateral transfers or relocations—to positions having different functional assignments, geographical locations, or organizational quarters (headquarters versus regional office)
- Layoffs, retirements, and resignations

Although only four types of internal moves are possible, the processes through which these internal moves occur are far more complex. Figure 1 presents a model, originally designed to reflect the complexities of selection design, that may prove helpful in deciphering the interactions underlying the internal placement process.[6]

Figure 1
A Model for Test Validation and Selection Research

Predictors [Individual Difference Measures] — Individuals — Job Behaviors — Situations — Consequences [Related to Organizational Goals]

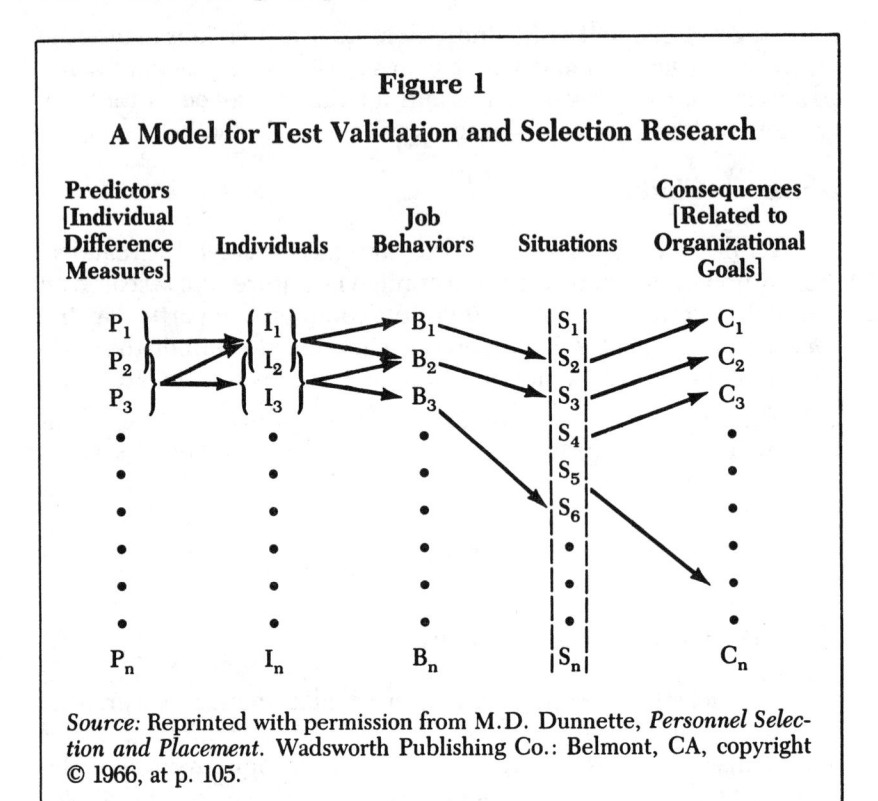

$P_1, P_2, P_3, \ldots P_n$

$I_1, I_2, I_3, \ldots I_n$

$B_1, B_2, B_3, \ldots B_n$

$S_1, S_2, S_3, S_4, S_5, S_6, \ldots S_n$

$C_1, C_2, C_3, \ldots C_n$

Source: Reprinted with permission from M.D. Dunnette, *Personnel Selection and Placement*. Wadsworth Publishing Co.: Belmont, CA, copyright © 1966, at p. 105.

Internal placement strategies attempt to measure as accurately as possible each person's unique characteristics, determine that person's profile of predicted job capabilities, and make placement decisions that balance this information with the employee's career goals and the organization's needs. The model depicted in Figure 1 demonstrates that complex interactions may occur between the characteristics used as predictors, the different groups or types of individuals, the different job behaviors, and the consequences of these behaviors on organizational goals. All of these factors can result in different conditions and complicate the internal placement process.

Types of Internal Placement Strategies

The complex interactions underlying the internal placement process help explain why the existing research focuses largely on alternative strategies for making placement decisions. Strategies for managing internal placements fall into three categories: pure selection, vocational guidance, and compromise placement.[7]

Pure Selection

The first type of internal placement strategy, pure selection, chooses the most qualified person for each position opening. This approach is maximally responsive to the organization. Organizations that use a pure selection strategy can rely on a number of mathematical formulas to assist their placement decisions. Examples include placement procedures that use multiple regression equations, statistical decision theory,[8] or discriminant function analysis[9] to guide decisions.

Vocational Guidance

The second type of placement strategy, vocational guidance, places the person in the position for which he or she is most qualified. This approach is maximally responsive to the individual.

One example of this strategy includes the assessment-classification model, which uses a profile of scores—rather than a composite score—to classify individuals.[10] This model, illustrated in Figure 2, has gained some validity through research supporting its concept that life experiences and employee interests contribute to predictions of industrial success in certain jobs.[11] This model has also focused attention on the development of biodata instruments to examine the accuracy of placement decisions. These biographical instruments have proved particularly useful in predicting career success for sales occupations, clerical jobs, and research competence.[12]

Compromise Placement

The pure selection and vocational guidance strategies for internal placement represent opposite ends of a continuum, and both extremes have drawbacks. If individual needs are ignored, as they are in pure selection, unwanted consequences, such as high turnover or lower productivity, will result. If organizational needs are ignored, as with the vocational guidance strategy, individual employees may be motivated and happy, but some critical jobs may be filled with individuals who are not the best qualified.

Figure 2
An Assessment-Classification Model

INDIVIDUAL ASSESSMENT | **MATCHING INDIVIDUALS WITH JOBS** | **JOB STRUCTURE**

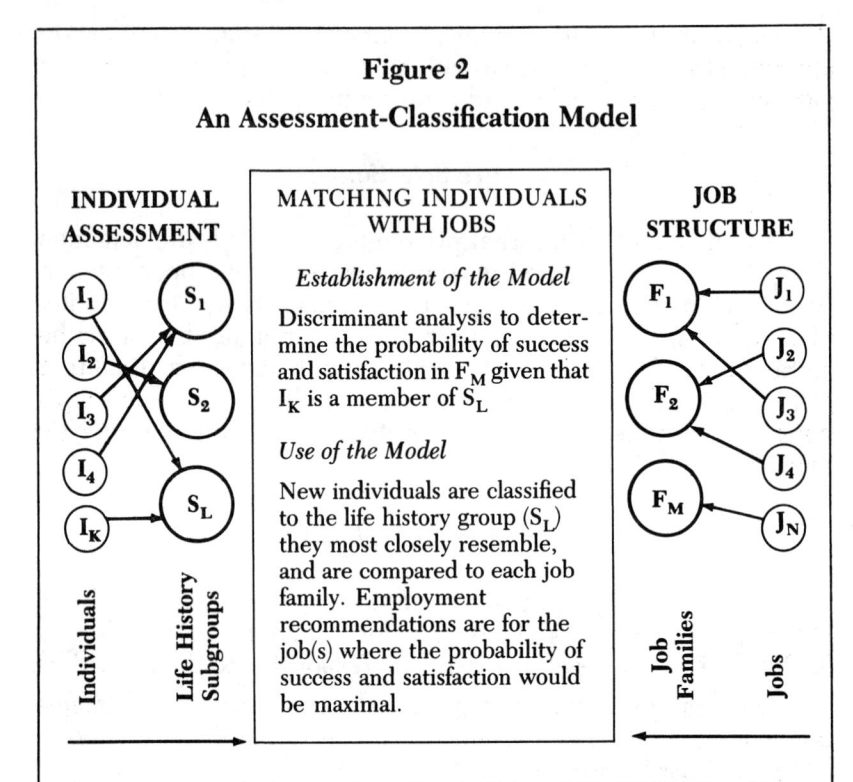

Establishment of the Model

Discriminant analysis to determine the probability of success and satisfaction in F_M given that I_K is a member of S_L

Use of the Model

New individuals are classified to the life history group (S_L) they most closely resemble, and are compared to each job family. Employment recommendations are for the job(s) where the probability of success and satisfaction would be maximal.

Individuals — Life History Subgroups — Job Families — Jobs

Source: Reprinted with permission from L. Schoenfeldt, "Utilization of Manpower: Development and Evaluation of an Assessment-Classification Model for Matching Individuals with Jobs." *Journal of Applied Psychology*, copyright © 1974, at p. 584.

The challenge to HR managers is to identify a compromise internal placement strategy that lies somewhere in the middle of this continuum. This strategy attempts to achieve the best allocation of available employees to position openings, while meeting individual and organizational needs. Compromise strategies place people in jobs so that all jobs are filled by individuals who meet at least some minimum standards of performance.

Strategy Selection

A number of factors affect the selection of the best type of internal placement strategy. In choosing an appropriate strategy, HR managers should consider the following conditions: the ratio of openings to applicants, the relative costs associated with performance in the position, and the nature of the interrelationship of one job to other jobs.

Selection ratio. When the number of applicants is large and the number of openings is small (a small selection ratio), the company is likely to maximize pure selection. In the reverse situation, when a company has many positions and few applicants (a large selection ratio), individuals will have more employment opportunities. In this case, a vocational guidance strategy may help lure the few eligible individuals into the organization, or convince those already in the work force to stay. In a situation with an equal number of openings and applicants, the compromise strategy will optimize the classifications and placements for both the individuals and the organization.

Performance costs. Another factor that will influence the selection of a specific internal placement strategy is the relative costs of error for the position.[13] If performance errors are extremely costly to the organization, a pure selection strategy based on scores or procedures with maximum validity will ensure the best person is placed in the job.

Type of job. A final factor affecting strategy selection concerns the type of position and its relationship to other jobs in the organization. For jobs that are successive and have dependent operations, the best strategy may well be to select several groups with similar output rates—slow, medium, and fast—rather than force three teams to work at the rate of their slowest worker.[14]

Succession Programs

Promotions are one type of internal move, and succession programs, involving planned placements to higher-level managerial positions within the organization, are a special kind of promotion program. A 1983 survey of parent companies found that organizations with management succession plans (just under 50 percent of those surveyed) outnumbered companies with HR plans (only 40 percent of those surveyed).[15] This finding is understandable, given the importance of management positions and the consequences associated with effective or ineffective managerial performance.

Career Management Programs

Another type of HRM program that results from the strategic planning process is a career management program. Such a program allows managers who view the strategic development of their organizations over a period of years to apply a similar perspective to the careers of individual employees to ensure adequate personnel.

Research Findings

While career management programs are gaining in popularity, the theoretical research needed to draw conclusions for program development and implementation has yet to emerge. The consequences of career planning for either individual employees or organizations have received surprisingly little attention, although some research does indicate that career systems lead to positive employee behavior and attitudes.[16] Nor have any research studies empirically evaluated the impact of alternative kinds of career systems or career management programs on organizational performance.[17] Instead, existing research focuses on identification of a career success cycle, evaluation of models of career stages, and development and validation of instruments to predict career success.

The Concept of "Career"

The components of a career management program can differ depending on the definition given the word "career." While some analysts have suggested that "there exists little consensus on defining a career,"[18] this chapter will adopt a narrow definition of career for the following discussion of career management:

> *Career:* A sequence of positions usually related in work content, having both length and a ceiling, with the movement through that sequence occurring at a certain rate and in a certain direction.[19]

This definition of career as a given sequence of positions leads to the concept of career paths, or what are also called career ladders or lattices. Employees and organizations have a common interest in determining what alternative careers or career paths represent possibilities for career development or advancement. Job analysis information provides the foundation for identifying progression possibilities, and movement may be lateral, diagonal, or vertical.[20]

Career Stages

A related concept that has received a great deal of attention concerns the identification of career stages for employees. Similar to the study of "life stages" or the various roles an individual assumes during a lifetime (one of which is "worker"),[21] theories about career stages concentrate on the phases experienced by a worker through his or her career. Four stages of professional career that have been identified include apprentice level, independent contributor, mentor, and sponsor.[22]

Several analysts have attempted to link career stages to specific chronological ages that are associated with stages in the adult life cycle.[23] While this linkage seems theoretically appealing, investigations are finding that chronological age is an increasingly unreliable predictor of what life stage a person will fit. In addition, differences in perspectives have arisen regarding the number of distinct stages through which an individual may pass, the overlapping tasks and issues faced in each stage, and the role of transition periods between stages.[24]

Career Success Cycles

A more useful model of career development reflects psychological theories and proposes a career success cycle in which success, once experienced, will lead to a desire for more success.[25] According to this model, a challenging job makes it possible for an individual to set difficult work goals, which in turn results in commitment to achieving those goals. Autonomy on the job enables the person to determine his or her own means of attaining those work goals and increases employee involvement. Support, defined as help or coaching from the boss and from peers, assists the employee in solving problems and in maintaining career motivation. Feedback provides the employee with information as to how well he or she is doing in attaining the job goals.

When people attain their goals, they experience psychological success and gain self-esteem and job satisfaction. When work behaviors (such as those behaviors that result in the accomplishment of job goals) are reinforced by increased self-esteem, those behaviors tend to be repeated. This process results in increased job involvement, motivation, and goal commitment, and the cycle is repeated over again.[26]

Career Planning vs. Career Management

As a type of internal placement program, career management programs require balancing individual needs and organizational needs to be successful. This distinction between individual needs and organizational needs is what separates career planning from career management.[27]

Career planning is a deliberate process in which the employee becomes aware of his or her unique opportunities, choices, and consequences. The employee establishes career-related goals and identifies programs, work, education, and other activities to achieve those goals.

Career management, on the other hand, reflects the organizational perspective. Organizations focus on planning their employees' careers in light of anticipated resource requirements.[28] Thus, career management is integrally related to the strategic HR plan of the organization. For the purposes of this chapter, career management programs are defined as systems that attempt to match individual and organizational needs through career planning and career management processes.

Factors Affecting Internal Placement and Career Management Programs

As one analysis has noted, "a person's career experiences and outcomes affect his or her performance, absenteeism, work quality, and turnover, all of which mean plus or minus dollars to the organization."[29] As a result, HR managers need to focus attention on those factors that determine the effectiveness of programs that influence career experiences and outcomes. Influences shaping the success of internal placement and career management programs include external factors, which shape society and the work force, and internal factors, which relate to the unique characteristics of a particular organization.

External Factors

The nature of the work force is evolving. In the late 1970s, about 3 million young adults entered the work force each year; by 1990, the number of entrants will drop to about 1.3 million per year, and by 1995, the work force will encompass about 7.5 million fewer workers ages 18 to 24.[30] Women are also joining the work force in record numbers, and employment opportunities for minorities and the handicapped have also expanded.

As the composition of the work force changes in terms of ages, sex, and other essential characteristics, accompanying changes take place in employee attitudes, motivations, and values.[31] HRM programs must adapt to ensure a highly motivated and productive work force as these new and changing perspectives and expectations evolve. The following discussion considers some career motivations and values of major groups that comprise the work force.

Integrating Women

The women's movement has created many new opportunities for women in the work force. To take two traditionally male fields as an example, women's share of medical degrees in the United States increased from 5 percent in 1967 to 26 percent in 1980, while the percentage of law degrees awarded women went up from 4 percent to 22 percent during the same period.[32]

But are women truly being integrated into the work force at all levels, including those of top management? Two interesting studies published in the *Harvard Business Review*, one in 1965[33] and one in 1985,[34] address this question. In 1965, women held 14 percent of all executive jobs; by 1985, 33 percent of all managerial and administrative positions were held by women.[35] While the percentage of respondents believing that women rarely expect or desire positions of authority dropped substantially,[36] more than half of the respondents in 1985 did not feel that women would ever be wholly accepted in business. While women's increasing numbers in the managerial ranks are encouraging, HR managers also must recognize the negative perceptions that women will not be accepted in management, and address these beliefs when undertaking career counseling. Managers must ensure that career opportunities are fairly publicized and that placements are made on the basis of the skills, knowledges, and abilities of the employees. Affirmative action initiatives, now condoned by the United States Supreme Court,[37] will also encourage women that their career aspirations can, in fact, be fulfilled.

Identifying Special Concerns of Minorities

The Civil Rights Act of 1964, as amended by the Equal Employment Opportunity Act of 1972, has banned employment discrimination on the basis of race for over 25 years. During this period, minorities have made some progress in moving up the corporate ladder. The Bureau of Labor Statistics found that the percentage of minority managers rose from 3.6 percent in 1977 to 5.2 percent in 1982.[38] Despite this increase, minorities are underrepresented in middle management and almost absent from board rooms and positions of corporate leadership.[39]

One 1986 survey of approximately 100 alumni of five top graduate business schools found that more than 98 percent of the respondents believed that corporations have not achieved equal opportunity for black managers.[40] Eighty-four percent thought that considerations of race have a negative impact on ratings, pay, assignments, recognition, appraisals, and promotions. Another 98 percent agreed that subtle prejudice pervades their own organizations.

These perceptions, whether or not they reflect reality, must be taken into account by HR managers when undertaking career counseling of minority employees. Only continued evidence of minority career progression will dispel the belief of discrimination and affirm the organization's commitment to equal employment opportunity.

Recognizing the Needs of Older Workers

In a special report on *Older Americans in the Workforce: Challenges and Solutions*, the Bureau of National Affairs, Inc. (BNA) reported that older workers are the fastest growing group in the work force. In fact, the report predicted that by the year 2000, more than half the work force will be over age 40.[41]

This aging of the work force makes it important for HR managers to recognize that evidence has documented a bias against older workers. One study conducted in 1986 found no overall improvement in attitudes toward older workers over a 30-year period.[42]

Accommodating Handicapped Employees

The Rehabilitation Act of 1973 helped to open corporate doors to the handicapped. Internal placement and career management programs should address the needs of both handicapped employees entering the organization and employees who become handicapped by an accident after being employed on the job.

Fortunately, HR managers are sharing their successful experiences in modifying jobs to accommodate the handicapped through the Job Accommodations Network.[43] This network, an outgrowth of the President's Committee on Employment of the Handicapped, has become a valuable resource for managers involved in internal placement and career management decisions for handicapped employees.

Integrating Cross-Cultural Employees

Multi-national corporations are adding new dimensions to internal placement and career management programs as their work forces comprise diversified cultures. To perform effectively, employees must learn important principles unique to multinationals, either through formal training sessions or through job experiences. Some analysts have suggested that even employees who do not move to other countries must begin to think globally. In addition, managers have to learn to look at United States management principles as only one way to do things, not as the only way.[44]

HR managers charting career ladders to management positions in multi-national corporations must ensure that employees receive the appropriate combination of training and development and suitable career placements to acquire the knowledges, skills, and abilities for effective performance in the higher-level positions.

Accommodating Dual-Career Couples

Organizations are now confronting the phenomenon of dual-career couples in which both individuals have strong identifications with their chosen professions. HR managers must be alert to the implications of an employed spouse when providing career counseling to an employee. Dual-career couples affect the organization's ability to move people geographically and often require dual-career management by the HR manager.[45] In addition, many dual-career couples may have problems arranging both work and family obligations.

Understanding the Values of the Majority

While the needs of women, minorities, older workers, and handicapped employees are important, HR managers must also understand the values of the young, non-disabled white males, the majority of the current work force. This group also is changing and adopting new values such as autonomy, self-development, entrepreneurship, and balance between work life and family life.[46] People want more meaningful work experiences and greater involvement in the decisions involving themselves. This change shows in a 1987 poll which found that Americans define success as "being a good parent" (95 percent), "having a happy marriage" (90 percent) or "relationship" (86 percent), and "having the respect of friends" (83 percent). Work values ranked fifth, with 80 percent defining the American Dream as "being one of the best at your job."[47]

Internal Factors

A number of influences within the organization can affect the success of internal placement and career management programs. Most of these factors concern procedures to ensure effective program implementation and should be addressed during the initial design stages.

Gaining Commitment of Top-Level and Line Managers

For an internal placement or career management program to succeed, it must have the ownership and involvement of top-level and line managers.[48] Consequently, HR managers must recognize both formal and informal power structures within their organizations, as well as the desire of people to maintain the status quo.[49]

Effective internal placement and career management programs give managers key responsibility in the development and career counseling of their employees. This responsibility helps to build ownership, while freeing HRM office staff to handle actual administration of the program.

Assessing Individual Capabilities and Interests

Prior to providing an individual with career counseling, HR managers must have an accurate assessment of each individual's capabilities and vocational interests, plus an accurate description of job requirements. With these two sources of data, decisions regarding the appropriate matching of individuals and particular career ladders will be made on a good foundation.

Data gathered to assist career counseling activities may prove useful later as part of the decision-making process in internal placement and career management programs. For example, if the assessment procedure used for an employment decision (such as promotion, or selection into a training and development program that leads to promotion) has an adverse impact on members of a protected class, then the HR manager will have to provide evidence of the job-relatedness of the procedure. The legal, regulatory, and professional mandates for accurate assessment of individual capabilities should govern placement programs and employment decisions.[50]

Determining Organizational and Job Requirements

Once the strategic plan has been developed, managers will need to translate goals and objectives into work or personnel requirements. Prior to assigning individuals to specific positions or job categories, HR managers must undertake some form of job analysis to identify the tasks or activities that must be performed and the prerequisite personal characteristics. Chapter 2.2 of this volume provides a thorough review of job analysis methodologies.

A comprehensive job analysis data base will assist HR managers in designing internal placement and career management programs, as well as other programs, if a multi-purpose technique is employed.[51] The job analysis data can be used to group related positions, to structure career ladders, and to sequence jobs according to the difficulty of their work requirements.

Some companies manage to achieve these ends without a formal job analysis. Sears and Roebuck, for example, uses job data provided through its point-factor job evaluation system to manage the careers of its employees.[52] Prior to a job transfer, the new position is compared to the individual's current position. The transfer is made if the new position requires at least (a) one additional skill area for effective performance; (b) a 10-percent increase in work demands as evidenced by the total number of job evaluation points; and (c) some assignments in different functional areas. The Sears Career Management Program places lesser emphasis on employee qualifications, as illustrated by the following assumptions: 1) The most important influences on career development occur on the job. 2) Different jobs demand the development of different skills. 3) Development occurs only when the person has not yet developed the skills demanded by a particular job. 4) By identifying a natural sequence of assignments for a person, the time required to develop the necessary skills for a chosen target job can be reduced.

Even large corporations that have two or more companies with different job evaluation systems can use the job data collected for career management purposes. Computer programs can convert the point values used in one job evaluation system to equivalent point values on an alternative job evaluation system.[53] This process facilitates career transfers across companies within the same corporation.

Once accurate data have been gathered on employees and jobs, the line manager and/or HR manager must undertake a "needs analysis." This analysis determines the most appropriate target job for a given individual, and the career ladder likely to facilitate attainment of that target job through the acquisition of needed knowledges, skills, and abilities.[54]

Designing Appropriate Support Systems

Many types of support systems can be designed to ensure the success of the new internal placement or career management program. Perhaps the most important support system is the use of computer-based information to provide line managers and HR managers with easy access to data relevant to their career decisions for employees. Integrated HR information systems are essential to facilitate the decision-making process, as successful companies seem to recognize. For example, IBM has created an Employee Development Planning System to help employees plan and manage their careers and personal growth within IBM.[55]

Another important support system for an internal placement or career management program is the financial or budgeting system. Funds must be allocated to ensure that planned training and development activities will occur, as needed, to facilitate career progression and to ensure organizational mobility.

Answering Key Policy Questions

With any new HRM program, managers should answer key policy questions through the publication of administrative rules, regulations, and procedures.[56] These policy documents outline the types of criteria used in the program, the levels of criteria, and the degree of uniformity used in applying those criteria to different internal placement or career management decisions.

This document should also address specific procedural concerns, including:[57]

- Guidelines for a "promotion from within" policy
- Safeguards for protecting the confidentiality of employee and career information
- Procedures for employee review of the information to ensure its accuracy

- The degree to which the program is voluntary or mandatory and

- The degree to which the program is tailored to the company's needs or canned

Examples of Internal Placement Programs

All internal placement programs can have an important influence on employees' careers and on organizational productivity levels. As the real-life cases described in this section illustrate, the type of impact and the effectiveness of a particular program can vary depending on the program's design and the organization's strategic goals. By highlighting useful features and possible drawbacks of different programs, the following discussion may prove helpful to HR managers when designing similar systems.

Downsizing Efforts

"Downsizing" is a fairly new term in HRM literature. As the number of internal placement programs directed toward downsizing has increased, the creativity of the methodologies designed to accomplish this goal has also grown.

Successful downsizing programs carry all the implications of layoffs but make jobs more financially bearable by offering employees early retirement programs and generous severance pay plans.[58] In addition, a number of the downsizing programs make out-placement decisions voluntary to reduce hard feelings among the work force. Such programs do not differentiate between individuals; rather, they target job cuts at a specific managerial level or geographical level.

DuPont's Downsizing Effort

One such voluntary downsizing program was designed at DuPont. It included a four-year effort as part of a long-term plan to eliminate some departments and create others, while refocusing work-force energies on customer treatment and growth markets.

DuPont's downsizing initiative relied on offering employees a choice of alternative attrition programs. While maximizing responsiveness to employees' needs, this strategy also recognized that some program initiatives would work better than others. In addition, a bonus program was added to support and enhance the entrepreneurial activities of employees who remained with the company.

Lessons Learned

While the voluntary nature of DuPont's downsizing program resulted in positive employee morale, the program also had a negative consequence. Talented managers who could easily find a new job sometimes left the organization to take advantage of the financially attractive severance program. By focusing downsizing efforts on certain departments and not on individuals, DuPont lost the opportunity to get rid of truly redundant employees while keeping the most productive. HR managers undertaking a downsizing program may wish to consider the tradeoff associated with voluntary versus mandatory programs.

Based upon the DuPont experience, one analyst concluded that an effective downsizing program should include the following features:[59]

- Mandatory cuts should implement the plan.
- Eliminations should be made decisively.
- Job cuts should appear sensible to those most affected.
- Employees should receive full communications.
- The plan should attempt to deal with the "survivors' syndrome" by counseling workers who remain as to their security and chances for career advancement.

Managerial Placement and Succession Programs

Systems that only concern personnel selection at the management level are a special type of internal placement program. The following examples illustrate two such programs, one that focuses mainly on candidate qualifications, and another that takes a more strategic and long-range view.

Honeywell's Participative Teams

Honeywell's Systems and Research Center employs 250 engineers and scientists, as well as individuals in marketing, administration, research, HRM, organizational development, communications, and information systems.[60] The center has practiced participative management since 1971, using a team of managers to make decisions in such areas as resource allocation, funds distribution, facility design, budgeting, and hiring. Honeywell believes that "a team effort yields better decisions, protects [the company] from arbitrary or careless actions and, above all, strengthens team members' commitment to . . . goals."[61]

The Honeywell Center Management Team has responsibility for choosing new managers by team consensus. While the decisions are subject to approval by top management, the team members recognize their accountability for the outcome of their decisions and consequently they take the task very seriously. The team approach consists of the following stages:

Stage 1: Brainstorming. Managerial candidates are either recommended by their superiors based upon earlier discussion of career growth, or they can apply for the positions themselves. During the team's brainstorming process, additional candidate names are added to the list.

Stage 2: Screening. After the brainstorming meeting, team members attempt to learn as much as possible about the candidates. Some evaluation criteria, such as candidate records or potential for growth, are important to certain team members, while other criteria, such as style or values, matter to other members. However, Honeywell suggests that the team consider the whole spectrum of criteria, thus reducing the likelihood of serious errors in judgment.

Stage 3: Interviewing. Each team member interviews a finalist for one hour. Prior to the interview, each candidate receives a list of the criteria to be used in making the decisions, a job description, the name of the interviewer, and information about the Systems and Research Center. Management and ethical problems are presented for the candidate to discuss during the interview.

Stage 4: Making the Choice. The team discusses the candidates and reaches a placement decision. Each member of the team must understand the decision, accept it, and be willing to implement it, even if the candidate selected is not his or her first choice. Team members must feel the decision is fair and represents either the best choice or close to it.

Stage 5: Selling the Decision. Along with providing feedback to candidates on the decision-making process, the team presents reasons for its choice to top management.

American Hospital Supply's Management Succession

For years, the American Hospital Supply Corporation was viewed as a leader in the development of HR planning programs, including internal placement programs for management succession. When American Hospital Supply was acquired by Baxter Travenol a few years ago, its HR planning programs were adopted with few refinements. This easy transition of the programs into the new parent company reflects the quality of the programs as first designed and implemented by American.

American Hospital Supply Corporation instituted HR planning to address management succession issues confronting the organization because of its expansive growth.[62] Net sales for the company increased from $467 million in 1969 to slightly more than $3 billion in 1982, and the corporation's focus shifted from sales and distribution to marketing research and development. In 1982, American had 33,000 employees across its 26 divisions in 275 domestic and 125 foreign sites. Within the company's five businesses—hospital, medical specialties, laboratory, internal, and marketing—the greatest proportion of exempt employees worked in sales and marketing, followed by manufacturing.

The internal placement program for management succession encompasses the following activities:

- Determine the number of senior managers needed.
- Identify domains of individual responsibility, skill, and activity.
- Work out the timing of needs.
- Develop career ladders.
- Identify back-up candidates for replacement of terminated or promoted employees.

American prepared a five-year strategic business plan and an annual operations plan, which specified a personnel ceiling for the organization. The vice presidents for personnel in each division, with input from line and staff managers, prepared initial personnel plans. Each plan took into account the personnel ceilings and data from computer simulations on retirements, terminations, resignations, promotions, lateral moves, demotions, and projected availabilities.

These divisional plans were reviewed and critiqued at the business level, then submitted in final form to the corporate director for management planning and development. Next, business-level personnel plans were prepared using the division plans, which underwent corporate review and analysis by the chief executive officer and chief operating officer. Finally, a comprehensive corporate personnel plan was developed.

The corporate plan included a discussion of the major strategic issues expected to arise during the term of the plan; an in-depth analysis of the year-to-year trends in back-up strength for the top 300 management positions; and a report on promotional, recruitment and executive development activities. In the case of executive development, American instituted a review program to discuss each executive in the context of strategic business and HR plans. Thus, executive development supported the management succession program.

Lessons Learned

The team approach to management succession at Honeywell has some real advantages in motivating team members and gaining their commitment to the final decision. The company supports the team approach on the belief that decisions reached by consensus get more support than decisions made by one individual. Honeywell also feels that the team process reduces suspicions of favoritism and arbitrariness, and protects the company from abrupt change.

The disadvantages cited by Honeywell to this internal placement program are the amount of time involved and the unpredictable nature of the process. Another more serious problem concerns the lack of a standardized information-gathering process regarding candidate qualifications. While team members are charged with gathering as much information as possible, this informal process could introduce biased information into selection decisions and could put Honeywell into a legally vulnerable position.

This lack of standardized criteria also affects the team decision-making process since team members differed on the relative importance of criteria. The importance of criteria is really an empirical question, and the weights associated with particular criteria should be based upon job analysis. For example, one of the candidates was nearly dropped because of his "autocratic style," yet this style was measured only through team members' observations.[63] Finally, the team's judgment may have been motivated by self-preservation and a desire to avoid suggesting a candidate whom top management would reject outright.

Honeywell's example provides a number of guidelines for HR managers who undertake management selection programs using team decisions:

- Candidate information should be gathered in a standardized manner.

- The decision-making process should be based on standardized criteria, measured objectively.

- Team decisions should be free from political pressure so that selections are based on candidates' merits.

In addition, the program at American Hospital Supply indicates the value of actively involving top-level and line managers in planning for management succession. Such top-level involvement and commitment undoubtedly contributed to the success and durability of the program.

Corporate Experiences With Career Management Programs

While research linking career management programs to organizational consequences is lacking, some evidence does indicate that the career management process improves employee behavior and attitudes. In fact, one observer has suggested that "career planning is important because the consequences of career success or failure are closely linked with each individual's self-concept, identity, and satisfaction with career and life."[64]

When career management programs produce these positive consequences for individual employees and thus impact job behavior, the programs no doubt will also affect organizational consequences, such as productivity levels. As a result, organizations have demonstrated an interest in learning more about how to support employees' careers through effective career management programs. In this section, four summaries of corporate experiences are presented.

Corporate Studies of Managerial Career Progress

Two corporations have undertaken long-term studies to identify employee characteristics that predict job success and promotion to managerial posts. The studies, two conducted by AT&T and another undertaken by Japanese department store chains, produced surprisingly similar findings despite the different corporate environments explored.

AT&T's Management Studies

AT&T has undertaken two longitudinal studies of managers in its various operating companies, one beginning in the 1950s and one in the 1970s. Both studies had a career development focus, examining changes occurring to the individual over time and career progression within AT&T.

The first investigation, the Management Progress Study (MPS), was undertaken in 1956. The original sample of 422 white males comprised 274 college graduates, who had been hired into first-level general management jobs, and 148 noncollege graduates, who had been hired into nonmanagement positions. The median age of the college graduates was 24, while the median age for the noncollege sample was 30.[65]

The second investigation, begun in 1977, was called the Management Continuity Study (MCS).[66] It parallelled the Management Progress Study and tracked differences in the characteristics and development of a new generation of Bell System managers. The MCS sample had 129 white males, 108 white females, 57 minority males, and 50 minority females. The median age of the sample was 25, and all were college graduates.

The MPS and MCS participants were put through a three-day assessment center evaluation at regular intervals over the years.[67] Using a variety of tests and exercises, assessors rated the participants on 26 dimensions and predicted who would advance to management ranks. Assessment center results were not made known to AT&T management, and consequently did not influence promotion decisions. A factor analysis of the ratings received by employees who advanced in management found the following dimensions to be most predictive of career success:

- Administrative skills, such as planning and organizing, decision making, and creativity

- Interpersonal skills, such as leadership, behavior flexibility, personal impact, oral communications, and social objectivity
- Intellectual ability, including range of interests

Japanese Career Progress Study

Another investigation of managerial career progress used a sample of 80 college graduates recruited by Japanese department store chains in 1972. Measures used in the study to evaluate employees included a battery of ability tests, administered prior to entry, and a rating of the quality of each recruit's working relationship with his or her immediate supervisor, obtained during the first year of employment.[68]

As with the AT&T studies, cognitive ability, as measured by tests, predicted a variety of career success criteria after a seven-year period. However, the seven-year follow-up found that the measure of the working relationship with the immediate supervisor had even higher correlations with success criteria, such as speed of promotion, bonuses, a promotability index, and job performance ratings.[69] In addition, the employee's working relationship with his or her immediate supervisor during the first year predicted the level of organizational commitment, role disillusionment, job needs, and job performance during the second and third years of employment.

Lessons Learned

The AT&T and Japanese studies all suggest that career success as a manager can be predicted early in an employee's career. As a result, career counselors and/or line managers would be wise to administer written ability tests to employees and to provide vocational guidance on the basis of these results. If available, managerial assessment center evaluations that tap administrative, interpersonal, and intellectual skills also should be taken into account in the career counseling process.

The Japanese Career Progress study also suggests that alternative measures of interpersonal skills, such as the employee's relationship with an immediate supervisor, can predict career success.

Executive Development Programs

The President's Council on Management Improvement concluded that competitive pressures on American corporations, coupled with the increasingly important role of HRM, require managers to update and develop their skills on a regular basis.[70] This conclusion clearly indicates that executive development programs will become an important component of any career management program.

A recent summary examined four executive development programs (at Motorola, Xerox, Federated Foods, and General Foods) that attempt to focus executive training and development on corporate strategy.[71] The analysis identified six common themes in these executive development programs:

- Top management support for the program
- Precisely articulated objectives
- Emphasis on the executive's role in achieving the company's goals
- Involvement of the senior managers in program design
- Instruction by senior executives (at three of the four programs)
- Custom-designed programs

Despite these shared themes, each company uses a different approach to emphasize the manager's role in achieving the company's goals. At General Foods, the trainee participates in personal action planning to identify one major action to facilitate goal attainment that the executive is committed to initiating. At Xerox, instruction in major business strategies and managerial styles teaches trainees how to improve their styles to implement a given strategy more effectively. At Motorola, the training is very results-oriented, focusing on the worldwide competitive threat to Motorola. At Federated, the trainees are taught how to thwart competition and emerge as a business leader.

Instruction by top executives is viewed as having a beneficial and substantial impact upon trainees. Executive presentations typically focus upon the vision for the company, the need for commitment to that vision, and what trainees can do to make the vision a reality.

The companies differ in the content of their executive development programs. At General Foods, the executives try to predict how the company will look and behave when it achieves its goal of becoming the world's premier food and beverage company. The comparison of the company currently to the futuristic vision provides a powerful learning experience.

Xerox covers eight areas within five-and-one-half days. Trainees learn about the desired role of Xerox in the world in the next decade, and they identify the hurdles that must be overcome to achieve that role.

Motorola's training includes an analysis of economic, political, and social factors in each Asian country to promote a better understanding of competitors. Federated's six-and-one-half-day program includes an analysis of the competitive forces surrounding an imaginary business.

Lessons Learned

These executive development training programs demonstrate that top-level executive commitment can result in an effective program. This top-level commitment can be enhanced by having executive participation as part of the actual content of the training program.

The training programs also succeed because of the results orientation and linkage to strategic planning. This success requires that the strategic plan is in fact valid and based on reasonable projections of internal and external factors affecting organizational productivity in the years ahead. If the strategic plan is faulty, then executive development programs designed to assist senior managers in implementing that plan will not be worthwhile.

A Career Development System

The previous examples have focused on investigations of the careers of managers in this country and abroad, and on executive development in particular. This section describes a comprehensive career management program that is fully operational at Coca-Cola USA. Known as the Career Development System, this example meets the definition of a career management program that balances the need of the individual and of the organization through career planning and career management processes.

The program, started in 1983, has four objectives:

- To promote from within whenever possible
- To develop talent in depth and in advance of staffing needs

Internal Placement & Career Management 2-225

- To give managers the responsibility for evaluating and assisting in the development of employees
- To expect individuals to take primary responsibility for their development

Program Components

As illustrated in Figure 3, Coca-Cola USA's Career Development System has four components: performance planning and review; individual career development discussions; department career development and succession planning reviews; and matching and selection criteria.[72]

Performance planning and review. The employees describe their past year's work and rate themselves on each performance objective and on each performance factor, as well as on an overall rating scale. The manager uses the employee's input, as well as discussion with managers at the next level, to determine final ratings of the employee on the objectives and factors. Each employee participates in an annual meeting with his or her manager to discuss the job performance rating.

Individual career development discussions. The employee completes a career interest form, giving interests and strengths to support them, as well as possible developmental activities. The employee and his or her manager participate in a career discussion that emphasizes growth, but not necessarily advancement. The manager provides feedback on the employee's interests and describes career opportunities. The manager provides comments on the employee's career interest form and submits it to the manager at the next level, who reviews the form and submits it to human resources.

Department career development and succession planning reviews (People Days). During these sessions, which are held for all employees in Coca-Cola USA, each employee is reviewed by two levels of management in departmental group meetings, with high-potential employees being reviewed by the company president. The performance reviews and career discussion documents are included to help identify how an employee's potential and readiness for promotion correspond to the company's development needs.

Matching and selection criteria. The information from the performance reviews, the career discussions and the department

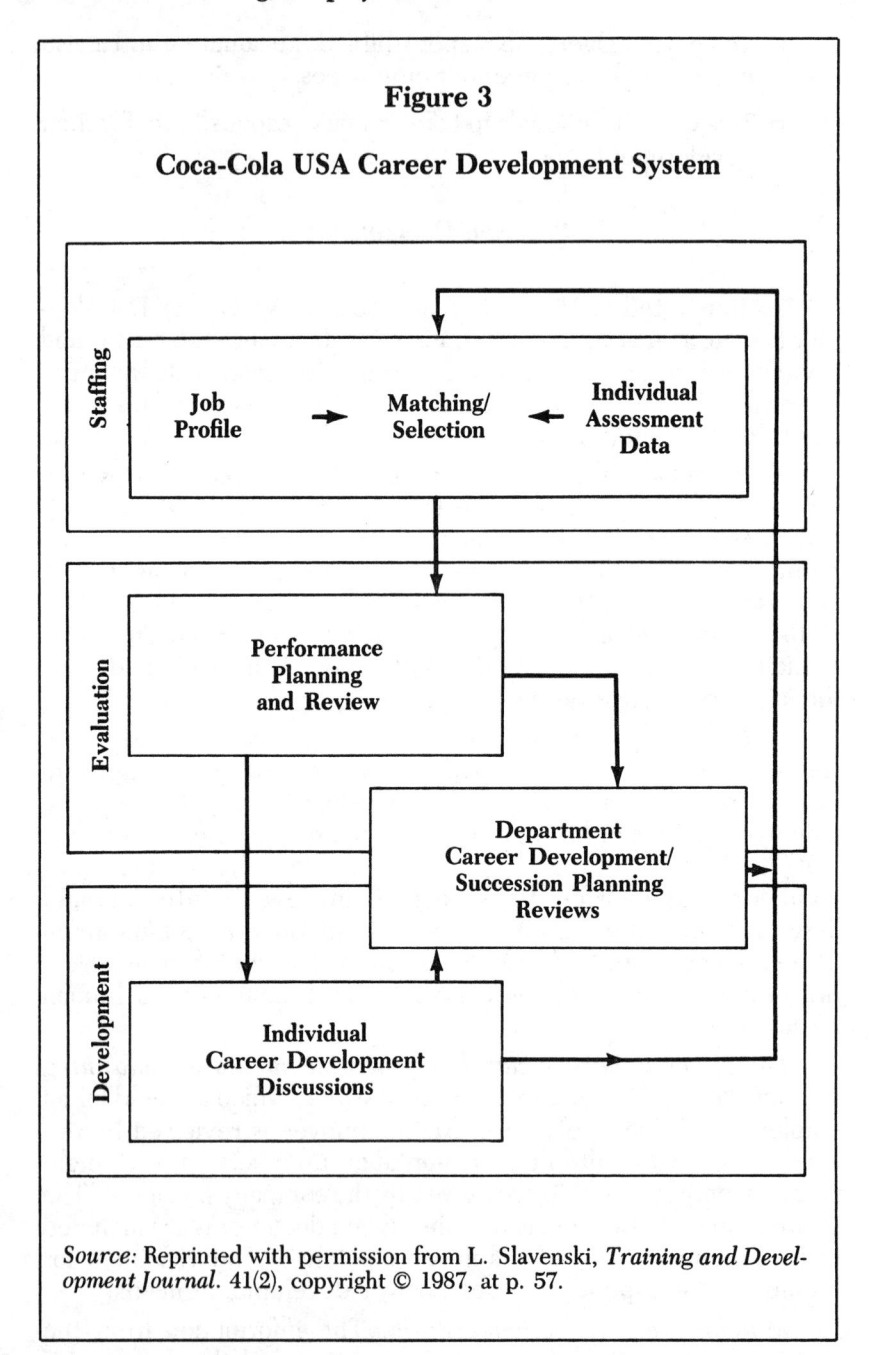

Figure 3

Coca-Cola USA Career Development System

Staffing
- Job Profile → Matching/Selection ← Individual Assessment Data

Evaluation
- Performance Planning and Review
- Department Career Development/Succession Planning Reviews

Development
- Individual Career Development Discussions

Source: Reprinted with permission from L. Slavenski, *Training and Development Journal.* 41(2), copyright © 1987, at p. 57.

career development and succession planning reviews form the basis for internal placement decisions. However, informal information (for example, what other mangers say about an individual's performance and potential) also plays a role in these decisions.

Program Operation

This career management system was gradually phased into Coca-Cola USA. In the first year, all managers were trained in performance appraisal. During the second year, all managers received training on how to implement career discussions, and career development and succession planning reviews were begun in the top levels of the company. In the third year, the career management program took effect at all management levels, and in the fourth year, it was applied companywide.

Communications to employees attempt to answer the following questions:

- Whom Can I Go To For Career Development Guidance?
  —The Manager
  —The Employee Relations Manager
- What Jobs Are There In The Company?
  —*Newsmakers:* monthly publication listing employee moves
  —Job Posting
  —Career Opportunities Booklets: overview of each department and qualifications for typical positions
  —Job Profile: extensive job descriptions; skills listed by importance; education and experience requirements
- How Can I Develop Myself?
  —30-Page *Career Planning Workbook*
  —2-day Career Strategies Workshop
  —Employee Training Catalog
  —100% Tuition Reimbursement
  —On-and Off-The Job Developmental Activities

Lessons Learned

The comprehensive career management program at Coca-Cola USA is successful for a number of reasons:

- Clearly stated objectives

- Integration of various components of the human resource management system. Selection and internal placement decisions are based upon the performance management system (performance review) and the career counseling process; and training and development activities are linked to the career counseling process.

- Incorporation of the employee perspective (individual career development discussions) and the organizational perspective (department career development and succession planning reviews)

- Effective and gradual introduction of the system. Coca-Cola introduced the Career Development System components gradually and trained all managers in the various aspects of performance appraisal and counseling. By using a top-down strategy of implementation, the company achieved manager buy-in before introducing the system companywide.

- Open communication to employees. Along with responding to employees' most critical questions, the career development system also opens communications between employee and manager, and between manager and manager.

- Distinct roles for the employee, the manager, and the HR department staff

- Involvement of line managers. The system belongs to line managers, not to the HR department.

- Realistic expectations—for growth of employees, but not necessarily for advancement

Conclusion

HR managers should review current policies and programs to ensure that internal placement and career management programs are operating effectively and meeting both individual and organizational needs. The following questions can help to direct this process and to strengthen the criteria used in program evaluation:

1. Is the internal placement/career management program a direct outgrowth of the HR planning process?

2. Is the HR planning process a direct outgrowth of the strategic planning process?

   ■ Does the internal placement/career management program have a strategic or long-term perspective to ensure personnel availability to meet the projected personnel requirements?

   ■ Do the training and development activities associated with the program have a results-orientation derived from the strategic plan?

3. Are program objectives clearly stated?

4. Is the program designed to adapt and respond to the changing motivations and values of the work force?

5. Does the program clearly define the roles and responsibilities of top-level management, line managers, and HRM professionals?

6. Is the program designed to gain the commitment of top-level and line managers? Are managers held accountable for their support of the program?

7. Is the program designed to provide equal opportunities for career advancement to members of all sex, racial, and ethnic groups? Does it accommodate the special concerns of women, minorities, older members, the handicapped, and dual-career couples? If the organization is cross-cultural, is the program sensitive to employees operating in this type of environment?

8. Are program policy statements (e.g., mandatory versus voluntary participation, programmatic criteria such as "promotion from within," procedures for safeguarding information) complete in their coverage and consistent with organizational goals?

9. Is the strategy underlying the program (i.e., pure selection, vocational guidance, or compromise strategy) appropriate in light of the selection ratio, the performance costs associated with the position, and the relationship of the position to other jobs?

10. Does the program integrate the other components of the HRM system (for example, performance management, training and development)?

- Is there a recognition of the need to link training and development activities with career placement decisions?

11. Are internal placement/career management decisions made on the basis of valid assessments of individual capabilities?

    - Does the program utilize valid assessment procedures to predict effective job performance (for example, ability tests, biodata instruments, peer evaluations, assessment center simulations, measures of work relationships between managers and their immediate supervisors)?

12. Are internal placement/career management decisions made on the basis of valid assessments of vocational interests?

13. Is information used to make decisions gathered in a standardized manner for each employee who is a candidate for a given position?

14. Are jobs accurately described in terms of their work behaviors and requirements? Are these descriptions used to identify appropriate training and development activities for those jobs? To establish rational career paths for linking jobs? To develop appropriate standardized criteria upon which to base internal placement/career management decisions?

15. Have adequate systems (for example, an automated HRM information system) been developed to support the program?

16. Have adequate funds been allocated in the budget to support program requirements (for example, training and development activities or organizational mobility)?

17. Has the program been introduced into the organization gradually with adequate training of all individuals in their program roles and responsibilities?

18. Has the program been introduced beginning with the top levels of the organization to help to gain program commitment from senior managers?

19. Have full communications been provided to all organizational employees? Do these communications clearly explain all program components? Facilitate the matching

of individual capabilities and job requirements? Ensure that realistic expectations are established?

20. Does the program allow career decisions to build employee motivation?

21. Does the program have the right level of complexity so as not to be an administrative burden to employees or to managers?

22. Is there a system established to monitor the program, to evaluate it periodically (including cost/benefit analyses) and to take corrective action, involving management where necessary?

The application of these questions to the organization's current policies and practices for Internal Placement/Career Management Programs will help to highlight programmatic strengths and deficiencies and to ensure that the program remains responsive to individual and to organizational needs.

◆

Notes

1. Marshall-Miles, Yarkin-Levin, and Quaintance (1985a), p. 22.
2. Hall and Morgan, p. 216.
3. Milkovich and Anderson, p. 374.
4. Guion, p. 780.
5. Cascio.
6. Dunnette (1975).
7. Dunnette (1966).
8. Cronbach and Gleser; Guion, p. 780. One drawback of this procedure is that it assumes jobs are entirely independent, with performance in one job having no relationship to performance on another job. However, in today's organizational settings, many jobs are successive (e.g., assembly-line work) or coordinate (e.g., task forces or team assignments) in nature.
9. This approach groups individuals on the basis of multivariate information that is combined in a linear manner. Placements are made on the assumption that people who are similar will work well together.
10. Schoenfeldt.
11. Owens, p. 272.
12. For a summary of research regarding the use of biodata to predict career success, see Quaintance (1981).
13. Cascio, p. 262.
14. Landy and Trumbo, p. 192.
15. Mills.
16. Milkovich and Anderson, p. 385.
17. Ibid., p. 383.
18. Ibid., p. 364.
19. Ibid., p. 378.
20. Burack and Mathys, p. 123.
21. Super.
22. See Simonson for a review of career stages originally identified by Dalton, Thompson, and Price.
23. See, e.g., Hall (1976), p. 57; Hall and Morgan, p. 219; and Rosenfeld and Stark.
24. Milkovich and Anderson, p. 367.
25. Hall (1986b), p. 134.

26. Hall and Morgan, p. 217.
27. Hall (1986a), p. 3.
28. Hall and Morgan, p. 214.
29. Ibid., p. 216.
30. Odiorne, p. 104.
31. Ibid., p. 103.
32. Rosenfeld and Stark, p. 63.
33. Sutton and Moore.
34. Bowman, Worthy, and Greyser.
35. The sample comprised 438 women and 348 men, with a response rate of 40 percent.
36. The exact percentages of respondents who believed women did not want positions of authority were 54 percent of men and 50 percent of women in 1965, and 9 percent of men and 4 percent of women in 1985.
37. Johnson v. Transportation Agency Santa Clara County, 480 U.S. 616, 43 FEP Cases 411 (1987).
38. Jones.
39. London and Stumpf, p. 40.
40. Jones.
41. Bureau of National Affairs, Inc.
42. Bird and Fisher.
43. Bowe.
44. Schein (1986).
45. Schein (1981).
46. Hall (1986a), p. 9.
47. The Executive Female.
48. Schein (1981), p. 102.
49. Burack and Mathys.
50. For discussions of fairness issues in assessment, see Quaintance (1984), pp. 73–112; Reilly and Chao; and Tenopyr.
51. Fleishman and Quaintance.
52. Wellback et al.
53. One such automated system is the Evaluation Assistance System for Effectiveness (EASE) developed by Laventhol and Horwath.
54. Burack and Mathys, p. 79.
55. Minor, p. 209.
56. Milkovich and Anderson, p. 381.
57. Wellback et al., p. 257.
58. Ropp.
59. Ibid.
60. Kizilos and Heinisch.
61. Ibid, p. 6.
62. Marshall-Miles, Yarkin-Levin, and Quaintance (1985b).
63. Kizilos and Heinisch, p. 7.
64. Cascio, p. 325.
65. Howard.
66. Ibid.
67. The MPS sample went through the assessment center in 1956 to 1960, 1964 to 1968, and 1976 to 1980. The MCS group went through the center in 1977 to 1979 and 1981 to 1982.
68. Wakabayshi and Graen.
69. The correlations between the measure of working relationship and other measures were r = .30 for speed of promotion, r = .24 for salary, r = .33 for bonus, r = .36 for the promotability index, and r = .35 for job performance ratings, with $p < .01$ for all correlations.
70. Harvey.
71. Bolt.
72. Slavenski.

Editor's Note: In addition to the References shown below, there are other significant sources of information and ideas on career management.

Books

Erikson, E.H. 1963. *Childhood and Society.* New York: Norton.

Hall, D.T. & Assocs. eds. 1986. *Career Development in Organizations.* San Francisco: Jossey-Bass.

London, M. and S.A. Stumpf. 1982. *Managing Careers.* Reading, MA: Addison-Wesley.

Schein, E.H. 1978. *Career Dynamics.* Reading, MA: Addison-Wesley.

Instruments

Hanson, J.C. and D.P. Campbell. 1985. *Manual* for the SVIB-SCII. Stanford, CA: Stanford University Press.

Zytowski, D.G. 1985. *Kuder Occupational Interest Survey Form DD Manual Supplement*. Chicago: Science Research Associates.

Manuals

Bolles, R.N. 1987. *The 1987 What Color Is Your Parachute?* Berkeley, CA: Ten Speed Press.

Holland, J.L. 1985. *The Self-Directed Search Professional Manual*. Odessa, FL: Psychological Assessment Resources.

♦

References

Bird, C.P. and T.D. Fisher. 1986. "Thirty Years Later: Attitudes Toward the Development of Older Workers." *Journal of Applied Psychology* 71: 515–517.

Bolt, J.F. 1985. "Tailor Executive Development to Strategy." *Harvard Business Review* 6: 168–176.

Bowe, F. 1985. "Intercompany Action to Adopt Jobs for the Handicapped." *Harvard Business Review* 1 (January/February): 166–171.

Bowman, G.W., N.B. Worthy, and S.A. Greyser. 1965. "Are Women Executives People?" *Harvard Business Review* 4 (July/August): 14.

Burack, E.H. and N.J. Mathys. 1980. *Career Management in Organizations: A Practical Human Resource Planning Approach*. Lake Forest, IL: Brace-Park Press.

Bureau of National Affairs, Inc. 1987. *Older Americans in the Workforce: Challenges and Solutions*. Washington, DC: BNA, Inc.

Cascio, W.F. 1982. *Managing Human Resources: Productivity, Quality of Work Life, Profits*. 2nd ed. New York: McGraw-Hill.

Cronbach, L.T. and G.C. Gleser. 1965. *Psychological Tests and Personnel Decisions*, 2nd ed. Urbana, IL: University of Illinois Press.

Dunnette, M.D. 1966. *Personnel Selection and Placement*. Belmont, CA: Wadsworth Publishing Company, Inc.

———. 1975. "A Modified Model for Test Validation and Selection Research." In *Organizational Behavior and Personnel Psychology*, ed. K.N. Wexley and G.A. Yukl. New York: Oxford University Press.

The Executive Female. 1987. "Americans and Success." (March/April): 25.

Fleishman, E.A. and M.K. Quaintance. 1984. *Taxonomies of Human Performance: The Description of Human Tasks*. Orlando, FL: Academic Press.

Guion, R.M. 1976. "Recruiting, Selection, and Job Placement." In *Handbook of Industrial and Organizational Psychology*, ed. M.D. Dunnette. Chicago: Rand McNally College Publishing Company.

Hall, D.T. 1976. *Careers in Organizations.* Palo Alto, CA: Goodyear.

———. 1986a. "An Overview of Current Career Development Theory, Research and Practice." In *Career Development in Organizations*, ed. D.T. Hall and associates. San Francisco: Jossey-Bass.

———. 1986b. "Breaking Career Routines: Mid-Career Choice and Identity Development." In *Career Development in Organizations*, ed. D.T. Hall and associates. San Francisco: Jossey-Bass.

Hall, D.T. and M.A. Morgan. 1983. "Career Development and Planning." In *Contemporary Problems in Personnel*, ed. K. Pearlman, F.L. Schmidt, and W.C. Hamner. New York: John Wiley & Sons.

Harvey, L.J. 1986. "Nine Major Trends in HRM." *Personnel Administrator* 31: 104.

Howard, A. 1986. "College Experiences and Managerial Performance." *Journal of Applied Psychology* 71: 530–552.

Jones, E.W., Jr. 1986. "Black Managers: The Dream Deferred." *Harvard Business Review* 3 (May/June): 84.

Kizilos, T. and R.P. Heinisch. 1986. "How a Management Team Selects Managers." *Harvard Business Review* 5: 6–12.

Landy, F.J. and D.A. Trumbo. 1980. *Psychology of Work Behavior.* Homewood, IL: Dorsey Press.

London, M. and S.A. Stumpf. 1986. "Individual and Organizational Career Development in Changing Times." In *Career Development in Organizations*, ed. D.T. Hall and associates. San Francisco: Jossey-Bass.

Marshall-Miles, J., K. Yarkin-Levin, and M.K. Quaintance. 1985a. "Human Resource Planning, Part I: In the Public Sector." *Personnel* (August): 22.

———. 1985b. "Human Resource Planning, Part II: In the Private Sector." *Personnel* (September): 38–44.

Milkovich, G.T. and J.C. Anderson. 1982. "Career Planning and Development Systems." In *Personnel Management*, ed. K.M. Rowland and G.R. Ferris. Boston: Allyn and Bacon.

Mills, D.Q. 1985. "Planning With People in Mind." *Harvard Business Review* 4: 97–105.

Minor, F.J. 1986. "Computer Applications in Career Development Planning." In *Career Development in Organizations*, ed. D.T. Hall and Associates. San Francisco: Jossey-Bass.

Odiorne, G.S. 1986. "The Crystal Ball of HR Strategy." *Personnel Administrator* 31: 104.

Owens, W.A. 1976. "Background Data." In *Handbook of Industrial/Organizational Psychology*, ed. M.D. Dunnette. Chicago: Rand McNally.

Quaintance, M.K. 1981. "Development of a Weighted Application Blank to Predict Managerial Assessment Center Performance." *Dissertation Abstracts International* 42 (Order No. DA 82-00399).

_____. 1984. "Moving Toward Unbiased Selection." In *Public Personnel Update*, ed. M. Cohen and R. Golembiewski. New York: Marcel Dekker.

Reilly, R.R. and G.T. Chao. 1982. "Validity and Fairness of Some Alternative Employee Selection Procedures." *Personnel Psychology* 35: 1–62.

Ropp, K. 1987. "Downsizing Strategies." *Personnel Administrator* 32: 61–64.

Rosenfeld, A. and E. Stark. 1987. "The Prime of Our Lives." *Psychology Today* (May): 62–72.

Schein, E.H. 1981. "Increasing Organizational Effectiveness through Better Human Resource Planning and Development." In *Public Personnel Management: Readings in Contexts and Strategies*, ed. D.E. Klinger. Palo Alto, CA: Mayfield Publishing Company.

_____. 1986. "A Critical Look at Current Career Development Theory and Research." In *Career Development and Organizations*, ed. D.T. Hall and Associates. San Francisco: Jossey-Bass.

Schoenfeldt, L.F. 1974. "Utilization of Manpower: Development and Evaluation of an Assessment-Classification Model for Matching Individuals with Jobs." *Journal of Applied Psychology* 59: 583–595.

Simonson, P. 1986. "Concepts of Career Development." *Training and Development Journal* 40: 70–74.

Slavenski, L. 1987. "Career Development: A Systems Approach." *Training and Development Journal* 41: 56–60.

Super, D.E. 1986. "Life Career Roles: Self Realization in Work and Leisure." In *Career Development and Organizations*, ed. D.T. Hall and Associates. San Francisco: Jossey-Bass.

Sutton, C.D. and K.K. Moore. 1985. "Executive Women—20 Years Later." *Harvard Business Review* 5 (September/October): 42–66.

Tenopyr, M.L. 1981. "The Realities of Employment Testing." *American Psychologist* 36: 1120–1127.

Wakabayshi, M. and G.B. Graen. 1984. "The Japanese Career Progress Study: A 7-Year Follow-up." *Journal of Applied Psychology* 69: 603–614.

Wellback, H.L., D.T. Hall, M.A. Morgan, and W.C. Hamner. 1983. "Planning Job Progression for Effective Career Development and Human Resources Management." In *Current Issues in Personnel Management*, 2nd ed., ed. K.M. Rowland, G.R. Ferris, and J.L. Sherman. Boston: Allyn and Bacon.

2.8

Outplacement

Donald H. Sweet

Outplacement has arrived, and it is here to stay. The use of outplacement services has increased dramatically over the past two decades, and the trend will no doubt continue. Indeed, outplacement may constitute the most significant employee relations tool to come along in recent years. It is the ultimate in "corporate caring": to assist a displaced employee through a very traumatic and emotional time.

What Is Outplacement?

At its most basic level, outplacement is an extension of the termination process. Typically it includes two elements: (1) counseling for emotional stress resulting from the trauma of termination, and (2) assistance with job search. These elements reflect a basic premise of outplacement—that the sooner a terminee is re-employed, the less time he or she has to become disgruntled, to file a lawsuit (warranted or otherwise), and possibly to upset employees who remain.

History

Initial development of the concept of outplacement has been attributed to Sol Gruner. In 1969 Mr. Gruner was approached by Standard Oil of New Jersey (now Exxon) to design a program to aid senior employees who were about to be laid off in a very large reduction of the work force.[1] This trend, to provide outplacement counseling for senior managers, continued for several more years. However, as the economic recession of the early 1970s forced companies to reduce the numbers of employees, outplacement was used to assist middle- and lower-level managers as well as senior executives who were facing layoffs. More recently, outplacement even has been used for those terminated for reasons of incompatibility and incompetence, as companies have come to realize the savings to be had with an outplacement program. Not surprisingly, therefore, outplacement as a profession has grown rapidly during the 1980s as changes in technology increased the emphasis on mobility and shifts in people.

While helping terminated employees is an admirable goal, it alone does not account for the growing popularity of outplacement services. As businesses have begun to discover, terminations and layoffs can produce effects that reach beyond the individuals fired. The time and cost of lawsuits brought by disgruntled former employees and the public relations damage done by massive layoffs can undermine an entire business. Morale among retained employees can also suffer if they feel that a terminated employee received unfair treatment or that the next layoff might target their positions.

Outplacement has become the answer for organizations seeking solutions to these problems. This chapter will review factors that spurred the growth of outplacement services, and examine how outplacement can benefit both terminated employees and organizations as a whole. It also will identify essential components of any outplacement program and options that organizations should consider when implementing outplacement services.

Factors Promoting Outplacement

As noted earlier, the concept of outplacement first arose in the late 1960s.[2] However, businesses did not adopt the practice until the mid-1970s. By the early 1980s, enough outplacement businesses had sprung up to merit formation of the Association of Outplacement Consulting Firms[3] and publication of a directory of outplacement firms. By 1988, this outplacement directory doubled to include about 200 firms whose gross earnings will likely total $250 to $300 million.[4]

This rapid expansion in outplacement services has paralleled changes in the business environment during the 1970s and early 1980s. The following section reviews several developments in this period that account for the growth of outplacement services.

The Termination Phenomenon

During the 1970s, terminations became commonplace as American industry started to feel the impact of foreign competition. The large influx of foreign goods, fluctuating interest rates, and economic ups and downs combined to undermine many businesses. Add to this trend the shift from manufacturing to service-oriented businesses and explosive advancements in technology, and the impact forced top managers to take long, hard looks at their organizations.

In many instances, these assessments led to organizational restructuring, paring down of staffs, plant closings, and layoffs. Everyone, from corporate chairmen to factory and office workers, felt the effect. Terminations were no longer something that only "happens to the other guy." In today's rapidly changing business world, the longer a person works, the greater the odds that he or she may suffer job loss.

Legal Challenges

As terminations became increasingly commonplace, employers also began to face increasing legal constraints on their right to fire someone. Former employees became more willing to challenge dismissals, and courts began to view these challenges with greater favor.

Until the 1970s, the traditional "employment-at-will" doctrine had allowed employers to fire someone at any time, for almost any reason, without any notice, provided the action did not violate special protective statutes or an express contract. This doctrine began to change in the 1970s as more and more courts began to apply "rules of fairness" restricting employers' right to terminate. Rules of fairness encompass a broad range of factors, such as public policy considerations, remarks made during the employment process or during performance appraisals, or statements made in company brochures and manuals.[5]

As some 60 million people—about 70 percent of the work force—are employed "at will," these legal developments have had far-reaching effects. In this age of litigation, any negative employment decision might result in a lawsuit. Employers now must closely examine HR policies and practices and ensure that all managers show sensitivity in hiring, evaluating, and terminating employees.

Work-Force Attitudes

As organizations began to adopt a bottom-line attitude toward employees, workers also began to view their employers in a new light. In today's business world, job performance alone does not guarantee job security. Instead, job security depends on an individual's ability to change jobs and to find employment in the open market. The person with a sought-after skill is the person with job security.

As a result, people tend to identify less with a particular company and more with a profession. Employees' loyalties have changed; the organization is no longer "Number One." This attitudinal shift has fueled the trend toward litigation by former employees, and it has made retention of sought-after workers more difficult.

The Value of Outplacement

All the changes outlined above have altered the employer-employee relationship and created new attitudes among both parties toward the duties that relationship engenders. The popularity of outplacement stems from its ability to address the needs of both employers and employees in this new relationship.

Benefits to Employers

Terminations rank among managers' most difficult and sensitive tasks. Whatever the reasons for the termination, the dilemma facing supervisors remains the same: how to dismiss employees with sensitivity, dignity, and efficiency, while adhering to fair employment procedures and minimizing the impact on the organization. Outplacement can address all of these concerns.

Universal Applicability

When ineffective performance results in a termination, supervisors can easily pinpoint reasons for the dismissal. But in today's changing and competitive economic environment, managers often must explain complex business concerns that necessitate laying off good performers. Reductions in work force can arise when organizations must rapidly adjust to decreased earnings, contract cancellations, or discontinuance of product lines or services. Mergers and acquisitions have become more commonplace and often require organizational restructuring and consolidation of employees. Expansion of services or relocation of plants can leave some employees out of work.

While terminations are never easy, putting good performers out of work creates additional stress for the fired employee, the firing manager, and the work force as a whole. By assuring fair treatment and transitional assistance to all terminees, regardless of the reasons for dismissal, outplacement can alleviate the emotional impact on all parties.

Public Relations

A hidden value in outplacement relates to an organization's image among the general public. By assisting departing employees and communicating openly with all interested parties, an organization will enhance its image as a good corporate citizen.

In addition, a company's outplacement policies can improve its standing within employment circles. Businesses known as "caring organizations" will facilitate their recruitment efforts, while organizations with a reputation for mishandling terminations will find hesitance among potential recruits.

Employee Relations

Terminations often create anxiety and/or resentment among remaining employees. Some workers may feel the departing employee received unjust treatment; others may doubt their own job security and question the organization's stability. Even when assured of job security, some employees may resent the upheaval and additional workload caused by a co-worker's departure.

A good outplacement program can help address these issues. It provides firing managers with training and procedures to minimize trauma to the terminee and disruption within the affected department. More important, the assistance given terminees assures that remaining employees will view their organization as a fair and considerate employer, despite any sympathy they may feel for their former co-worker.

Objectivity

By providing a uniform system for handling dismissals, outplacement reduces the prospect of potential litigation. Allegations of discrimination and other sensitive issues become less likely when dismissal procedures no longer vary from case to case and manager to manager.

An objective system for handling terminations also can lower termination-related expenses for organizations. Without clear and established termination procedures, managers may delay dismissing poor performers, with resulting productivity losses. In addition, companies without an outplacement program often offer excessive severance payments to make up for the lack of other assistance.

Benefits to Departing Employees

Whatever the reasons for dismissal, all terminees experience anger, fear, self-pity, and shock. The degree and impact of these emotions depends heavily on how effectively the organizations handle the termination. An outplacement program can play a critical part in lessening termination trauma.

Effective outplacement is a two-pronged process: First, outplacement provides emotional support to alleviate the immediate trauma of termination. Second, it supplies professional assistance to facilitate the terminee's job search and eventual re-employment.

Emotional Support

Before terminees can begin job search activities, they must first accept their job loss. Outplacement can help individuals to defuse their hostility toward former employers, to understand the reasons behind the termination, and to regain the self-confidence and motivation necessary for effective job hunting.

Outplacement can also mitigate the damaging effects of unemployment on family life by including the terminee's spouse in counseling sessions. Recent evidence indicates that such concern for the impact of terminations on families is well founded. In fact, when outplacement consultants were asked to describe the first thought to strike an executive who has just been fired, almost none mentioned financial worries or job-search issues. Rather executives' first concern is "What will the reaction be at home?" Executives worry about what their spouses and children will think, about what their teenage children will tell their friends, and about the reaction among members of their extended families. Conversely, when a fired woman is the major breadwinner, a husband may feel threatened if she doesn't rush out to find a new job.[6]

Professional Assistance

Outplacement services usually include a thorough career assessment and assistance in job search activities. Terminees receive help reviewing their accomplishments, skills, and career preferences—tasks that can prove difficult without objective feedback. In addition, a good outplacement program provides training on the specifics of job hunting—from résumé writing to interviewing techniques. Finally, outplacement assists individuals to evaluate potential employment sources, negotiate job offers, and select the best placement.

What about the impact of termination on women as opposed to men? A recent report from the Association of Outplacement Consulting Firms concluded that after outplacement counseling, women tend to approach the job search in a better, more positive frame of mind.[7] One possible reason for this, according to the report, is that the terminated women are typically younger and lower down the executive ladder than men. Women also seem to be more flexible than men in terms of the kinds of jobs they will accept. Men tend to want positions that match what they were doing before. But a positive attitude and flexibility do not necessarily speed the process of reemployment. Women don't find jobs any faster than men do.

The Termination Process

Contrary to popular perception, the outplacement process does not begin with a decision to terminate. Instead, effective outplacement begins with the employer-employee relationship and the duties engendered by that relationship. Organizations that fail to establish clear and fair employment practices will create problems that an outplacement program cannot overcome.

Organizational Policies

For any outplacement program to operate effectively, the HR department must develop organizational policies to govern all dealings with employees that could impact terminations. Almost every stage of employment can affect the outplacement process: For example, poor hiring practices often lead to increased—and more difficult—terminations. HR managers should make this linkage clear when developing termination-related policies.

In addition, organizations should implement systems to assure clear understanding and uniform application of these procedures. Managers must understand the impact their actions can have on the termination process, and every supervisor should receive training on how to handle terminations. Several basic policies that can facilitate the outplacement process are outlined below.[8]

Employment Policies

HR managers should review and, if necessary, rewrite all relevant documents, such as personnel manuals and company handbooks. Any wording in these documents that appears to guarantee permanent employment should be removed. In a similar fashion, HR managers should include a disclaimer on employment applications to clarify that the organization will honor only written agreements and not any oral promise regarding duration of employment or termination standards.

Written termination policies should cite specific examples of which offenses will provoke warnings and which ones will merit discharge. Disciplinary standards should specify the number of warnings allowed for each offense and provide a system for recording offenses and warnings. Organizations should also require that supervisors submit every termination decision to review by a designated executive, preferably a lawyer or knowledgeable personnel manager.

Performance Appraisal Policies

Employment engenders joint obligations on employers and employees. Employees must help their companies succeed by devoting their best efforts toward achievement of organizational objectives. Employers, on the other hand, must help employees become successful contributors by providing them with the necessary tools and guidance. Regular and honest performance appraisals play a key role in fulfilling these joint responsibilities.

To be effective, performance appraisals should take place continually, not just once a year. Policies should set forth objective performance standards and goals, and formal appraisals should specify corrective actions when needed. Supervisors should review performance ratings with employees and obtain their signatures on all records generated during these reviews.

Each department should maintain written copies of all performance appraisals, since these records will play a critical role in the outplacement process and in wrongful discharge actions. Line managers should avoid "papering" an employee's file with complaints, especially trivial ones, lest they give the impression of wanting to "get" a particular employee.

Termination Procedures

The joint responsibilities created by the employment relationship also extend to dismissals. When terminations occur, the affected employees share blame with the managers who hired or promoted them. Much like a no-fault divorce, a termination often results from incompatibility rather than incompetence: Neither party is entirely at fault, both parties suffer to some degree, and both sides benefit from ending an unproductive relationship.[9]

Recognition of this shared responsibility is central to successful outplacement. Organizations must establish termination procedures and provide managers with training that reflects employers' obligations. The following discussion identifies some methods that can facilitate the termination process.

Training Managers in Termination Techniques

While most managers are capable of hiring qualified people, many supervisors lack the skills necessary to fire employees effectively. Training managers in termination techniques can protect organizations from potential litigation, while preserving the employee's rights and self-respect. In addition, such training helps to minimize delays and stress to the firing manager.

Termination training should familiarize supervisors with company policies and provide a termination checklist for managers to use when conducting dismissals. A sample termination checklist appears in Exhibit 1. The program should also use role-playing to prepare managers for different dismissal situations. Useful points to cover in termination training programs include the following:

- Methods of conducting a termination interview, typical questions to anticipate, and suggested responses to these queries.
- The emotions experienced by terminees and firing managers, and how to cope effectively with these emotions.
- Termination policies, such as who handles the exit interview, how to continue benefits, what medical and security arrangements are feasible, and the like.
- Outplacement services available and the value of these services to the employee.

Conducting Termination Interviews

Before deciding to dismiss an employee, managers should conduct a detailed review of all relevant facts, including the employee's side of the story. To assure consistent treatment, the supervisor also should examine how the organization handled comparable cases.

Once a decision in favor of dismissal has been made, the termination interview should minimize trauma to the affected employee. The following obligations to terminees should govern the firing manager's actions:[10]

Timely action. Employers often waste months looking for nonexistent alternatives to delay a termination decision. Continued employment of someone who has lost the boss' confidence can only elevate job stress to the employer, the employee, and department co-workers. Once the situation has exceeded reasonable limits, further delay does disservice to the employee and the organization.

Respect. The actual termination interview should take place in private, and it should provide the employee with accurate reasons for discharge. However, the interview should not degenerate into detailed reviews of past performance appraisals or into a discussion of the employee's personal quirks or attitudes. Instead, the manager should recognize the mismatch, identify missing factors, and review strong points that could further the terminee's career elsewhere.

Exhibit 1

The Termination Checklist

DOCUMENTATION
____ If the job is eliminated, gather supporting evidence of a company or department reduction in head-count.
____ If poor performance is the reason, the file should contain copies of several successive poor appraisals that were transmitted to (and usually signed by) the candidate at the time they were prepared.

CLEARANCES
____ Who needs to approve the termination?

PRIOR NOTICES
____ Safeguards to prevent leaks to the public
____ Key staff members
____ Board members
____ Key customers
____ Regulatory agency officers

PRECAUTIONS FOR NEW LEAKS
____ Ignore the leak
____ Advance the date of termination to immediate
____ Delay the termination with no comment

TERMS OF TERMINATION
____ Resignation
____ Transfer to special assignment
____ Early retirement
____ Outright termination

LEGAL PRECAUTIONS
____ Salary
____ Bonuses
____ Benefits
____ Other obligations
____ Scientists and inventors
____ Noncompete agreements

PUBLIC ANNOUNCEMENTS
____ Should it be a standard press release?
____ What should the content of the statement be?

PERSONAL CONSIDERATIONS
____ Medical data
____ Significant dates
____ Family circumstances
____ Personal emotional state

Exhibit 1 continued

THE TERMINATION INTERVIEW
____ Think through details.
____ When? Not late on Friday.
____ Who? It's the line manager's responsibility.
____ Where? Best place is in a neutral area or the candidate's office.
____ Outplacement consultant on hand?
____ Termination letter prepared?

ORDERLY TRANSITIONS OF COMMITMENTS
____ Reassign internal assignments and projects
____ External activities to be reassigned:
- Customer servicing;
- Convention or professional meetings;
- Speeches and public relations commitments;
- Civic and professional commitments;
- Club memberships;
- Board memberships, e.g., of subsidiaries.

REGROUPING THE STAFF
____ Announcement to immediate colleagues and support staff
____ What they are to be told
____ Transfer of assignments
____ References
____ Reassurances.

TERMINATION LETTERS
____ Written evidence to verify the termination
____ Summary of important information the candidate may not have listened to, or remembered.
____ Brief and business-like confirmation of the facts and the details.
____ Include:
- Termination date
- Severance of bridging pay allowance
- Vacation pay

____ Continuation of benefits:
- Regular benefits
- Special benefits, such as pension rights

____ Job Search Support:
- Logistical
- Financial
- Outplacement
- Transfer of responsibilities
- Continuation of responsibilities
- Return of company property
- Legal documents
- Conditions of termination?

Source: Reprinted with permission from James J. Gallagher, chairman, J.J. Gallagher Associates, New York, NY.

When incompatibility rather than incompetence is the reason for dismissal, the firing manager should volunteer to provide good references.

Financial assistance. Even organizations with realistic termination and outplacement policies struggle over the issue of severance pay for departing employees. Most termination policies use length of service or salary level as the basis for determining severance pay levels. However, these policies overlook the real purpose of severance pay: to provide a financial bridge until the terminee gains new employment.

Instead, the financial settlement should reflect a realistic appraisal of the time needed to regroup. Using this concept, lower-level employees should receive a minimum of three to four months of severance payments, middle-level executives should qualify for six months of severance pay, and top-level executives should earn slightly more. In exchange for these benefits, the terminee should consent to sign an agreement releasing the organization from further financial or legal obligations.

Publicizing Termination Decisions

Communicating reasons for dismissals and layoffs to concerned audiences forms an important, but often overlooked, aspect of the termination process. All too often, the people leaving the organization get more attention than those individuals who remain, and the public at large receives no attention at all.

After terminations or layoffs, remaining employees may suffer from low morale, loss of confidence in departmental or organizational leadership, or doubt about the company's goals and objectives. Managers should pay particular attention to better performers, who may face additional job pressures as a result of the resulting vacancies. Other personnel in need of support include the terminee's secretary or administrative assistant.

Public disclosure of termination practices usually generates apprehension at all levels of an organization. However, companies that communicate their dismissal policies may enhance their image as concerned employers. Public disclosure can also assist employees displaced in layoffs since it assures potential employers that economic factors—not individual shortcomings—caused the dismissals.

The Mechanics of Outplacement

The preceding discussion identified essential termination policies that organizations should implement regardless of any assistance offered to individuals following termination. This section will review different types of outplacement services, factors that organizations should consider when selecting outplacement services, and essential features of effective outplacement programs.

The Make-or-Buy Dilemma

After deciding to offer outplacement assistance, organizations must choose whether to develop an in-house program or retain an outplacement consultant. Key issues to examine in the "make or buy" decision include personnel qualifications and cost.

Personnel Qualifications

To implement an in-house program, the organization must have competent and available HR personnel who can handle all facets of outplacement. Given the time, effort, and individual follow-up involved in the outplacement process, the other responsibilities of in-house personnel may constrain their ability to provide effective assistance.

Along with fewer time constraints, outside consultants frequently have greater expertise and resources to offer terminated employees. Moreover, former employees may prefer to deal with an objective third party, particularly when the termination has aroused feelings of bitterness and resentment. Table 1 provides a checklist to use in evaluating the services and skill of outplacement firms.

Cost

The cost of hiring an outplacement consultant varies, depending on the type of outplacement service retained. While the expense can prove substantial, the recent proliferation of outplacement firms and resulting competition has made price negotiation possible.

Businesses offering individual counseling usually charge 5 percent of the terminee's total annual compensation. The client organization also could pay another $500 to $1,500 for printing, telephone, and mailing expenses, as well as pick up any travel expenditures.

Table 1

Evaluation of Outplacement Consultants

Evaluation Criteria	Related Factors
Compatibility	Chemistry between organization and consultant firm
	Chemistry between terminees and counselor assigned to organization
Knowledgeability	Years of experience of firm and of counselor
	Range of contacts and clients served by firm and counselor
	Background in the particular job market, disciplines, and job levels involved
Time Commitment	Extent of assignment and likelihood of establishing an effective relationship
	Length of job searches for specific disciplines, position and compensation levels, and in particular locations
	Availability of counselor for duration of job search
Extent of Assistance	Specific responsibilities of terminee and consultant
	Help with job search vs. assistance with job placement
	Length of follow-up activities

SERVICES	EXECUTIVE SEARCH FIRMS	EMPLOYMEMT AGENCIES
Time Commitment	Consultant invests 40 to 50 hours per month on each search	Limited investment of time on any one client, due to lack of guaranteed payment
Referral Rates and Guarantees	Two to four highly qualified candidates recommended to each client	Large number of applicants referred to increase odds of a placement
	Recruitment and evaluation efforts target broad range of candidates, most of whom are not in job market	Recruitment focuses mainly on candidates actively seekly new employment
	Process- and results-oriented	Placement-oriented
	Reputable firms offer a professional guarantee and commitment to thorough, ethical practices	Contingency fee arrangement eliminates any obligation to produce results

Table 1 continued		
SERVICES	EXECUTIVE SEARCH FIRMS	EMPLOYMEMT AGENCIES
Level of Client Involvement	Minimal HR and management time involvement required	Considerable HR time required to screen, interview, and evaluate candidates

Outplacement firms that specialize in group counseling usually charge daily or per-terminee rates, plus related expenses. Placement support centers typically base rates on the weekly cost per counselor, plus expenses.

Outplacement Services

Most outpatient consultants offer a choice of individual or group counseling services. While the two services share many of the same features, each offers some unique components.

Individual Counseling

The advantage of individual counseling is that it assures personalized service to the terminee. Techniques that may prove effective for one individual do not always work for other people, and individuals may differ in the amount of time and resources they need to make successful readjustments.

Any outplacement program should also reflect the unique characteristics of the firing organization. Services should take into account the type of industry, the level of employees involved, and the organization's corporate culture.

Despite these individualized components, the process of one-on-one outplacement counseling should encompass the following steps:

Phase One: Acceptance. Counseling should assist the individual to gain emotional and intellectual acceptance of job loss. This step must take place to ensure the terminee can adopt the positive attitude needed to communicate his or her strengths and abilities during the job hunt. The terminee's spouse should also receive orientation to ensure thorough understanding of the situation.

Phase Two: Career Assessment. The outplacement counselor should help the terminee conduct a thorough self-analysis covering business experience, salary history, educational background, strengths, limitations, attitudes, and motivations. This information should form the basis for an individualized job hunting plan that considers the terminee's functional area or discipline, financial requirements, interests, aspirations, and career options.

Phase Three: Search Preparation. The outplacement program should provide thorough training in the job search process. Along with developing résumés and cover letters, this training should identify employment sources, proven approaches to these sources, and contacts within the organizations. Finally, the counselor should role-play interviews with the terminee and provide feedback on ways to improve interviewing techniques.

Phase Four: Offer Evaluation. As the terminee begins to receive job offers, the outplacement counselor should provide guidance on how to negotiate the conditions of the job offer through knowledge of the company's position levels, salary ranges, and other data. Once the candidate receives a final offer, he should receive assistance in evaluating the hiring organization and the specific job against his job search goals.

Phase Five: Follow-up. Finally, the outplacement consultant should conduct follow-ups to offer professional and emotional support while the individual readjusts to a new employer.

Group Counseling

Outplacement firms that specialize in group counseling usually offer one- to two-day workshops covering all aspects of job hunting, with some individual counseling provided for a specific duration. One common type of group outplacement firm is the placement support center. This facility offers terminated employees a base of operations where they can conduct research, place phone calls, and prepare résumés and correspondence.

While many of the topics covered in group outplacement sessions resemble those of individual counseling, participants receive less personalized advice. By necessity, each workshop must address a narrow aspect of the outplacement process. A typical outplacement seminar might follow the following format:

Self-Analysis and Career Assessment. This session would cover the same points outlined in phase one of an individualized counseling service.

References and Party Line. Topics addressed in this workshop might include preparation and proper use of references, and how to establish a "party line," or standard response when asked about reasons for dismissal.

Résumé Preparation. This discussion should help participants develop complete and concise résumés that emphasize specific accomplishments.

Resource Appraisal. Participants should receive a thorough appraisal of all potential job sources and guidance on how to maximize use of these sources in local and national job markets.

Correspondence. This session should teach letter-writing techniques that catch employers' eyes and open the door to an organization.

Interviewing. Issues addressed might include a review of the interview process and tips on presenting oneself in ways that maximize skills and abilities.

Salary Negotiation and Offer Acceptance. This workshop would identify data that individuals can use in salary negotiations, and offer tips on determining which job or organization best fits their needs.

The New Job. The seminar should close with advice on how to start off on the right foot in a new organization.

Outplacement in Practice

Ever since oil prices collapsed in early 1986, oil firms and firms that provide related services (such as geologic studies, rigs, and oil field supplies) have been forced to terminate many employees. Representatives of 18 of these companies, along with a sample of employees who had been laid off from them were interviewed in depth to determine the workings of their outplacement programs.[11] While the findings to be reported here cannot be assumed to generalize, they do provide insight into the practical side of outplacement services.

All 18 of the companies provided severance pay to the terminated employees. Some allowed terminated employees to choose whether to receive the money in a lump sum or spread out over a period of time. Twelve of the 18 companies also provided help with résumé preparation, secretarial support, office space, and phone use for limited periods of time. Seven of the firms provided outplacement counseling.

Reasons given by the companies for offering outplacement programs include: helping the ex-employee to deal psychologically with the layoff, to dissipate negative feelings toward the company, to help the terminated employees to assess their skills, and to teach job-search skills. Of the 18 companies, 17 reported that terminated employees did use the outplacement services that were offered, and all the terminated employees interviewed felt that the process was beneficial to them.

One suggestion made by a number of the terminees was to offer a "cafeteria style" approach to outplacement benefits, particularly the financial ones. The "most useful benefit" varied greatly across terminees. Those with families preferred extended medical insurance over longer severance pay. Some felt that the purchase of a company car was most important. Still others considered tuition reimbursements for continued education to be most important. To the extent that various outplacement benefits are roughly equally costly, therefore, firms might consider offering choices among available benefits.

Cost/Benefit Analysis

Despite the cost savings claimed for outplacement in the professional literature, none of the 18 company representatives mentioned "saving money" as a reason for instituting an outplacement program. Indeed, none had any idea of the total costs of their programs or of the values of benefits to be expected. The following costs were therefore estimated for one of the 18 firms in the study, a 100-employee firm that does its own outplacement and terminated 10 percent of its staff—three clerical and seven professional employees. Costs and benefits for that program were as follows:

Cost to Company		Benefit to Employees
	$30,000	Severance Pay
	56,000	Unemployment Compensation
	2,300	Insurance Continuation
	300	Secretarial Services
	200	Postage, Miscellaneous
Total	88,800	

One alternative to this arrangement is to hire an outside firm to conduct the outplacement program. Such a program will include office space, phones, résumé service, counseling, seminars, and miscellaneous services. Costs for this option were estimated to be:

Cost to Company	Benefit to Employees
$30,000	Severance Pay
56,000	Unemployment Compensation
2,300	Insurance Continuation
40,000	Consultant's Fees
5,215	Other Costs*
Total 133,215	

*Other costs were computed as follows:

Supervisors' lost time = 5 @ 4 hours each	$1,500	(salary)
	610	(benefits)
Survivors' lost time = 90 @ 1 hour each	2,250	(salary)
	855	(benefits)
	5,215	

A third option is to conduct an outplacement program, including counseling and seminars, by using the company's own human resources staff. Costs and benefits for this package are:

Cost to Company	Benefit to Employees
$30,000	Severance Pay
56,000	Unemployment Compensation
2,300	Insurance Continuation
2,100	Office Space
1,200	Clerical
1,000	Phone
11,683	In-House Counseling*
Total 104,283	

*These costs were computed as follows:

Two in-house HRM staffers for one week	$3,600	(salary)
	1,368	(benefits)
Travel expenses	1,500	
Supervisors' lost time = 5 @ 4 hours each	1,500	(salary)
	610	(benefits)
Survivors' lost time = 90 @ 1 hour each	2,250	(salary)
	855	(benefits)
	11,683	

The costs of the company's present program, $88,800, was considered to be the minimum amount to be spent for this analysis. Any savings from the other alternatives to reduce their cost to an equal or lesser value would make the alternative programs cost effective. Such savings might be realized in several different ways.

For example, if one terminated geologist is rehired within one year, the training costs saved are roughly equivalent to six months salary plus benefits, or $25,000 + 38%, for a total savings of $34,500. This saving easily justifies the cost of the in-house program, and almost makes the outside consultant's program equal to the present plan as well.

Other possible opportunity savings might be realized from litigation that is avoided. Even if just one major case could be avoided, this would justify any of the alternative programs. One major adverse judgment against the company could cost $50,000 just in attorneys' fees, plus damages awarded to the plaintiff (e.g., another $100,000, two years' back pay for a terminated geologist who successfully sues under Title VII).

A final way to look at cost savings is in terms of increasing survivors' productivity following a layoff of their fellow employees. If three days of lost time could be reduced 50 percent through counseling, the gains would be considerable. For the 100-employee firm described earlier, consider the possibilities:

90 survivors with daily salaries of	$9,375
plus 38% benefits of	3,563
Total cost per day:	$12,938
1.5 days saved = 1.5 × $12,938 =	$19,406

Obviously, as the size of the affected group of survivors increases, the dollar amount of the savings from counseling also increases. Whether outplacement is offered in-house or by an outside firm, counseling of survivors is a valuable benefit that should be offered when a layoff occurs.

Conclusion

Just how far outplacement has come in its brief history becomes evident from a recent survey of company termination practices.[12] Of the 150 organizations surveyed, 70 percent offered some outplacement assistance, whether through external consultants (72 percent), internal personnel (16 percent), or a combination of the two (12 percent).

The percentage of employers offering outplacement services will likely grow if industry trends continue at the current pace. From 1985 to 1987, some 500,000 white-collar jobs were eliminated from large companies due to downsizing, mergers, and the like.[13] The resulting shift in employee loyalty and increased litigation over termination implies a need to rewrite the basic social contract between employers and employees.

Outplacement provides one method to address the shared interests, mutual benefits, and differing rights of both parties. As one observer has noted, "Because outplacement can prove the genuine concern of an employer with the human investment which the individual and the organization have made, it will become increasingly more sophisticated and it will gain greater acceptance by a broader spectrum of business."[14]

With more widespread acceptance of outplacement, the process should gain greater sophistication. One HR manager predicts, "As corporations' need for third-party assistance is accepted, the emphasis will shift to the proper handling of potential termination cases earlier . . . making those terminations that are inevitable less of a shock to the employer."[15]

In short, outplacement has become a management tool, and the tool of choice for dealing with terminations. Outplacement has brought a conscience to terminations that recognizes the financial and emotional obligations created by the employer-employee relationship.

♦

Notes

1. Bearak.
2. Along with the author, early advocates of the outplacement concept include Dr. J.J. Gallagher, the late Thomas Hubbard, and Sol Gruner.
3. This association was founded in 1983.
4. The *Directory of Outplacement Firms*, published by Kennedy and Kennedy of Fitzwilliam, New Hampshire, first appeared in 1982 and contained about 100 listings.
5. Alsop.
6. Solomon.
7. Labor Letter.
8. Policies discussed in this section are adapted from recommendations made by Paul Grossman of the Los Angeles firm of Paul, Hastings, Janofsky and Walker.
9. Dr. J.J. Gallagher, chairman of J.J. Gallagher Associates, coined this analogy comparing terminations to no-fault divorce.

10. These guidelines are adapted from "What Do You Owe the Executive You Fire?" by James J. Gallagher.
11. Cerrone et al.
12. Reported in the 1985 *Directory of Outplacement Firms*.
13. Hallett.
14. John Bramlage, director of recruiting and placement, Mead Corporation.
15. Robert Tate, manager of placement resources, Dow Chemical.

Editor's Note: In addition to the References shown below, there are other significant sources of information and ideas on outplacement.

Articles

Adams, D.N. Jr. 1980. "When Laying Off Employees the Word is 'Out-Training'." *Personnel Journal* (September): 719–721.

Babcock, C. 1986. "AT&T Succeeds in Helping Laid Off Employees Find Jobs." *Computerworld* (March 17): 132.

Bailey, T. 1980. "Industrial Outplacement at Goodyear: The Company's Position." *Personnel Administrator* (March): 42, 44–45.

Barkhaus, R.S. and C.L. Meek. 1982. "Practical View of Outplacement Counseling." *Personnel Administrator* (March): 77–81.

Branham, L.F. 1983. "How to Evaluate Executive Outplacement Services." *Personnel Journal* (April): 323–326.

Broussard, W. and R.J. DeLargey. 1979. "The Dynamics of the Group Outplacement Workshop." *Personnel Journal* (December): 855, 873.

Brown, L. 1982. "Take the Sting Out of Losing Your Job." *Black Enterprise* (October): 83–86.

Business Week. 1974. "How Consultants Make Firing Easier." (July 20): 67–68.

Camden, T.M. 1982. "Using Outplacement as a Career Development Tool." *Personnel Administrator* (January): 35–37.

Carroll, A.B. 1984. "When Business Closes Down: Social Responsibilities and Management Actions." *California Management Review* 26, 2: 125–140.

Challenger, J.E. 1982. "What You Should Know About Outplacement." *Management World* 11, 12 (December): 26–27.

Driessnack, C.H. 1982. "Outplacement: A Benefit for Both Employee and Company." *Personnel Administrator* (April): 24–26, 29, 99.

———. 1980. "Outplacement—The New Personnel Practice." *Personnel Administrator* (October): 84–93.

English, C. 1983. "New Growth Industry: Help for Fired Workers." *U.S. News & World Report* (August 1): 63.

Forbes. 1982. "Viva Unemployment." (May 10): 200–201.

Friedman, M. 1982. "Outplacement: Taking Out the Sting." *Chain Store Age Executive* (October): 18–20.

Fulmer, W.E. and C. Fryman. 1985. "A Managerial Guide to Outplacement Services." *SAM Advanced Management Journal* (Summer): 10–13.

Gooding, J. 1979. "Out-Placement. . . ." *Across the Board* (April): 14–22.

———. 1981. "Firing at the Top." *Across the Board* (October): 17–21.

Harrick, E.J., M. Hansel and R.E. Schutzius. 1982. "Outplacement Training: Process, Content and Attitudes." *Training and Development Journal* 36, 2 (February): 79–85.

Hastings, R.E. 1982. "No-Fault Career Counseling Can Boost Middle and Upper Management Productivity." *Personnel Administrator* (January): 22–24, 26, 27.

Henriksen, D. 1982. "Outplacement: Program Guidelines That Ensure Success." *Personnel Journal* 61, 8 (August): 583–589.

Jacobs, B. 1980. "Recycling Rescues Laid-Off Executives." *Industry Week* (June 23): 17–18.

Klein, H. 1982. "Sometimes Corporate Generosity Is Just a Way to Get Rid of the Boss." *Wall Street Journal* May 5: 33.

Latack, J.C. and J.B. Dozier. 1986. "After the Ax Falls: Job Loss as a Career Transition." *Academy of Management Review*, vol. II: 375–392.

Management Review. 1981. "Outplacement Is Not Being Outplaced." (October): 67.

Mendelson, J.L. 1975. "Does Your Company Need Outplacement?" *SAM Advanced Management Journal* 40, 1 (Winter): 4–13.

Meyer, H.E. 1977. "Flourishing New Business of Recycling Execs." *Fortune* (May): 328–330, 334–338.

Oliver, A., M.D. 1985. "Outplacement Plans Cut Losses." *National Underwriters (Lifehealth)* (89)(24): 13–24.

Shahzad, N. "Outplacement Services Generate Good Will." *Healthcare Financial Management* (39)(8): 71–72.

Silverman, E.B. and S.D. Sass. 1982. "Applying the Outplacement Concept." *Training and Development Journal* 36, 2 (February): 70–77.

Stybel, L.J. 1982. "Negotiating Your Own Severance Arrangements." *Business Horizons* (January/February): 77–80.

Tavernier, G. 1980. "Easing Redundant Executives on to the Job Market." *International Management* (March): 12–16.

Van Duesen, D. 1984. "Inside Outplacement." *Duns Business Month* (January): 87–90.

Western Oil World. 1986a. "Amoco Production Co. Reducing E&P Staff by 15%, 1560 Jobs." *Oil World*. (43)(6): 12.

———. 1986b. "Atlantic Richfield to Slash Denver Staff." (43)(3): 15.

Books

Bolles, R.N. 1986. *What Color Is Your Parachute?* Berkeley, CA: Ten Speed Press.

Bostwick, B.E. 1977. *How to Find the Job You've Always Wanted.* New York: John Wiley.

Buskirk, R.H. 1976. *Your Career—How to Plan It—Manage It—Change It.* Boston: Cahners Books.

Cascio, W.F. 1987. *Costing Human Resources: The Financial Impact of Behavior in Organizations* 2nd ed. Boston: Kent Publishing Co.

Deutsch, A.D. 1979. *The Human Resources Revolution.* New York: McGraw Hill.

Irish, R.K. 1975. *If Things Don't Improve Soon I May Ask You to Fire Me.* Garden City, NY: Anchor Press, Doubleday.

Kingsley, D.T. 1984. *How To Fire An Employee.* New York: Facts on File Publications.

Lewis, J.A. and M.D. 1986. *Counseling Programs for Employees in the Workplace.* Monterrey, CA: Brooks/Cole Publishing Co.

Maurer, H. 1979. *Not Working: An Oral History of the Unemployed.* New York: Holt, Rinehart and Winston.

Morin, W.J. and Yorks, L. 1982. *Outplacement Techniques: A Positive Approach to Terminating Employees.* New York: AMA COM.

Sweet, D.H. 1975. *Recruitment: A Guide for Managers.* Reading, MA: Addison-Wesley Publishing Co.

Tarrant, J.J. 1974. *Getting Fired: An American Ordeal.* New York: Van Nostrand Reinhold.

Organizations

The Association of Outplacement Consulting Firms, 364 Parsippany Rd., Parsippany, NJ 07054.

The Directory of Outplacement Consultants, Kennedy and Kennedy, Inc., Templeton Rd., Fitzwilliam, NH 03447.

◆

References

Alsop, R. 1980. "Some Basic Rules for Managers to Follow When an Employee Has to Be Dismissed." *Wall Street Journal* (October 23): 37.

Bearak, J.A. 1982. "Termination Made Easier: Is Outplacement Really the Answer?" *Personnel Administrator* (April): 63–71, 99, 104.

Cerrone, M., S. Erickson, G. Trouth, D. Wikstrom, and J. Wilson. 1987. "Lay-Off Outplacement Programs." Unpublished manuscript, University of Colorado-Denver (January).

Gallagher, J.J. 1986. "What Do You Owe the Executive You Fire?"

Grossman, P. "Eleven Steps an Employer Might Take to Minimize Their Involvement in Wrongful Termination Suits." *Chemical Week Magazine* (June 22, 1983).

Hallett, J.J. 1987. "Worklife in America: Changing Times." *Personnel Administrator* (April): 21.

Labor Letter. 1988. "Getting Fired: It's Different for Women than Men." *Wall Street Journal*, October 25: A1.

Solomon, J. 1988. "Fired Executives Worry How It Plays at Home." *Wall Street Journal*, October 18: B1.

———— ♦ ————

Author Index

Authors appearing in this Index appear in the Notes and References at the end of each chapter. The individual authors of the chapters appear here also. Anyone referenced in the body of the text will appear in the Subject Index.

Adams, D.N., Jr. 2–258n
Administrative Management
    Society 2–129n, 2–133
Alsop, R. 2–257n, 2–260
American Psychological
    Association 2–156n, 2–157
American Society for Personnel
    Administration 2–100n,
    2–101
American Society for Training and
    Development 2–31n, 2–31
Anderson, J.C. 2–231n, 2–232n,
    2–234
Anthony, W.R. 2–31n, 2–32
Arvey, R.D. 2–156n, 2–157, 2–196n,
    2–198
Asher, J.J. 2–197n, 2–198
Avner, B.D. 2–69n, 2–69

Babcock, C. 2–258n
Bailey, T. 2–258n
Baratta, Joseph E. 2–159—2–199
Barkhaus, R.S. 2–258n
Barron, J. 2–31n, 2–31
Bayley, G. 2–197n, 2–198
Bayley, S. 2–197n, 2–198
Bearak, J.A. 2–257n, 2–260
Beer, M. 2–69n, 2–69
Belenky, A.H. 2–69n, 2–69
Belt, J.A. 2–157n, 2–157
Bemis, S. 2–69n, 2–69
Bennett, A. 2–31n
Bentz, V.J. 2–156n, 2–158
Berger, L.A. 2–69n, 2–70
Bird, C.P. 2–232n, 2–233
Bolles, R.N. 2–233n, 2–260n
Bolt, J.F. 2–232n, 2–233
Borman, W. 2–196n, 2–198
Bostwick, B.E. 2–260n

Boudreau, J.W. 2–157n
Boulding, K.E. 2–31n, 2–32
Bowe, F. 2–232n, 2–233
Bowes, L. 2–131n
Bowman, G.W. 2–232n, 2–233
Bramlage, J. 2–258n
Branham, L.F. 2–258n
Bray, D.W. 2–197n, 2–198
Broussard, W. 2–258n
Brown, L. 2–258n
Brumback, G.B. 2–69n, 2–70
Burack, E.H. 2–69n, 2–70, 2–231n,
    2–232n, 2–233
Bureau of National Affairs,
    Inc. 2–131n, 2–232n, 2–233
Busch, C.M. 2–157n, 2–157
Business Week 2–31n, 2–32, 2–258n
Buskirk, R.H. 2–260n
Byham, W.C. 2–197n, 2–199

Calvert, R., Jr. 2–131n
Camden, T.M. 2–258n
Campbell, D.P. 2–233n
Campion, J.E. 2–156n, 2–157,
    2–196n, 2–198
Campion, M.A. 2–157n, 2–157,
    2–158
Carley, W.M. 2–31n, 2–32
Carroll, A.B. 2–258n
Cascio, W.F. 2–1—2–33, 2–69n,
    2–70, 2–156n, 2–157n,
    2–157, 2–197n, 2–198,
    2–231n, 2–232n, 2–233,
    2–260n
Caskey, D.T. 2–69n, 2–71
Cerrone, M. 2–258n, 2–260
Challenger, J.E. 2–258n
Chao, G.T. 2–156n, 2–157n, 2–158,
    2–232n, 2–235

HR Planning, Employment & Placement

Christal, R.E. 2-69n, 2-70
Clothier, R.C. 2-196n, 2-199
Cole, K.W. 2-131n
Conference Board 2-129n
Costello, Erdlen & Co. 2-100n, 2-102
Coyle, B.W. 2-196n, 2-199
Cronbach, L.T. 2-231n, 2-233
Cunningham, J.W. 2-69n, 2-71

Decker, P.J. 2-157n, 2-158
DeLargey, R.J. 2-258n
Deutsch, A.D. 2-260n
Deutsch, Shea & Evans 2-129n
Devanna, M.A. 2-69n, 2-72
Dozier, J.B. 2-259n
Driessnack, C.H. 2-258n
Drucker, P.F. 2-69n, 2-70
Dunnette, M.D. 2-196n, 2-198, 2-231n, 2-233
Dyer, L. 2-69n, 2-70

Eaton, N.K. 2-157n, 2-157
Ehrenhalt, S. 2-31n, 2-32
Employment Management Association 2-129n, 2-133
English, C. 2-258n
English, J.W. 2-69n, 2-70
Erickson, S. 2-258n, 2-260
Erikson, E.H. 2-232n

Farish, Philip 2-103—2-134, 2-129n, 2-133
Field, H. 2-197n, 2-198
Fine, S.J. 2-69n, 2-70
Fisher, T.D. 2-232n, 2-233
Flanagan, J.C. 2-69n, 2-70
Fleishman, E.A. 2-69n, 2-70, 2-71, 2-232n, 2-233
Fombrun, C.J. 2-69n, 2-72
Forbes 2-258n
Frantzreb, R. 2-132n
Freedman, A. 2-129n
Freeman, R.B. 2-31n, 2-32
Friedman, M. 2-258n
Fryman, C. 2-259n
Fullerton, H.N., Jr. 2-31n, 2-32
Fulmer, W.E. 2-259n

Gade, P.A. 2-156n, 2-158
Gael, S. 2-197n, 2-198

Gallagher, J.J. 2-257n, 2-258n, 2-260
Garner, W.R. 2-156n, 2-158
Gatewood, R.D. 2-69n, 2-70
Geller, A. 2-69n, 2-70
Ghiselli, E.E. 2-197n
Glass, H.E. 2-69n, 2-70
Gleser, G.C. 2-231n, 2-233
Gooding, J. 2-259n
Gooding, R.Z. 2-196n, 2-197n, 2-199
Gordon, G.C. 2-69n, 2-71
Gordon, M.E. 2-197n, 2-198
Gottier, R.F. 2-197n
Graen, G.B. 2-232n, 2-235
Grant, D.L. 2-197n, 2-198
Greyser, S.A. 2-232n, 2-233
Gridley, J.D. 2-69n, 2-71
Groneman, C. 2-129n, 2-133
Grossman, P. 2-257n, 2-261
Gruner, S. 2-257n
Guion, R.M. 2-196n, 2-197n, 2-198, 2-231n, 2-233
Gustafson, D.J. 2-31n, 2-32

Hakel, Milton D. 2-135—2-158, 2-156n, 2-157
Hall, D.T. 2-231n, 2-232n, 2-232, 2-234, 2-235
Hallett, J.J. 2-258n, 2-261
Hamner, W.C. 2-232n, 2-235
Hansel, M. 2-259n
Hanson, J.C. 2-233n
Harrick, E.J. 2-259n
Harris, M.M. 2-157n, 2-158
Harvey, L.J. 2-232n, 2-234
Hastings, R.E. 2-259n
Heinisch, R.P. 2-232n, 2-234
Henriksen, D. 2-259n
Heyer, N.O. 2-69n, 2-70
Hodes, B. 2-129n, 2-133
Hodgkinson, H.L. 2-31n, 2-32
Hogan, J. 2-157n, 2-157, 2-197n, 2-198
Hogan, R. 2-157n, 2-157
Holden, P.B. 2-157n, 2-157
Holland, J.L. 2-233n
Hough, L.M. 2-157n, 2-157
Howard, A. 2-197n, 2-198, 2-232n, 2-234

Author Index 2-265

Hubbard, T. 2-257n
Hudock, A.W. 2-69n, 2-71
Hunter, J.E. 2-156n, 2-157n, 2-158, 2-197n, 2-199
Hunter, R.F. 2-156n, 2-157n, 2-157, 2-197n, 2-198

Irish, R.K. 2-260n

Jackson, G.R. 2-156n, 2-158
Jacobs, B. 2-259n
Jacobs, Rick 2-159—2-199
Jeanneret, P.R. 2-69n, 2-71
Jones, E.W., Jr. 2-232n, 2-234

Kandola, R.S. 2-197n, 2-199
Keller, L.S. 2-156n, 2-158
Kennedy, J. 2-129n, 2-133
Kiechel, W., III 2-31n, 2-32
Kingsley, D.T. 2-260n
Kirsch, M. 2-196n, 2-197n, 2-199
Kizilos, T. 2-232n, 2-234
Klein, H. 2-259n
Kleinman, L.S. 2-197n, 2-198
Klimoski, R.J. 2-157n, 2-158
Knowles, A. 2-132n

Labor Letter 2-257n, 2-261
Landy, F.J. 2-196n, 2-198, 2-231n, 2-234
Latack, J.C. 2-259n
Latham, G.P. 2-157n, 2-158
Lear, R. 2-129n, 2-133
Levine, E.L. 2-69n, 2-71
Lewis, J.A. 2-260n
Lewis, M.D. 2-260n
London, M. 2-232, 2-232n, 2-234
Lord, J. Scott 2-73—2-102
Lordeman, A. 2-132n

Management Review 2-259n
Manzini, A.O. 2-69n, 2-71
Marshall-Miles, J. 2-231n, 2-232n, 2-234
Mathys, N.J. 2-69n, 2-70, 2-231n, 2-232n, 2-233
Maurer, H. 2-260n
McCormick, E.J. 2-69n, 2-71
McEvoy, G.M. 2-197n, 2-198
McKenzie, R.C. 2-197n, 2-199

Mecham, R.C. 2-69n, 2-71
Meek, C.L. 2-258n
Mendelson, J.L. 2-259n
Meyer, H.E. 2-259n
Miles, R.E. 2-31n, 2-32
Milkovich, G.T. 2-231n, 2-232n, 2-234
Miller, E.R. 2-129n, 2-133
Miller, T.I. 2-31n, 2-32
Mills, D.Q. 2-231n, 2-234
Minor, F.J. 2-232n, 2-234
Morin, W.J. 2-260n
Moore, B.E. 2-69n, 2-71
Moore, K.K. 2-232n, 2-235
Moore, R.W. 2-129n, 2-133
Morgan, M.A. 2-231n, 2-232n, 2-234, 2-235
Morgan, P.V. 2-31n
Morrison, M.H. 2-31n, 2-32
Muldrow, J.W. 2-197n, 2-199

Narayanan, V.K. 2-31n, 2-32
Nath, R. 2-31n, 2-32
Needle, D. 2-31n, 2-32
Noe, R.A. 2-196n, 2-197n, 2-199
Nye, D. 2-31n, 2-32

Ochsner, R.C. 2-69n, 2-70
Odiorne, G.C. 2-232n, 2-234
Olian, J.D. 2-157n, 2-158
Oliver, A., M.D. 2-259n
Owens, W.A. 2-157n, 2-158, 2-231n, 2-234

Page, Ronald C. 2-34—2-72, 2-69n, 2-71
Peat Marwick 2-129n, 2-134n
Peters, T. 2-31n, 2-32
Pfeffer, J. 2-31n, 2-32
Phillips, N.F. 2-156n, 2-157, 2-197n, 2-198
Pinto, P.R. 2-69n, 2-72
Podgorski, R. 2-129n
Prien, E.P. 2-69n, 2-71
Primoff, E.S. 2-69n, 2-71
Pursell, E.D. 2-157n, 2-158

Quaintance, Marilyn K. 2-156n, 2-200—2-235, 2-231n, 2-232n, 2-233, 2-234
Quigley, A. 2-197n, 2-198

Rabby, R.   2–129n, 2–134n
Rafaeli, A.   2–157n, 2–158
Ralston, D.A.   2–31n, 2–33
Reilly, R.R.   2–156n, 2–157n, 2–158, 2–232n, 2–235
Resource   2–31n, 2–32
Reynolds, D.   2–100n
Ritchie, R.J.   2–197n, 2–198
Robertson, I.T.   2–197n, 2–199
Rockmore, B.W.   2–69n, 2–70
Romashko, T.   2–69n, 2–71
Ropp, K.   2–31n, 2–32, 2–232n, 2–235
Rosenfeld, A.   2–231n, 2–232n, 2–235
Ross, J.D.   2–69n, 2–71
Roy, T.S., Jr.   2–69n, 2–71
Ryan, A.M.   2–157n, 2–158

Saari, L.M.   2–157n, 2–158
Sackett, P.R.   2–157n, 2–158
Sands, W.A.   2–156n, 2–158
Sass, S.D.   2–259n
Schein, E.H.   2–232n, 2–232, 2–235
Schmidt, F.L.   2–156n, 2–158, 2–197n, 2–199
Schmitt, N.   2–156n, 2–157n, 2–158, 2–196n, 2–197n, 2–199
Schoenfeldt, L.F.   2–157n, 2–158, 2–231n, 2–235
Schutzius, R.E.   2–259n
Sciarrino, J.A.   2–197n, 2–198
Scott, W.D.   2–196n, 2–199
Serrin, W.   2–31n, 2–32
Shahzad, N.   2–259n
Siegel, L.   2–31n
Silverman, E.B.   2–259n
Simonson, P.   2–231n, 2–235
Slavenski, L.   2–232n, 2–235
Snow, C.C.   2–31n, 2–32
Society for Industrial and Organizational Psychology   2–156n, 2–158
Soder, D.A.   2–69n, 2–69
Solomon, J.   2–257n, 2–261
Sparks, C.P.   2–197n, 2–199
Sperling, J.   2–69n, 2–72
Spriegel, W.R.   2–196n, 2–199
Stanton, E.S.   2–133n
Stark, E.   2–231n, 2–232n, 2–235
Sternberg, R.J.   2–156n, 2–158

Stumpf, S.A.   2–232n, 2–232, 2–234
Stybel, L.J.   2–259n
Sullivan, A.   2–31n, 2–33
Super, D.E.   2–231n, 2–235
Sutton, C.D.   2–232n, 2–235
Sweet, Donald H.   2–100n, 2–102, 2–133n, 2–236—2–261, 2–260n

Tarrant, J.J.   2–129n, 2–134n, 2–260n
Tate, R.   2–258n
Tavernier, G.   2–259n
Tenopyr, M.L.   2–232n, 2–235
The Executive Female   2–232n, 2–233
Theologus, G.C.   2–69n, 2–71
Thornton, G.C.   2–69n, 2–71, 2–197n, 2–199
Tichy, N.M.   2–69n, 2–72
Time   2–31n, 2–33
Tornow, W.W.   2–69n, 2–72
Trouth, G.   2–258n, 2–260
Trumbo, D.A.   2–196n, 2–199, 2–231n, 2–234

Uhrbrock, R.S.   2–196n, 2–199
Ulrich, L.   2–196n, 2–199
U.S. Bureau of the Census   2–31n, 2–33
U.S. Department of Labor   2–69n, 2–72
U.S. General Accounting Office   2–129n, 2–134n

Vale, C.D.   2–156n, 2–158
Van De Voort, David M.   2–34—2–72
Van Duesen, D.   2–259n

Wagner, R.K.   2–156n, 2–158
Wakabayshi, M.   2–232n, 2–235
Walker, J.W.   2–69n, 2–72
Wall Street Journal   2–31n, 2–33
Wellback, H.L.   2–232n, 2–235
Western Oil World   2–259n
Wigdor, A.K.   2–156n, 2–158
Wikstrom, D.   2–258n, 2–260
Wiley, W.W.   2–69n, 2–70
Williams, J.E.   2–69n, 2–69
Wilson, J.   2–258n, 2–260
Wilson, T.B.   2–69n, 2–72

Worthy, N.B.   2–232n, 2–233
Wortman, M.S., Jr.   2–69n, 2–72

Yarkin-Levin, K.   2–231n, 2–232n, 2–234

Yorks, L.   2–260n
Yoxall, G.   2–133n

Zammuto, Raymond F.   2–1—2–33
Zytowski, D.G.   2–233n

Subject Index

A

Administrative Management
    Society 2–107
Advertising, recruitment
    budget 2–122
    direct mail 2–120—2–121
    newspapers and magazines 2–120
    other media 2–121
    trends in 2–121—2–122
    use of advertising agencies 2–92, 2–119
Affirmative action organizations, as recruitment source 2–124—2–125
Age Discrimination in Employment Act 2–10
Amalgamated Clothing and Textile Workers Union 2–22
American Express 2–119
American Hospital Supply Corporation 2–218—2–219, 2–220
American Management Association 2–43
American Newspaper Publishers Association 2–120
Apple Computer 2–29
Armco 2–127
Assessment centers
    cost estimates
        administration costs 2–188
        cost-benefit analysis 2–188—2–189, 2–196
        legal implications 2–189
    effectiveness 2–186—2–187
    in employee selection 2–150—2–151
    use of by AT&T 2–221
    when to use 2–186
Association of Executive Search Consultants 2–110
Association of Newspaper Classified Advertising Managers 2–120
Association of Outplacement Consulting Firms 2–237, 2–242
Atlantic Richfield 2–115
AT&T 2–16, 2–151, 2–185, 2–189, 2–221—2–222
Attraction, employee
    effect of organizational restructuring 2–21
    minority recruitment 2–20
    single-parent and two-earner households 2–20—2–21
Automation
    educational trends and 2–12—2–13
    effect on employee selection 2–21—2–22
    ethnic composition and 2–13—2–15
    impact on age groups 2–12
    shift to service industries 2–15—2–16

B

Bank of America 2–29
Baptist Medical Services 2–115
Baxter Travenol 2–218
Bernard Hodes Advertising 2–115
Biographical information, in employee selection 2–146—2–147
Boulding, Kenneth 2–4
Bramlage, Jack 2–111—2–112
Bureau of Labor Statistics 2–210
Bureau of National Affairs, Inc. (BNA) 2–210

C

California State University of Los Angeles 2–123
Campus recruitment 2–84—2–85
Career Development System, at Coca-Cola USA 2–224—2–228

2-269

Career Directions Program 2-50—
2-53
Career fairs
fees 2-91
history of 2-123—2-124
open house 2-124
selection of 2-91—2-92
Career management programs
career stages 2-206—2-207
career success cycles 2-207
corporate experience with
AT&T 2-221—2-222
Coca-Cola USA 2-224—2-228
Japanese 2-222
definition of career 2-206
executive development
programs 2-222—2-224
external factors affecting 2-208—
2-212
internal factors affecting 2-212—
2-215
versus career planning 2-207—
2-208
CBS 2-29
Chase Manhattan 2-66
Civil Rights Act of 1964 2-40,
2-136—2-137, 2-153, 2-209,
2-256
Coca-Cola USA 2-224—2-228
CODAP. *See* Comprehensive
Occupational Data Analysis
Programs
Cognitive abilities tests
cost estimates
administration expenses 2-172
cost-benefit analysis 2-173—
2-174
outcome analysis costs 2-172—
2-173
preliminary expenses 2-172
effectiveness 2-171
legal implications 2-174—2-175
College Placement Council 2-113,
2-114—2-115, 2-116
College recruiting
alumni associations 2-116—2-117
cooperative education
programs 2-117—2-118
internships 2-118
Ph.D. programs 2-117

tools for 2-115
trends in college relations 2-113—
2-117
Compensatory model 2-155—2-156
Comprehensive Employment and
Training Act 2-123
Comprehensive Occupational Data
Analysis Programs
(CODAP) 2-47—2-48
Computers
applications of 2-12
as interview aids 2-146
as recruitment tool 2-81—2-82
computer-based name
banks 2-125
in executive search firms 2-88—
2-89
in test administration 2-142—
2-143
office communications 2-25—2-26
telecommuting and 2-24
Control Data Corporation 2-53—
2-54, 2-64, 2-68
Co-op and work study
programs 2-95, 2-117—
2-118
Cooperative Education Association,
Inc. 2-118
Critical incident technique 2-43—
2-45

D

Deregulation and
decentralization 2-16—
2-19
Deutsch, Shea & Evans 2-108
Dictionary of Occupational
Titles 2-45—2-46
District of Columbia 2-45
Downsizing 2-28—2-29, 2-113,
2-126, 2-215—2-216, 2-257
Drexel Institute 2-118
Drug tests 2-153—2-154
DuPont 2-29, 2-215—2-216
Dynamic network 2-15—2-16

E

Employee attraction. *See* Attraction,
employee

Subject Index 2-271

Employee development 2-39—2-40
Employee leasing 2-23
Employee referral programs
  award systems 2-108
  guidelines for effective
    operation 2-97—2-99
  suggestions for
    implementing 2-108
Employee Relocation Council 2-127
Employee retention. *See* Retention,
  employee
Employment agencies
  code of ethics 2-109—2-110
  fees 2-90
  government 2-95, 2-123
  types of 2-109
Employment function
  history of 2-1—2-2
  overview 2-2—2-4
Employment Management
    Association 2-107, 2-109—
    2-110, 2-111, 2-122
Environmental Scan 2-62
Environmental scanning 2-62
Environmental Scanning
    Association 2-62
Equal Employment Opportunity
    Act 2-209
Equal Employment Opportunity
    Commission 2-189
Equal Pay Act of 1963 2-41, 2-67
Executive Recruiter News 2-112
Executive search firms
  characteristics of 2-110—2-111
  current trends 2-112—2-113
  evaluation of 2-89
  fees 2-86
  in-house function 2-111—2-112
  role of consultant 2-89
  selection of 2-88—2-89
Experience and past performance, of
    employment candidate
  as a predictor 2-189
  cost estimates 2-191—2-192
  effectiveness 2-190
  legal implications 2-192
  when to use 2-190
External recruitment sources
  advertising 2-84, 2-92, 2-119—
    2-122

affirmative action
    organizations 2-124—2-125
alternative sources 2-92—2-95
associations and professional
    societies 2-125
career fairs 2-84, 2-91—2-92
college recruiting 2-113—2-118
computer-based name
    banks 2-125
employment agencies 2-84, 2-90,
    2-109—2-110
executive search firms 2-84,
    2-86—2-89, 2-110—2-113.
temporary agencies 2-126
unemployed youth 2-118—2-119
university relations 2-84—2-85
See also names of specific sources
Exxon 2-29, 2-236

F

Fair Credit Reporting Act 2-149
Fair Labor Standards Act of
    1938 2-41, 2-53, 2-67
Family Educational Rights and
    Privacy Act 2-149
Federated Foods 2-223—2-224
First Chicago Corp. 2-23
Ford 2-29
Fortune 2-26

G

Gannett Company, Inc. 2-106
General Accounting Office
    (GAO) 2-123
General Electric 2-66
General Foods 2-223—2-224
General Motors 2-22, 2-117
Genetic screening 2-152—2-153
Griggs v. Duke Power 2-136—2-137
Gruner, Sol 2-236

H

Handwriting analysis 2-152
Harvard Business Review 2-209
Harvard University 2-117
Hay Group 2-62

Hay Management Consultants 2–54
HAY VALUE 2–54—2–58
Honesty tests, in employee
 selection 2–148—2–149
Honeywell's Systems and Research
 Center 2–216—2–217,
 2–219—2–220
HR FOCUS 2–53—2–54
HR (human resource) information
 systems 2–41
HRM (human resource management)
 functional responsibilities
  changing role of 2–60
  implications of 2–19—2–30
  overview 2–2—2–4
 implications of future
  trends 2–19—2–30
 organizational policies 2–243—
  2–244
 societal trends and staffing
  policies 2–1—2–33
HR managers. *See* Managers, HR
HR planning
 definition of 2–60—2–61
 future directions of 2–68—2–69
 importance of 2–34—2–35
 job analysis and 2–34—2–72
 process 2–62—2–66
HR programs
 policy documents and 2–214—
  2–215

I

IBM 2–64—2–65, 2–214
Inducements, as recruitment tool
 relocation aid 2–127
 sign-on bonuses 2–127—2–128
Inroads, Inc. 2–124
Integrated personnel system 2–49—
  2–58
Internal placement programs
 examples of
  American Hospital Supply
   Corp. 2–218—2–219, 2–220
  DuPont 2–215—2–216
  Honeywell 2–216—2–217,
   2–219—2–220

external factors affecting 2–208—
 2–212
internal factors affecting 2–212—
 2–215
process 2–201—2–202, 2–228—
 2–231
strategies for managing
 placements 2–202—2–205
succession programs 2–205
Internal recruitment
 employee referral program 2–97—
  2–99, 2–107—2–108
 in-house temporary pool 2–99
 job posting programs 2–96—2–97,
  2–103—2–106
 process 2–96
 retirees 2–106—2–107
International Foundation of Employee
 Benefit Plans 2–118
Interview applicants
 attractiveness and age of 2–165
 competency of 2–164
 expenses of 2–168—2–169
 sex of 2–165
 verbal fluency of 2–164—2–165
Interviewers
 consistency among 2–169—2–170
 multiple 2–164
 similarities to interviewee 2–162
 skills of 2–162
 stereotyping 2–161
 stress during interview 2–161
Interviews
 arranging 2–76—2–77
 as job analysis method 2–43
 computerized 2–146
 contrast effect 2–166
 cost estimates of 2–167—2–169
 history of 2–160
 legal implications 2–169—2–170
 primacy and recency effects 2–166
 reliability and validity of 2–166—
  2–167
 situational 2–146
 structured vs. unstructured 2–145,
  2–163
 termination 2–245—2–248
 types of questions 2–163—2–164,
  2–170

Subject Index 2-273

J

Japan 2–221, 2–222
Job Accommodations
   Network 2–210—2–211
Job analysis
   applications of 2–36—2–41
   as basis for employee
      selection 2–137—2–139
   components of 2–35—2–36
   future directions of 2–68—2–69
   importance of 2–34—2–35
   in internal placement and career
      management 2–213—2–214
   methods 2–41—2–58
Job posting programs 2–96—2–97,
   2–103—2–106
Job previews, realistic
   cost estimates 2–194
   effectiveness 2–193—2–194
   legal implications 2–194—2–195
   when to use 2–193
Job-relatedness 2–137—2–139,
   2–169, 2–174
Job Service 2–123, 2–125
Job sharing 2–95
Job Training Partnership Act
   (JTPA) 2–123
Job try-outs 2–137
JobScope 2–50—2–53
Jordan, Mark 2–116
Journal of Applied Psychology 2–156

K

Kemper Group 2–128
Kennedy, James 2–112
Kodak 2–29

L

Labor force
   age distribution of 2–9—2–10
   gender composition of 2–9
   post-1995 2–10—2–11
Lendmen, Ernest 2–124
Life Insurance Marketing and
   Research Association 2–147

Lockheed Missiles & Space
   Company 2–108, 2–114

M

Management information systems
   (MIS) 2–82
Managers
   HR 2–2, 2–4—2–19, 2–25, 2–28,
      2–30, 2–155, 2–200—2–231
   line 2–4, 2–21, 2–25, 2–28, 2–30,
      2–212
Mead Corp. 2–111, 2–127
Merck 2–29
Metropolitan Area Transition
   Clearinghouse
   (MATCH) 2–117
Mobil 2–114
Monsanto 2–29
Moore, Richard 2–117
Motorola 2–223—2–224

N

National Academy of Sciences 2–144
National Action Council on Minorities
   in Engineering 2–124
National Alliance of Business 2–119,
   2–123
National Association for the
   Advancement of Colored
   People 2–119
National Association of Corporate and
   Professional
   Recruiters 2–110
National Association of Minority
   Engineering Program
   Administrators 2–125
National Association of Personnel
   Consultants 2–110
National Association of Private
   Industry Councils 2–123
National Cash Register 2–127
National Commission on Cooperative
   Education 2–118
National Urban League 2–119
Nationwide Insurance
   Companies 2–39, 2–50,
   2–68

New York University 2–117
Newspaper Advertising
 Bureau 2–120
Northeastern University 2–118

O

Occupational Safety and Health
 Act 2–41, 2–153
*Older Americans in the Workforce:
 Challenges and
 Solutions* 2–210
Organizational and Strategy
 Information Service
 (OASIS) 2–66
Organization development
 (OD) 2–40
Outplacement
 at Exxon 2–29
 benefits to employers 2–239—
  2–241
 benefits to terminees 2–241—
  2–242
 consultant costs 2–249—2–251
 cost/benefit analysis 2–254—2–256
 counseling 2–251—2–253
 definition of 2–236
 factors promoting 2–237—2–239
 firms 2–92, 2–113
 history of 2–236—2–237
 practical side of 2–253—2–254
 termination process 2–242—2–248

P

Pacific Bell 2–24
Pacific Telesis 2–66
PAQ. *See* Position Analysis
 Questionnaire
Peat Marwick 2–128
People Express 2–28
Performance standards and reward
 systems 2–39
Personality and interest inventories
 cost estimates
  administration expenses 2–178
  cost-benefit analysis 2–178
  development costs 2–177
 effectiveness 2–176—2–177
 legal implications 2–178—2–179
 when to use 2–147, 2–175—2–176

Personnel Journal 2–121—2–122
Personnel Psychology 2–156
Phillips, H.A. 2–108
Physical abilities tests
 cost estimates
  administration costs 2–181
  cost-benefit analysis 2–181
  development costs 2–180—
   2–181
 effectiveness 2–179—2–180
 legal implications 2–182
 when to use 2–179
Pickwick Group 2–109
Polly Bergen Jewelry, Inc. 2–23
Polygraphs 2–147—2–148, 2–154
Population projections 2–6—2–8
Position Analysis Questionnaire
 (PAQ) 2–46—2–47, 2–48
President's Committee on
 Employment of the
 Handicapped 2–210—
 2–211
President's Council on Management
 Improvement 2–222—
 2–223
Private Industry Council 2–123
Proctor & Gamble 2–108

Q

Quality of work life programs 2–16

R

Recruiting Trends 2–116
Recruiters
 business sense of 2–84
 communications skills of 2–82—
  2–83
 familiarity with the
  organization 2–83
Recruitment
 government sources 2–95, 2–123
 history of 2–73
 inducements 2–127—2–128
Recruitment, external. *See* External
 recruitment sources
Recruitment function
 assessing recruitment
  needs 2–78—2–79
 staffing 2–82—2–84

Subject Index 2-275

structure for implementing
 hiring demands 2-79—2-81
 resources committed to 2-81—2-82
Recruitment, internal. *See* Internal recruitment
Recruitment process
 control of offers and
  acceptances 2-77—2-78
 requisitions 2-74—2-75
 résumés 2-75—2-76
Rehabilitation Act of 1973 2-153, 2-210
Résumés
 controlling flow of 2-75—2-76
 source of 2-78
Retention, employee
 communications
  technology 2-25—2-26
 corporate reorganization 2-26—2-27
 shift to service jobs 2-26
 telecommuters 2-23—2-25
Retirees, as recruitment
 source 2-95, 2-106—2-107
Runzheimer International 2-127

S

Santa Fe Braun Company 2-123
Sara Lee 2-66
School Match 2-127
Sears and Roebuck 2-143, 2-213
Selection, employee
 choosing measurement
  methods 2-154—2-155
 combining preemployment
  information 2-155—2-156
 effect of automation 2-21—2-22
 establishment of job-
  relatedness 2-137—2-139
 laws concerning 2-136—2-137
 selection tools 2-139—2-154
 temporary workers 2-23
 See also Tests, employee selection
Senior Job Bank 2-107
Severance pay 2-248, 2-253
Smith, Roger 2-117
Social Security 2-10
Societal trends and staffing policies, in HRM

factors affecting future HR
 managers 2-4—2-19
 implications for HRM 2-19—2-30
Society of Women Engineers 2-124
Staffing decisions, tools for 2-159—2-199
Staffing policies, in HRM 2-1—2-33
Standard Oil of New Jersey. *See* Exxon
Stanford University 2-116

T

Task inventory method/
 CODAP 2-47—2-48
Telecommuters 2-23—2-25
Temporary agencies 2-126
Termination
 impact on women 2-242
 procedures 2-244—2-248
 See also Outplacement
Tests, employee selection
 cognitive and personality 2-142—2-143
 future developments 2-143—2-144
 honesty 2-148
 limitations on 2-144—2-145, 2-148—2-149
 medical, physical, and
  drug 2-153—2-154
 performance 2-142
 personality and interest 2-147
 See also name of individual test
Title VII. *See* Civil Rights Act of 1964
Trade shows, as recruitment
 source 2-95
Training Research
 Corporation 2-117
Transamerica Life Companies 2-106
Travelers Corporation 2-20, 2-107

U

Uniform Guidelines on Employee
 Selection Procedures 2-67, 2-170
University of Texas–Austin 2-117
University of Virginia 2-117
University relations, as recruitment
 source 2-84—2-85

USA Today 2–106
U.S. Bureau of the Census 2–6
U.S. Civil Service Commission 2–46
U.S. Department of Labor 2–27, 2–46
  job analysis procedure 2–45—2–46
  See also Bureau of Labor Statistics
Utility analysis 2–155

W

Wharton School of the University of Pennsylvania 2–117
Work force
  analysis 2–40—2–41
  attitudes toward employers 2–239
  cross-cultural 2–211
  dual-career couples 2–211
  handicapped 2–210—2–211
  minorities in 2–209—2–210
  older workers 2–210
  values of the majority 2–211—2–212
  women in 2–209
Work in America Institute Inc. 2–119
Work samples
  as selection tool 2–182—2–183
  cost estimates 2–184—2–185
  effectiveness 2–183—2–184
  legal implications 2–185—2–186
  when to use 2–183

X

Xerox Corp. 2–25, 2–223—2–224

DATE DUE			
DEC 1 0 1998			
DEC 1 2 1999			
JUN 0 9 2002			
NOV 1 0 2003			
REC'D NOV 0 6 2003			
			Printed in USA

HIGHSMITH #45230